Espionage and Exile

Espionage and Exile

Fascism and Anti-Fascism in British Spy Fiction and Film

Phyllis Lassner

Univcrsity Prcss

Edinburgh University Press is one of the leading university presses in the UK. We publish academic books and journals in our selected subject areas across the humanities and social sciences, combining cutting-edge scholarship with high editorial and production values to produce academic works of lasting importance. For more information visit our website: edinburghuniversitypress.com

© Phyllis Lassner, 2016

Edinburgh University Press Ltd
The Tun – Holyrood Road
12(2f) Jackson's Entry
Edinburgh EH8 8PJ

Typeset in 10.5/13 Adobe Sabon by
Servis Filmsetting Ltd, Stockport, Cheshire

A CIP record for this book is available from the British Library

ISBN 978 1 4744 0110 4 (hardback)
ISBN 978 1 4744 0111 1 (webready PDF)
ISBN 978 1 4744 1673 3 (epub)

The right of Phyllis Lassner to be identified as the author of this work has been asserted in accordance with the Copyright, Designs and Patents Act 1988, and the Copyright and Related Rights Regulations 2003 (SI No. 2498).

Contents

Acknowledgments	vi
Introduction: Exile – The Heart of the Secret World	1
1. Eric Ambler: Espionage Chronicler of the 1930s	16
2. Double Agency: Women Writers of Espionage Fiction	69
3. Leslie Howard: Propaganda Artist	118
4. John le Carré's Never-ending War of Exile	166
Conclusion	217
Bibliography	223
Index	239

Acknowledgments

I am deeply grateful to the people and institutions that have encouraged and supported me throughout my research, writing and the production of this book. Jackie Jones' enthusiasm for *Espionage and Exile*, the guidance of Adela Rauchova, James Dale's meticulous instructions, Nicola Wood's rigorous copyediting and Rebecca Mackenzie's brilliant work on my cover have been models of editorial support from start to finish. As in the past, Bob Gundlach supported my work by encouraging me to create courses on espionage fiction and film and to apply for travel grants to research libraries and conferences. Generous funding by Northwestern University allowed me to examine the papers of Eric Ambler at the Howard Gottlieb Research Center at Boston University, Helen MacInnes' papers at the Department of Rare Books and Special Collections at Princeton University, and Leslie Howard's radio scripts at the BBC written archive at Reading. The help of the archivists and staff at each of these libraries made research an enormous pleasure.

Throughout the entire process of thinking through the issues that coalesced as *Espionage and Exile*, I had the great good fortune to reap the benefits of supportive and brilliant colleagues and friends who read various chapters and whose knowledge, insights and suggestions enriched my thinking and writing, and nudged me to contextualise, clarify and extend my nascent ideas. In particular, I wish to thank Elizabeth Maslen, Allan Hepburn, Margaret Stetz, Clare Hanson, Mike Williamson, Laurie Baron and Nathan Abrams. I am very grateful to Clare Hanson, Will May and James Jordan for sponsoring my award of the International Diamond Jubilee Fellowship at Southampton University, UK. Their generous hospitality and friendship gave me ten blissful days of scholarly activities and conversations focused on my research and so many topics that enriched my thinking for this book, including the symposium on espionage representation, the seminar on Holocaust history and representation co-taught by James Jordan and

Shirli Gilbert, Will May's MA workshop on women writers and Karen Robson's guided tour of the Parkes Institute archives where I hope to work during my next two visits. Other opportunities to share my work on this book spurred me on with demonstrations of support, including Allan Hepburn's gracious organisation of my talk at McGill, Toby Manning's invitation to keynote at his 'Spying on Spies' conference in London and the Space Between annual conference, my scholarly home that has nurtured lifelong friendships.

I would like to express appreciation to Andrew Boose at Davis Wright Tremaine LLP for permission to quote from Helen MacInnes' letter to Mrs Enid Cosgriff. Peters Fraser and Dunlop granted non-exclusive licence on behalf of the Estate of Rebecca West to quote from Rebecca West's unpublished typescript of her introduction to Pamela Frankau's novel *Colonel Blessington*, held at the Burns Library, Boston College. Credit for images from *Pimpernel Smith*, 1941 goes to Leslie Howard, British National/Anglo-Amalgamated. Many thanks to Marika Lysandrou for granting permission to quote the untitled poem from Charlotte Delbo's *Auschwitz and After*, Copyright 1995 by Yale University Press.

Far more than illustrative, Ava Kadishson Schieber's remarkable drawings express the intertwined, contradictory and multiple identities and relationships produced by an experience of exile, finding home and homelessness everywhere ever since she went into hiding from the Nazis in 1941 and emerged four years later to build a new life, a family and to become an artist and writer in Israel and in Chicago. Ava's art offers a way of seeing what I could only suggest in a scholarly study. I will always be grateful for the gift of her art, her wisdom and friendship. Years of sharing the murky pleasures of decoding spy thrillers with Jacob Lassner has been one of the great pleasures of thinking, researching and writing this book.

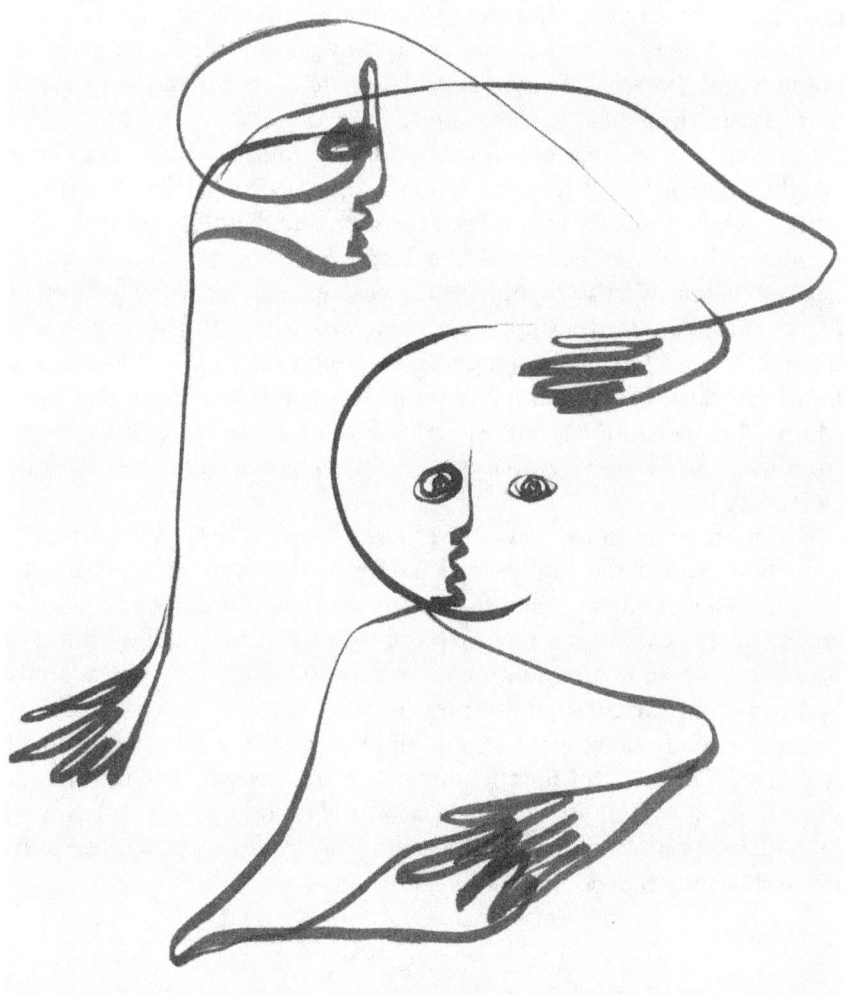

Introduction

Exile – The Heart of the Secret World

On 9 July 2010, the FBI completed an investigation called 'Operation Ghost Stories' and arrested ten Russian spies acting as sleeper agents in the United States.[1] The FBI Illegals Program discovered that these agents were trying to acquire secret intelligence by masquerading as ordinary Americans while socialising with corporate executives, academics and government officials. Newspaper stories highlighted the agents' disguise as middle-class suburban families, upsetting popular images of spies as turbo-driven loners in covert wars against megalomaniac enemies. The 'Ghost' story, with its bizarre but reality-based context, combining familiar tropes of the spy thriller with a defamiliarising political narrative, has been transformed into an acclaimed American TV series, *The Americans*. As I write, the series is going into its fourth season, continuing to entice viewers as the 1980s KGB protagonists/antagonists become ever more sympathetic to viewers, even while committing their dastardly deeds.

One of the series' key surprises is its focus on romantic and family tensions in the protagonists' marriage of political convenience. While casting women in spy thrillers as protagonists and antagonists has become more prominent in recent years,[2] the intensity with which Elizabeth commits her assassinations compared to Philip's increasing doubts calls attention to gender as a category of espionage and exile, and in so doing, unsettles the genre's contrasting representations of masculinity and femininity. With the possibility of returning to Russia an ever-receding promise and premise, the conflicting responses of Elizabeth and Philip Jennings to being Americans heighten their gendered differences as well as the series' suspense. The focus has shifted from the genre's high speed chases to the couple's working and domestic roles and troubled responses to their irrevocable exile. For Elizabeth, exile threatens her devout Russian identity and politics, while for Philip, exile incites his critical questioning. Kader Konuk offers an analytical framework for viewing the place of exile in espionage fiction: 'Exile has typically been analysed not as a site for the contestation of hegemonic identity formations, but as a site for the development of critical consciousness. More so than diaspora, exile has served as an epistemological category, drawing attention to the ways in which knowledge is produced and transformed under exilic conditions' (31). For these Soviet spies in America, as with so many British agents in the fictional field, there can be no diaspora, no reconstruction, adaptation, or construction of a community with shared values, history and customs – no celebratory cosmopolitanism. There is only displacement, conceptual and cultural disorientation, the loss of native languages and cultural traditions.[3] As season three ended, no heroes emerged, begging a critical question of the genre: will the liminal position of the KGB protagonist spies solidify into villainy or victimisation or will exile revise this dichotomy by creating conflicted, complicated spies who have more in common with those created by Eric Ambler and John le Carré than with Jason Bourne and his evil adversaries?

Spy Thrillers and the Question of Political Art

This book will examine the narrative interweave of spy fiction and exile to show how each is a political discourse and critically heuristic perspective that illuminates the other. The pervasive presence of exiled conditions and characters in British spy fictions from the 1930s onwards demonstrates the historical and political importance of spy thrillers to modern literature and to the genre's formalist innovations, as proffered by Clive Bloom: 'In many respects the spy genre like the world it depicts is a form attempting to exist in disguise' (1). As recent scholarship demonstrates, the forms of the genre are being integrated into major literary trends, including modernism and the middlebrow.[4] The interchange of espionage and exile will also refute Michael Denning's claim that although spy fiction is 'one of the most "political" of pop fiction genres', dealing with 'the Empire, fascism, communism, the Cold War, terrorism', its 'political subject is only a pretext to the adventure formulas and the plots of betrayal, disguise, and doubles [. . .]' (2).

Espionage and Exile brings together six British writers of spy fiction whose plots are constituted as Britain's political and ethical relation to Europe and North America from the 1930s through World War II and the Cold War. My rationale for this selection derives from my own reading and film-going experiences, when I began to notice that the figure of the exiled Jew and other refugees kept appearing in the 1930s fictions of Eric Ambler and Pamela Frankau, the 1940s fictions by Helen

MacInnes and Ann Bridge and filmmaker Leslie Howard, and in the Cold War novels by Frankau and John le Carré. Even when these exiled figures were featured as minor characters or killed off early on, they became a significant presence, complicating the genre's conventional plotting by raising political questions about their characterisations and fates. Once I began to investigate this phenomenon, I saw that each of these writers situates exile as a political condition and state of being and identity. Whether enforced or voluntary, exile is endemic to the secret worlds of espionage and to the character of spies.[5] These spy fictions fuse context and content, representing contemporaneous international crises as the foundation of plots, characters, imaginative analysis and polemical positions. The significance of this thematic and structural amalgam is that it overturns Denning's assessment, enters debates about the relationship between the remits of art and political polemics and deploys the genre's conventions to perform as both entertainment and political analysis. Eva Horn argues for the analytical acuity that spy fiction brings to the secret worlds of politics:

> Fiction [. . .] is the most lucid way of shedding light onto the structure of the modern political secret. Since fictions do not, like works of journalism and history, claim to offer the *one* historical truth of an event, they are better suited to analyzing how secrecy functions; they can explore *possible* versions of an event but refrain from settling on an 'ultimate' solution. Fictions illuminate secrecy's structure because they reconstruct its logic, its subtle and mysterious economy of light and dark, truth and lies, presence and absence. (25)

I argue that the writers gathered together in this book expose and critically question the secrets that imperil both citizens and victims of international conflict. In so doing, they create political art that represents, dissects and warns their audiences about the violence inherent to Fascism, Nazism and Communism and the contradictory responses of the liberal democracies.[6] Although this discordance has been studied by historians, its fictional representation adds probing insights from both contemporaneous and retrospective perspectives. In concert, these fictions construct a multivocal form of cultural production that commingles propaganda, popular entertainment and cultural history.

Of course the infusion of political polemics into fiction is not exactly breaking news. The rise of Fascism, Italy's invasion of Abyssinia, the Spanish Civil War, the consolidation of Nazi power, its takeover of the Sudetenland and then the Anschluss drove many British writers in the 1930s to debate the responsibility of their nation and themselves regarding the possibility of another and more horrifying world war.[7] As Janet Montefiore notes, 'The 1930s are remembered, for better or worse, as an intensely political decade' (4). For example, Storm Jameson, Phyllis

Bottome, Rebecca West, Katharine Burdekin and Naomi Mitchison expressed their ambivalences about a war against Fascism and Nazi Germany's conquests.[8] But unlike Vera Brittain, Aldous Huxley and others, when these women confronted the escalating persecutions of Nazism's designated *untermenschen* (subhumans), they felt it necessary to yield their pacifist convictions to rally for the defeat of Germany. Because of this support for the war, their writing did not fit any literary or feminist paradigms that portrayed women as passive victims, war resisters or 'complicit with the power of a masculinist war machine' (Lassner, *British Women*, 4). Instead, these writers are most productively situated within intermodernism, a literary history that affirms the significance of liminal twentieth-century writers who exploit but critique narrative techniques associated with modernism, realism and speculative fiction by foregrounding historical and political analysis.[9]

Debates then and now express the worry that a primary goal of waging World War II was to preserve the British Empire. Absent from discussion are the racialist ideology, laws and practices of the Third Reich, a key concern of this book's authors. Most significantly, my research revealed that drawing attention to the fate of Hitler's victims and linking this to supporting a war effort is highly exceptional among canonical modernists and some literary critics today.[10] Empathy for the persecuted forms a literary, political and ethical bond among the writers studied in this book, but it is exceptional, not only for canonical writers but for conventional spy fictions where cool detachment from political victims is a key rule of the game.

The spy fictions studied here are certainly not the only ones whose narrative focus interweaves espionage and exile as political art. Examples include Graham Greene's 1949 screenplay *The Third Man*, set in immediate post-war Vienna, which dramatises the opportunism and displacement arising from the fertile but unstable grounds created by the detritus of a war-torn Europe. More recently, John Banville's *The Untouchable* explores the gendered meanings of national identity and interests, citizenship and belonging, through a homosexual narrator based on the conflicted loyalties of Anthony Blunt, one of the Cambridge Five. Like those fictions, my selected texts and films offer a range of political approaches to twentieth-century international crises, but foreground exile as the perspective and discourse. My inclusion of unduly neglected women writers shows how the gendered representation of these issues and the voices of women agents make a difference to interpreting states of belonging and dispossession.[11]

A core feature of these writers' political art is its polemical armature, a distinction from modernists who mandated the separation of art and politics. Virginia Woolf began her career by inveighing against realist conventions, which in her view falsely presumed the stability and authenticity of iconographic detail and could therefore depict individuality only superficially, as opposed to exploring the flux of individual consciousness. For other writers, political crisis demanded art that could represent the documented experiences of displacement, incarceration, torture and the threat of state-sponsored murder. As Ambler, MacInnes and Howard assert and Frankau and Bridge strongly suggest, their remit was to alert their British and North American audiences to the imminent threat of Fascism to human rights and national sovereignty in Europe and beyond. The warning would take the form of dystopian espionage fiction.

Graphic depictions of Fascist and Nazi terror do not, however, mean a return to the Georgian style realism so despised by Woolf. For example, Eric Ambler's 1938 novel *Epigraph for a Spy* uses photography to depict the exile's identity as a matter of representation, an image in the eye of the beholder to be interpreted, lacking contextual or corroborating evidence to authenticate its lived reality. Like other writers in this book, Ambler also combines the psychologically inflected style of the Gothic and German Expressionist film to convey the political entrapment faced by the stateless refugee. For example, to convince the French police that the tenuousness of his exiled status can become a useful weapon, Ambler's refugee protagonist in *Epigraph*, Vadassy, becomes a spy and at least for the moment, avoids deportation to his former homeland, Fascist Hungary. The urgent actuality of a refugee's plight leads Ambler to develop a hybrid narrative form that reflects the political psychology of the historical moment. Other writers would create revisionary propaganda art through such techniques as characters' anti-Nazi perorations or the more elliptical method of portraying European cities and London as Expressionist sites of defeat and destruction committed by Nazi and Communist terror. Le Carré's Cold War fiction is infused with personified memories of Nazi Germany's crimes against humanity. His Holocaust perpetrators and survivors appear as embodied memory traces of the Third Reich who infiltrate Britain, having morphed into East German Communists. The memory work of le Carré's novels, like that of Ann Bridge's *A Place to Stand* or Frankau's *Colonel Blessington*, does not serve a mimetic function. Instead these fictions disrupt temporal linearity, points of view and the comforts of plot-driven resolution.

In their polemical forms, these writers also distinguish and relate the journeys of characters into political and ethical consciousness and the narrative's political trajectory. In both instances, the search for ethical politics is never certain as their narratives juggle relationships between espionage as a fictional genre, individual agency and as State driven. The result dramatises the worry that as intelligence gathering becomes an act of witness, it bears responsibility for the fate of individuals who are victimised or villainised by the secret world. Combined with their polemical and propagandist rhetoric, these narratives defamiliarise conventions of espionage, modernist and realist fiction, creating a political art that challenges readers intellectually and politically while entertaining them. Interestingly, by the time bombs destroyed Virginia Woolf's London home, she had shaped her 1943 essay 'Thoughts on Peace in an Air Raid' with mimetic detail to register the need to defeat Nazi Germany.

Charting Exile as a Condition of Espionage Fiction

Even before the Holocaust, enlightened humanism had wavered. Since 1933, the experience of exile had undermined its founding principle, that is the notion of the 'human being', as it had been turned by the Enlightenment into the Kantian 'subject', namely 'the individual'. (Perriaux, 83)

The twentieth century revolutions have set loose unprecedented migration which includes people of every race, every social class, every [. . .] profession: Russian aristocrats, and, more lately, Russian technicians; Italian liberal professors and Austrian socialist workmen; German individualists [. . .] capitalists and anti-capitalists; the flower of the prosperous Jewish bourgeoisie; and inhabitants of the East European half-ghettoes; non-conformists of every race and every social, religious, and political viewpoint. (Thompson, 376)

Exile, I learned very early on, was about telling a story. (Borinsky, 3–4)

Multiple meanings of exile emerge across genres, including memoirs, histories, and theories of exile, studies of artists, political dissidents and intellectuals who fled to Britain and the United States to escape Nazi and Communist oppression. Like its resident Others, the word exile serves so many different interests, from the historically contingent to universal ascription. Eva Hoffman, for example, assigns exile existential meaning, experienced as ejections from 'our first homes and landscapes, from childhood, from our first family romance, from our authentic self' (55). In light of my book's timeline and the centrality of Central Europe from the 1930s through to World War II and the Cold War, it is instructive to begin this discussion with Hannah Arendt's linkage between the Rights of Man, exile and the stateless refugee, which she forged in 1951:

The first loss which the rightless suffered was the loss of their homes, and this meant the loss of the entire social texture into which they were born and in which they established for themselves a distinct place in the world [. . .] What is unprecedented is not the loss of a home but the impossibility of finding a new one. Suddenly, there was no place on earth where migrants could go without the severest restrictions, no country where they would be assimilated, no territory where they could found a new community of their own [...] Nobody had been aware that mankind, for so long a time considered under the image of a family of nations, had reached the stage where whoever was thrown out of one of these tightly organized closed communities found himself thrown out of the family of nations altogether. ('Perplexities', 34)

Arendt's analysis is based on demolition of the right to asylum established in the wake of World War I and the Russian Revolution by the Council of the League of Nations. By the 1930s, not only did European nations withdraw support for refugees, but the United States and Canada refused them entry.[12] Arendt situates the stateless exile in an imprisoning no man's land where there is no negotiation for an acceptable identity.[13] In its absolute stasis, individuality and belonging are crushed. The only possibility for the refugee's rescue is the nation, as Timothy Snyder argues: 'Statehood matters because it ensures that certain paths to survival, though difficult and uncertain, might remain open' (365).[14]

Arendt's analysis is grounded in juridical, philosophical and experiential terms, while Andrea Hammel links the experiences of exile to their literary incarnations, where is a 'tension between exile as reality and exile as metaphorical concept and the gendered aspects of both real and metaphorical displacement [...]' (201). Barbara McCloskey theorises that

> Modernist conceptions of exile tend to emphasize those who are politically persecuted and excluded. [T]hese individuals possess a subjective coherence [...] grounded and fixed in some kind of origin – ethnic, linguistic, national, historical [...] from which they have been driven out, but to which they are irrevocably tied, and from which they ultimately derive their identity. In postmodern thought, however, the exile becomes a favored figure for capturing the condition of the human subject under late capitalism – displaced rather than coherent; dispersed rather than fixed; and rootless and migratory in an increasingly globalized world where technology, communications, travel, and the machinations of capital render the idea of nations and origins more and more obsolete. For the modernist, the exile is the exception; for the postmodernist he or she epitomizes the contemporary human condition. (136–7)

Benjamin Robinson questions this dichotomy by asking whether reading exile writers is a search for 'witnesses to modernity's intrinsic injustice – the injustice for which we moderns are responsible' or should we be viewing this claim as 'ironic and poised for subversion?' (178).[15] Eva Hoffman expresses a related concern about interpretations of exile in warning against 'the idealization of exile – its, so to speak, theoretical seductions', especially postmodern approaches that redefine it 'as somehow interesting, morally heroic, even glamourous' (57).[16]

My study will intervene in these representations by demonstrating that espionage fiction creates a critical relationship between the loss of subjective coherence and universality suffered by the twentieth-century European refugee and the construction of fictional character. The tenuous, alien presence of the exiled, like that of Ambler's Vadassy, Frankau's Philip Meyer, Ann Bridge's Litka Moranska and le Carré's Elsa Fennan, challenges both modernist and postmodern versions of exile, nationhood and subjectivity by reversing each of their above definitions. The novels under consideration form a mélange of 1930s, World War II and Cold War imagined history that reveals the disjunctive, fluctuating sites of exile created by the 'fixed', dominant position of totalitarian nationalism. Framing these exilic conditions, Sophie Perriaux asserts that 'Being free to choose one's own community means consequently that the chosen identity prevails over the received identities' (84). But in the context of Nazi domination, she asks: 'How did the experience of exile question the conception of the individual? By defeating both notions: firstly, the Republic of Letters proved to be largely a myth, and secondly, it became nearly impossible to escape from the identities imposed upon the exiles' (84).

Throughout the elongated timespan of *Espionage and Exile*, the borders of Central European nations are both heavily guarded to assert their sovereignty and threatened with dissolution. In either case, whether the nation becomes aligned with or occupied by Nazi Germany or the Soviet Union, the consequence for the unwanted or dissident throughout the region is an intensified threat to individual subjectivity. In so many cases, individual subjectivity becomes obsolete, not the nation. Enforcing their hegemony, Fascist nations obliterate the exile's cultural origins, reducing native languages and customs to memory traces. The amalgam of exile and spy questions the modernist–postmodern division because each role exacerbates the instability of the other's meaning. Whereas the exile is victimised by 'modernity's intrinsic injustice', being a spy incorporates the profession's intrinsic risks, and so the secret agent cannot be considered a victim. John le Carré, for example, worries that espionage sacrifices the individual by exploiting the rhetoric that declares the principle of doing whatever necessary to protect the nation's citizens. Nowhere are these concerns more evident than in the reflexive portrayals of protagonists and antagonists as spies in exile and exiles in espionage.

Defying the privileged position afforded by the popularity of spy thrillers, the authors studied in this book create agents whose heroism is at best tentative or defeated by ethical compromises, unresolved allegiances, weak resolve and anxieties about enemy forces far more outward looking than their own nation and therefore more purposeful and powerful. Interestingly, unlike James Bond or Jason Bourne, none of the spies featured in these fictions ever became a prototype or generated a series franchise. Le Carré's George Smiley is a prime example. He appears in several novels but is always portrayed differently, easily recognisable in his ill-fitting tweeds but impossible to fathom in his inscrutable, almost uncanny recalibrations.

By definition, spies occupy a position of Otherness, as Erin Carlston notes, 'pass[ing] as something other than what they are', expected 'to lie and deceive, to perform loyalties that they do not actually feel' and in the case of double agents, unknowable and dangerous (4). Hepburn puts it succinctly: 'In effect, a spy belongs nowhere' (11). In the fictions I examine, the displacement and inscrutability of the spy share critical and historical terrain with the exile. Besieged by the distinctive yet overlapping oppressive practices of Fascism, Nazism and Communism, in their efforts to defy and yet mimic official and social codes, spy and exile often seem like secret sharers, uncanny presences within each other – frightening and threatening to others and even to themselves. To become visible as an adopted persona but with undetectable origins, they complicate the figure of the double agent. As Carlston notes about spies, Jews and homosexuals, 'invisible Others passing as the Same, they could act like, and on behalf of, both the "us" within the nation and the "them" outside it' (5). Whether or not the fictions studied in this book borrow elements of historically based characters, their entwined conditions and characterisations of spy and exile are compelled by anxieties about immediate or forthcoming historical crisis.

Of principal concern to this book is how the character of the spy and that of the stateless refugee can converge to highlight the political and historical implications of belonging, national and ideological loyalty. In exile from a nation's sense of unified self, the spy shares contested political and ethical terrain with the refugee, the outsider, the alien and the unprotected, and even with citizenship, cannot be integrated into a national culture. Like the exiled Other, spies are suspect even when their forged identity papers and masquerades bear the stamp of authenticity. It is as though the characters of spies and exiles are inherently disjunctive and displaced. No context, contingency, extenuating circumstance or relationship secures them or generates sympathy within the text. As not so free floating signifiers, they cannot be assigned coherent or stable meaning.

Historical Crisis, Espionage and Exile

The 1930s was crisis ridden. A global economic depression persisted throughout the decade along with mass unemployment. The rise of Fascism exacerbated the refugee crisis that began in 1918 while Soviet Communism and its international vision loomed as both an egalitarian ideal and an ideological and military threat to democracy. As Janet Montefiore proffers, 'the inescapable politicization of European life' meant 'the steady disappearance of ordinary private lives and choices' (147). The dissolution of the Austro-Hungarian Empire resulted in shifting national boundaries that destabilised national identities and citizenship for so many in Central Europe who found themselves exiled in their own or newly established polities, such as Czechoslovakia. The Central European countries in Ambler's 1937 novel *Background to Danger* are all sites of displacement. Lethal competition for oil and other resources exploits the transnational politics of Fascism, obliterating national borders while using nationalism as a weapon against its unwanted Others. Competition for Romania's oil fields makes the nation a pawn of international intrigue.[17] Hungary, a pawn of the Axis powers, expels Ambler's Vadassy and imprisons the Polish refugees who swarm 1941 Budapest in Ann Bridge's 1953 novel *A Place to Stand*. From her postwar perspective, Bridge imbues the city with her memory of the terror that would lead to the Nazi-led deportation of almost all of Hungary's Jewish and Roma population to be gassed in Auschwitz. Nazi Germany, the leader of the Axis, is also shaped by historical memory in the novels of Helen MacInnes and John le Carré. Four years after the passage of the Nuremberg Laws, writing in 1939, Pamela Frankau depicts Nazi Germany's targeted Jewish and disabled victims as central to her plotting. In 1941, MacInnes constructs the medieval city of Nuremberg as a torture chamber for its 1939 Jewish victims, already rendered stateless; without protection, they face expulsion and murder. Le Carré's 1961 novel *Call for the Dead* imagines Jewish Holocaust victims as ghostly avengers who are betrayed and exiled by another despotic ideology and polity, Communism.

This book is structured chronologically, according to the publication dates of each novel. The purpose of each of its four chapters is to demonstrate a trajectory of political anxiety beginning with the spread of Fascism in the 1930s. For many modernists and their critics, the Spanish Civil War is a defining moment of Fascism's threat. Graham Greene's 1936 novel *The Confidential Spy* is its canonical espionage fiction. The writers I study situate the Fascist danger further to the east, where its persecutory intentions emerge. Forming a geographical and political relationship, these writers dramatise Britain's relationship to the fate of Central and Eastern Europe as Fascist governments begin their rule, Nazi Germany plans its conquests and the Soviet Union sends its spies westward to stake out its geo-political role. Eric Ambler's novels of the 1930s create a European landscape infested with an omnivorous offspring of Fascism: Fascist capitalism. Unaligned with any nation state at the time, renegade corporate entities and individuals use all the classic methods of espionage and sabotage to expropriate the natural and human resources necessary to consolidate their power. This chapter sets the agenda for the book by establishing Ambler's fiction of this period as both historical analysis and propaganda, coalescing as the dystopian art of the spy thriller. As his amateur agents return to Britain, they carry stories that warn of dire consequences resulting from ignoring the mutually exploitative relations between Fascist capitalists and governments. His messengers and narrators recount stories of agents and victims who become exiles in a Euroscape where the idea and reality of national boundaries are being crushed and the ensuing political chaos is used as an instrument of terror.

The following chapter, focusing on British women writers of spy fiction, introduces their importance to the genre and World War II literature. These are writers who have been unduly neglected in studies of any twentieth-century fictional genre. Just as women scholars continue to demonstrate the analytical acuity and narrative innovations of women writing middlebrow and crime fiction, so I hope to inspire continued work on those who wrote spy fiction.[18] A major contribution of Helen MacInnes, Pamela Frankau and Ann Bridge is their creation of the woman character as historical subject, spy and exile. Unlike the characterisation of women characters in more conventional spy thrillers as ornamental sidekicks, villainous or dispensable sex objects and a sideshow to the main event, the women characters in this study motivate and activate the plot. Like other British women writers of the 1930s and World War II, their writing and activism represent challenges to extant dichotomies between liberal or left and conservative. In the face of Fascist and Nazi persecution of targeted victims, these women, like others previously mentioned, do not support the war to preserve imperialism in any form or traditional social codes, but because they see the defeat of Fascism and Nazism as an opportunity to progress towards a more egalitarian society. These writers show how the threats of Fascism climax in the emergence of Nazism and its designs for European conquest. Pamela Frankau's 1939 novel *The Devil We Know* charts the political and psychological relationship between antisemitism as an internalised form of persecution and its construction of the Jewish exile. Helen MacInnes narrates the fears and forms of Nazi persecution and its human suffering while Ann Bridge dramatises the terrors being perpetrated by Nazi Germany on the conquered. Like Ambler and Leslie Howard, they become propaganda artists, hoping, as Helen MacInnes would say about non-intervention, 'we've come out of the ether [. . .]' (*AS*, 93).

Chapter 3 examines Leslie Howard's radio broadcasts and two films from 1940 to 1941. Howard came to this work as an avowed propagandist, on behalf of rallying support for Britain's war effort. Working with the Ministry of Information and the BBC, Howard projected his voice to North Americans, deploying his popularity as a Hollywood film star. Combining familiar elements of his screen persona, Howard used his broadcasts to describe the material conditions and responses of Britons to the Blitz and Battle of Britain. Whereas his 1941 film *Pimpernel Smith* employs satire to defang the Nazi higher command and show their vulnerabilities, his role in *49th Parallel*, for which he wrote his part, adopts an angry and more insistent polemic against the myth and ideology of the Master Race. In all these endeavours, Howard includes portraits of Hitler's targeted victims as necessary to the civilisation he envisioned as democratically inclusive and empathetic.

The last chapter studies only two of John le Carré's novels in a career that began in 1961 and is still going strong. I chose *Call for the Dead* and *The Spy Who Came in from the Cold* as the focus because they plot le Carré's continuing concerns about the political and ethical ambivalences of the western democracies as Britain's espionage responses to totalitarian power. Le Carré is not, in any sense, writing propaganda, but these are political novels in which his narrative methods include polemical voices that issue warnings about the ethical risks of espionage in defining and carrying out missions. That he labels British Secret Intelligence a 'Secret World' attests to its position beyond public or media knowledge or even official government scrutiny. Its position and that of its agents is one of political and cultural outlier, metaphorically and institutionally in both voluntary and involuntary exile from ethical codes of loyalty, trust and honesty. A significant consequence of this outsider position is a challenge to reading twentieth-century fiction from the 1930s onwards in which victims and villains can either change places or combine in the historical crises produced by Nazi Germany and Soviet and East German Communism. Men and women characters in all the novels studied in this book share the power of making strategic and ethical choices that change the twentieth-century fictional landscape from narrative adventure to political theatre.

Notes

1. See Charles Savage and Scott Shane, and James Barron.
2. Rosie White observes that by the late twentieth century, female spies feature 'as protagonists and heroes, rather than the marginal love interest or villain [. . .] representing both the power of the individual and the power of the state', p. 3.
3. Anthony Coulson's survey of political and psychoanalytic theories of exile critiques Enlightenment thinking for removing the Other from dominant cultural and political structures, but this could be corrected by sharing the migrant's historically divided situation: strangers to self and other, embarked on a journey between we and they, between memory and hope. As my subsequent chapters will show, refugee and exiled subjects occupy a more complicated relationship to Enlightenment universalism.
4. The literary value of spy fiction has now been firmly established by Allan Hepburn, Erin Carlston, Robert L. Snyder, Michael Denning and Eva Horn.
5. Hepburn argues persuasively that although spies always extend their 'innate human curiosity to realms of political intrigue', their 'identities are historically contingent, not essential categories', p. xiii.
6. Without considering the plotting of actual historical crises, David Seed argues that spy fiction 'veers toward a paranoid vision of violation by outside and inside agencies', p. 115.
7. Wesley Wark notes that 'the real equivalent of early spy fiction's fantasies' was Fascism, p. 5.
8. See my *British Women Writers of World War II* for fuller discussion of these and other women writers.
9. Kristin Bluemel's theory of intermodernism is also important because of its fluidity that allows writers to position themselves among a range of cultural and political categories instead of being incorporated into modernist templates and eliding their distinct modes of writing and concerns.
10. Some modernist scholars have concluded that 'world war shrank [late modernist] writers' horizons [and] curtailed the possibility of literal and imaginative departure – between the late 1930s and late 1940s [with] an anti-humanism emerging from both', Mackay, p. 1601. Jed Esty maintains that canonical modernists turned inward, enclosing cultural agency within 'national or ethnolinguistic borders', pp. 2–3. Such claims are challenged by the British writers in this book and by Phyllis Bottome and Storm Jameson, whose European settings show that imperilled Jewish characters were stuck, not the writers. To his credit, Adam Piette addresses how British wartime propaganda created a vicious cycle of antisemitic justification for neglecting the fate of Europe's Jews, p. 195. Although he argues that victory over Nazism was necessary, he also asserts that the war 'traumatized postwar British culture', particularly writers whose 'private stories worry about being manipulated by propaganda, hardly think about Germany at all, conceive of the war as a drudge and an incomprehensible duty', p. 5. Contrary to the writers in this book and research by Elizabeth Maslen, Mia Spiro, Judy Suh and Alexis Pogorelskin, Piette hopes that 'the literary record will

convince people once and for all that the Second World War was a very great evil for everybody concerned', p. 7.
11. The volume *Women's Writing in Exile* edited by Mary Lynn Broe and Angela Ingram is a model of feminist recovery and explication of women writers' cultural, racial and political exile. It does not, however, include World War II writers or subjects.
12. For documented historical research, see Tony Kushner, *The Holocaust and the Liberal Imagination*.
13. Bernard Schweizer observes that adapting to 'forced exile and voluntary expatriation' entails similar difficulties; like Arendt, many intellectuals 'wrote their best work under conditions of displacement', pp. 392, 394.
14. Timothy Snyder's archival research on Eastern Europe as the site where the Holocaust began, shows that it is necessary to study 'the issue of statehood [as] an absolutely fundamental one', including the consequences in pre-war states being 'destroyed or displaced' and in those that allied with Germany or that were overtaken by the Soviet Union, p. 365.
15. Among other scholars, Linden Peach notes that fictional references to 'modernity' are 'ambivalent' about urban expansion, centralised 'socio-economic power' and 'traditional perspectives', pp. 4, 55.
16. Further complicating these distinctions, Michael Gluzman notes that 'not all Jewish modernists advocated exile or found it intellectually liberating', questioning 'the critical tendency to read modernist practices as essentially antinationalist' (232).
17. For historical background of Central Europe from 1914 to 1945, see Stanley G. Payne.
18. See for example, Erica Brown and Mary Grover, Nicola Humble, Victoria Stewart and Gill Plain.

Chapter 1

Eric Ambler: Espionage Chronicler of the 1930s

In the 1951 'Footnote' to a reprint of his 1938 novel *Epitaph for a Spy*, Eric Ambler affirms the staying power of espionage as an institution and as a story:

> Longer before Moses sent spies into Canaan [. . .] and Joshua's agents were hidden by Rahab in Jericho, the Sumerian rulers of Mesopotamia, who flourished a thousand years or so before the traditional date of Adam, were sending out undercover operators to bedevil their opponents. There seems, in fact, to have been no period in recorded history during which secret agents have not played a part in political and military affairs. (261)

Although this epic history suggests normative statecraft and a popular cultural tradition, Ambler wants no part of either. Instead of aligning his own espionage stories with heroic tales of undercover operations, Ambler's novels of the 1930s 'bedevil' these tales by dramatising the question of how espionage fiction can represent and analyse recorded and undocumented political history. For Ambler, the 'political and military affairs' that shaped this crisis-filled decade exerted pressure on the genre to reject allegorical universalising. Instead he would revise the thriller's conventional forms to situate Britain's responses to the rise of European Fascism as the historically specific but speculative fulcrum of his plots. His method would emphasise the visual, including the mechanisms of photography, the ambiguous materiality of photographs and literary evocations of German Expressionist film.

Debunking the trajectory of his aesthetic influences, Ambler mocks his first efforts at playwriting 'in the manner of Ernst Toller', as having 'nothing to commend it except a plot; and that was probably stolen from another source' (*Here Lies*, 102). Yet his spy novels of the 1930s resound with Toller's mordant German Expressionism.[1] Despite his focus on the historical moment and use of extensive graphic detail, Ambler offers no stylistic gestures towards mimesis or verisimilitude.

His aesthetic choice may be explained in part by his early career as a playwright when he

> was all for thinking of the theatre as a place in which to reveal 'the inner beauty and the meaning of life', [but] I could not bring myself to believe that Gordon Craig's 'total' theatre was going to reveal anything but handsome set designs. I thought that Wedekind and the German Expressionists had the right ideas. I set out to speak with their voices. (*Here Lies*, 102)

In their combination of uncanny refugees, 'the motif of the journey' and dark visions of modernity, Ambler's espionage novels of this period coincide with the concerns and stylistics of Gothic Expressionism (Haltof, 447).

With various narrative permutations, Ambler created literary images of claustrophobic, labyrinthine spaces to represent the present as portending an oppressively uncertain political future. Combining the trope of witness testimony with these images, his 1930s novels examine political and ethical tensions arising from appeasement towards Fascist and Nazi oppression. The question of whether political or military intervention was even possible from 1936, when his first novel was published, is represented by propelling male protagonists, villains and victims into frenetic and often thwarted attempts to cross the contested, militantly guarded borders of Central Europe and the Balkans. Trapped in imprisoning places or on a tour bus, in getaway cars and on foot, Ambler's spies and their ambiguous cultural identities are figured as the places and political plots in which they are embroiled. As a persistent and mutually destabilising combination, this narrative trajectory addresses the question of how to plot the tenuousness of an immediate and combustible history.[2]

Narrating the Mixed Messages of the 1930s

> In most human beings, ideas of spying and being spied upon touch fantasy systems at deep and sensitive levels of the mind. (Eric Ambler, 'Epitaph for an Espione', np)

Ambler's preface to the 1990 reprint of his 1936 novel *The Dark Frontier* maintains that he was exploiting 'the old secret service thriller as written by E. Phillips Oppenheim, John Buchan, Dornford Yates and their crude imitators; and I meant to do it by placing some of their antique fantasies in the context of a contemporary reality' (xvi).[3] The narrative construction and negotiated meanings of this context become especially significant as the identities, allegiances and motivations of Ambler's spies become increasingly entangled or unravel under the pressure of seeking the information and safety that will remain elusive beyond the novels' endings. In contrast to the clearly marked road signs that lead readers through the vertiginous rides of earlier espionage fiction, Ambler's novels provide neither clues nor explanatory bridges as guides through disjointed labyrinths. Rather than satisfy the stressful search for knowledge, these novels suspend solutions and present the fate of modern Europe as a threatening global problem and a challenge to a genre known for its gift-wrapped resolutions. Ambler's 1939 novel *The Mask of Dimitrios* notes the comforting conventions of the genre: 'the menace across the frontier is a typical phrase' (*A Coffin*, 166). A 'typical phrase' indicates the outworn portrait of a generic enemy territory.

Elizabeth Maslen analyses the historical background that so concerns Ambler as Britain's ambivalence toward Europe: 'there were powerful voices in favor of fascism in the early thirties, some equating it with Russian communism, some uneasy' ('Military Tales', 4). By 1936 'mixed messages' abounded in Britain: 'pacifism, pro-and anti-fascism – as well as the vacillating attitudes of the Communist Party and popular front as they responded to changes in Soviet policy' ('Military Tales', 9). In their multi-faceted uncertainties, Ambler's novels depict British debates about the nation's role in the fate of Europe and impassioned warnings about the attractions and dangers of Fascism. Although Fascism lost its appeal in Britain once Hitler's expansionist plans and persecutions were reported widely, these dangers did not rally either official or popular opinion on behalf of Hitler's victims. In addition to indifference and antisemitism, the legacy of World War I's catastrophic losses produced an active pacifism that was a constant reminder of the costs of meddling in Europe's self-destructive conflicts.

Ambler's depictions of anxious travels, confusing incidents, identities, national interests and testimony dramatise the shifting political perspectives that represented the increasingly unsettling decade.[4] Brett Woods summarises Ambler's turn to the spy novel where

> he found the ability to encompass international action and topical themes, such as the economic conflict between capitalism and socialism, and the political battles between the Right and the Left. It could, therefore, transcend contemporary closed-world, middle class biases and engage the major political issues of the day. (np)

Ambler's autobiography records his sense of urgency:

> The year was 1936, the year in which Italy invaded Abyssinia, Civil War broke out in Spain and Hitler ordered the German Army to reoccupy the Rhineland. It was a year of yet more refugees and of marriages arranged to

confer passports. It was also the year in which the League of Nations was at last seen plainly to be impotent. (*Here Lies*, 124)

Ambler fictionalises his critique of political impotence into a panoply of stateless refugees, false papers and identities as well as interplays between passive, indifferent and autocratic governmental or corporate powers. In his 1937 novel *Background to Danger*, where the narrator warns against this precarious Euroscape of 'Fascism in Italy, National-Socialism in Germany, the Croix de Feu in France, Rexism in Belgium, and Nationalism in Spain', tensions between the Soviet Union and Germany over claims for crucial energy resources and exploitation of the powerless threaten to explode (*BD*, 132).

At the moment of this spy thriller's publication, when the Spanish republicans are being defeated by Nazi support for Franco's legions, and many writers and intellectuals see the Soviet Union as the only bulwark against a Fascist takeover of Europe, Ambler's political position is hesitant. Recalling his politics in the late 1930s, he told interviewer Joel Hopkins: 'I suppose theoretically I was a socialist. Anyway, I was certainly anti-fascist, but that was an easy thing to be. Anybody can be anti-fascist. It's being pro something that's difficult' (Hopkins, 287).[5] His hesitancy here responds to the passive responses to Fascism that he found so troubling and to his own ambivalence about Communism as an alternative political ideology and system.

Ambler is definitive, however, about how to transform both his anti-fascist stance and hesitancy into a politicised model of characterisation. From his first novel, this would mean abandoning the thriller's standard fare:

> It was the villains who bothered me most. Power-crazed or coldly sane, master criminals or old-fashioned professional devils, I no longer believed a word of them. Nor did I believe in their passions for evil and plots against civilization. As for their world conspiracies, they appeared to me no more substantial than toy balloons, over-inflated and squeaky to the touch, with sad old characters rattling about inside like dried peas. The hero did not seem to matter much. He was often only a fugitive, a hare to the villain's hounds, prepared in the end to turn pluckily and face his pursuers. He could be a tweedy fellow with [. . .] gun pads on both shoulders or a moneyed dandy with a taste for adventure. He could also be a xenophobic ex-officer with a nasty anti-Semitic streak. None of that really mattered. All he really needed to function as hero was abysmal stupidity combined with superhuman resourcefulness and unbreakable knuckle bones. (*Here Lies*, 120–1)[6]

Ambler's fiction recoils from the qualities listed above. In contrast to straw villains, his novels feature antagonists who possess considerable intelligence and historically documented goals. Applying their talents strategically from within serpentine corporate structures, Ambler's moguls and their agents intervene in international politics for capital gain. As Michael Denning notes, Ambler's protagonists participate in this 'figuration of fascism and capitalism' as 'a class of professionals and managers, engineers and technicians. It is a class which is in many ways the hired guns of capital' and also constituted 'the readership of these "serious", "literate" thrillers [. . .]' (78–9).

In Ambler's fiction of the 1930s the consequences of Fascist and capitalist manipulations will threaten international instability and even war, but the villains' passion for power is less concerned with global *coups d'état* and star wars than with global exploitations for profits. The politics of combining Fascist oppression with free range capitalism suggests the term 'fascist capitalism', fusing politics and economics that constitutes their method and goal and eschewing the more formulaic megalomaniac villains of earlier spy fictions by William Le Queux and E. Phillips Oppenheim.[7] In Ambler's novels, the success of fascist capitalism relies on the muscular promise of economic triumph over the impotent will of the Western democracies. To assert his anti-fascist convictions, Ambler confronts the conventions that confuse action with heroism in so many spy novels. Instead of '"heroes dressed in black shirts [who] went around beating up Bolsheviks and Jews, all with the total approval of the author I decided to turn things round"' (qtd in Oram, 6). In narrative rebuttals to Fascism and the passive complicity that enabled its expansion, Ambler transfigured the genre's oppositions between enemies and saviours. As Michael Denning asserts, 'the anti-fascism of the thriller [reverses] the earlier codings of heroes and villains' (65). Ambler's novels of this darkening decade reveal a trajectory of narrative investigations that created the vexed role of bystander or spectator whose uncommitted position threatens to become complicit with fascistic practices. In this fashion, agents could be both protagonist and antagonist.

In his introduction to a 1943 omnibus edition of four Ambler novels, Alfred Hitchcock highlighted the 'material of reality' that distinguished the author from his predecessors:

> His heroes are anything but heroic, nor are they startlingly wise, or even daring. They are ordinary, rather pleasant people [. . .] who want to stay out of trouble and live comfortably [. . .] In only one of these four novels does the hero *do* anything; in others, things are done to him. [Ambler's villains] are not only real people, they are actually the kind of people who have generated violence and evil in the Europe of our time. (qtd in Kingra, np.)

A key measure of Ambler's revisionary realism or speculative dystopias is his personification of the immediate political contexts in which his novels of the 1930s are set. Constituted as a tumultuous Europe, with dangerously unstable borders and regimes, these settings are far distant from a mythic little England or even, as represented by John Buchan, a wish-fulfilling united Great Britain. Addressing a political reality that British officialdom would resist throughout the decade, Ambler's European settings become vibrant players in themselves. A combination of political analysis and Expressionist character, Central Europe is figured as villainy and victimisation in concert and in conflict. To highlight the threat of this political and ethical disorientation, Ambler exploits the gritty realism so often associated with espionage fiction, only to transform it with an Expressionist method that portrays Central European Fascism as palpably monstrous and ineffably expansive. Ambler's Europe becomes not only the site of villainy, but the progenitor and perpetrator of international conflict. In so doing, his visual method fuses Expressionist and Gothic tropes to represent the unappeasable malevolence of Fascism and Nazism.

Ambler's Gothic Expressionism

I have no character, I am a fantasist. (Ambler, qtd in Amory, 30)

The word 'thriller' [...] converts from a comparatively inoffensive noun into a blunderbuss term of abuse. Lumped together with detective and crime novels and there in the field of fire will be the neo-Gothic romance, vampire horror tales, black-magic, pornography. (Ambler, 'A Better Sort of Rubbish', 1, 7)

The eyes of the victims of the post-war world might be said to stare through German expressionist art. (Spender, *The God that Failed*, 234)

Ambler's personification of ominous Fascist spaces coincides in method and motivation with the German Expressionist films produced during 'the political disarray' of the Weimar period (Turner, 148). As Graeme Turner observes, such Expressionist filmmakers as Fritz Lang 'employed low-key lighting, geometric shapes, oblique camera angles, and sharp juxtapositions of light and dark' to depict the 'essence' of an object, situation or state of being (149). Although these films did not foreground the erosion of Weimar attempts at democracy and the rise of Nazism, politics are embedded 'in the narrative structure and images, myths, conventions, and visual styles, in melodramatic stories and Gothic images' (149). 'The films produced in Germany during those years captured the cry of a broken nation and a people horrified by the every-day' (151). German Expressionist film evokes mystery, alienation, disharmony, hallucination and destabilisation, lending confusion to distinctions between the real and the dream. Sets are stylised, with sharply angled street images representing the outdoors as a lost and forgotten space, closed in and imprisoning, while extreme camera angles suggest interminable surveillance of all spaces. The point of view resulting from this cinematography is paranoid and obsessed, foretelling irrevocable doom.

Ambler's Gothic Expressionism differs from modernist and earlier Gothic concerns with fractured subjectivity as an existential response to modernity's destabilising transformations. Instead his novels dramatise a polemical call to feel anxiety as a precursor to political activism. From his first novel through to the last of the decade, hallucinatory scenes of an atomic laboratory, labyrinthine buildings, claustrophobic open spaces and indeterminate images register the need to fear an unprecedented threat by the unstoppable and brutally oppressive realities of Fascism. Thomas Elsaesser's discussion of Expressionist space, as blurring conventional demarcations between detective and spy films delineates its political inferences. His reference to 'a conspiracy thriller' includes elements of German Expressionism that intersect in Ambler's 1930s spy fiction: 'contiguous, separate or overlapping action spaces, the generation of suspense, and the uneven distribution of knowledge' (90). Elsaesser sees such space as representing a bourgeois crisis in which 'agency is make believe, causality becomes role-play, and action becomes reaction' (96).

Like the Expressionist films Turner and Elsaesser discuss and the emotional extremes and sinister spaces of the Gothic aesthetic, Ambler's graphic images of ominous physical space represent false or misleading clues – epistemological dead ends. Such spaces are disorienting, leading only to partial or generalised explanations of the dread that pervades all of Central Europe as it is being choked by fascistic forces operating within accepted forms of capitalism. Yet as Elaesser explains,

> a climate of lawlessness and violence [suggests] more than monetary inflation, the disintegration of values, and pervasive cynicism. Each situation or encounter demands dissimulation and disguise, everyone operates by means of messenger and messages, uses corrupt sellers, and engages middlemen to produce effects, all this in the absence or ignorance of its (real) causes. (96)

The thrills, chills and chases of Ambler's spy fiction are not diluted by his political and epistemological concerns with the historical moment. Instead, his novels' suspense and political arguments gain narrative power through their dramatic interweaves of undetectable fascist capitalist plots that entrap protagonists, witnesses and villains. Marlow, the narrator protagonist in *Cause for Alarm*, uses Gothic Expressionist tropes to explain how fascistic greed has blurred national boundaries to create a global dystopia:

> It used to be the custom to commemorate moments of national humiliation or disaster by applying the adjective 'black' to the day of the week concerned. The pages of European history are, so to speak, bespattered with the records of Black Mondays and Black Thursdays. It may be that, in this twentieth century, almost daily acquaintance with large-scale catastrophe has deprived the custom of its point. Black and white have tended to merge into a drab grey. (CA, 47)

Circuitous train journeys, undulating streets, buildings and rooms and dank, blind and twisted passageways signify the autocratic politics of fascistic greed, the flaccid politics of confused, drifting and paralysed national perspectives as well as political ignorance and indifference. The marriage of political and epistemological impotence and uncertainty generates only unrelieved tension, depicted as his male protagonists are continuously crossing borders to confront danger on all sides and becoming ensnared in physical, political and metaphorical mazes.

That every side of every unstable border leads to heightened danger marks these novels as speculative dystopias, warnings about increasingly bad times that question their own epistemological grounding and investigative methods.[8] As Thomas Elsaesser notes, German Expressionist film 'highlights the strategic role of the detective film', as in *The Cabinet of Dr Caligari* (1919), where 'a multi-stranded narrative, sustained by mutually interdependent sources of knowledge, is woven around a detective plot'.[9] Infused with confusion emanating from mutually destabilising knowledge, shadowy settings, unknowable or mistaken identities and monstrous masculinity, Ambler's Gothic Expressionism reflects his concerns with the disorienting integration of political and economic oppression into conventional moral pieties and plots.

Linking observations of Europe's tumultuous present with dystopian warnings constructs a political and ethical indictment of appeasing Fascism. Because these speculative dystopias caution readers about a Fascist present and future but do not create a causal trajectory emanating from the past, their analysis would not be considered teleological according to Anton Kaes' definition. Kaes criticises Siegfried Kracauer's view of Weimar Expressionist cinema as teleological because it predicted a future that could not be known in the 1920s, a future suffocated by the inconceivable horrors of the Nazis' Final Solution. Kaes argues that the serial killers, undead and suffocating spaces of Weimar cinema are inspired by the horrors and after-effects of trench warfare in World War I. Whereas Weimar filmmakers dramatised the lingering effects of soldiers' traumatic, emasculating wounds and Germany's memory of the immediate past, a decade later Ambler responds to the threatening consolidation of European Fascist power as it was emerging from the political and economic instability that marked post World War I Europe. From Mussolini's Italy to Nazi Germany and across Central Europe and the Balkans, he depicts the oppression resulting from dictators filling the power vacuums left by transitions from imperial rule to yearnings for democracy. Reading political signs that so many would ignore or rationalise, such as the 1935 Nuremberg Laws, Hitler's 1936 occupation of the Rhineland and the Czech crisis, Ambler takes stock of unfolding events and warns his readers to recognise Fascism's enveloping dangers.[10] His novels encapsulate these dangers by representing them in metaphorical extremis as overpowering, explosive spaces and as spectral characters, all of which encodes the villainy of Fascism and its victims.

The conceptual discord between disguised and overdetermined images of absent or ambiguous causes leads Ambler to combine his Gothic Expressionism with another visual medium. Thus he merges indeterminacy and irresolution with the epistemological ambiguities produced by photography. In almost all of his novels of the 1930s, cameras, photographs and the uncertain meanings of visual images are central to the questions of political intrigue, identity, evidence and unsettled conclusions. Cameras construct Ambler's Gothic Expressionist space by calling attention to its framed artificiality as congruent with his multifaceted meanings of betrayal. Susan Sontag analyses how viewing photographs as narratives is an inherently unstable process, betraying any expectation of capturing the reality of their subjects: 'A photograph is only a fragment, and with the passage of time its moorings come unstuck. It drifts away into soft abstract pastness, open to any kind of reading (or matching to other photographs)' (71). Yet for Ambler, the photographic image intervenes in the process of intelligence gathering as it only reinforces the duplicity of information. The word 'intelligence' becomes an oxymoron; rarely do secret missions yield any useful information, in effect casting doubt on the viability of espionage and counterespionage, as well as the ratiocinative powers of those thrust into international intrigue.

Like prototypical spies, Ambler's protagonists are often set up for betrayal, not simply by human duplicity or treacherous spaces, but by the very idea that they can rescue themselves and their nation through investigation and discovery of the source of danger. Whatever realism is promised in grim and gritty detail is betrayed by the presumption that by dint of their experience and insight, spies and readers can decipher a plot's dissimulation. In his review of John le Carré's 1965 novel *The Looking Glass War*, Ambler comments that while the average reader has little means of assessing the 'level of realism' in spy fiction, 'they do expect secret service operations to be carried out with a reasonable display of cunning, foresight and professional expertise. A little bungling is acceptable – supermen are uninteresting – but only a little, and it must be the bungling of able men, not of the stupid and inept' (8). All of Ambler's accidental, professional or involuntary spies lose control over their lives, overwhelmed as they are thrust into the web of European 'political and military affairs'. This adventure offers no promise of satisfaction or release. Betrayed by national and corporate intrigue, the spy's self-determination is lost. Whether he is a refugee like Vadassy in *Epitaph for a Spy* or a multicultural Englishman like Kenton in *Background to Danger*, the British writer Latimer in *The Mask of Dimitrios* or Marlow, the British engineer in *Cause for Alarm*, Ambler's accidental spies reside in epistemological, political and existential exile. Even if the race for self-reclamation seems to parallel the suspended hope of triumph over Fascism, this is an open and suspect possibility. Ambler's interweave of identity construction, espionage, exile and the treachery of deluded national self-interest allows each of these categories to provide a critical gloss on the other.

Expressionist Exile

As all of Ambler's novels of the period show, the condition of the refugee, the alien, afflicts all his male characters, protagonists and antagonists, villains and victims.[11] All are disposable, strangers whose unsettled personae convey a sinister threat wherever they travel. Stripped of a definitive masculinity, they also represent an increasingly threatening question as the 1930s bleeds into the 1940s: who deserves to be designated human? Ambler's men embody a liminal status of being, between creature and character; they are both empowered and powerless. Even when their intentions are benign, most have been plunged into circumstances that unhinge their identities and as a result become suspect, whether their motives are to investigate, to find respite or employment or to manipulate. The innocent but stateless Hungarian, Vadassy, in *Epitaph for a Spy*, is an easy object of suspicion and pawn in a counter-espionage plot because his identity papers reflect the shifting borders of his national origins and are therefore questionable, his ambitions indefinite. He is radically alone, with no family, friend or lover. Even British subjects abroad are treated like refugees. In *Cause for Alarm*, barely has the protagonist Marlow arrived in Milan to begin his legally sanctioned job when the police take his passport and like the stateless Vadassy, he must report weekly to them. In both *Background to Danger* and *Cause for Alarm* the Russian agent Zaleshoff has no home. His orders emanate from Russia but do not endow him with any power. He may be savvier than Kenton, the hapless protagonist, but he is just as vulnerable against the forces of Fascism. Like Elizabeth and Philip Jennings in *The Americans*, both Zaleshoff and his sister sidekick Tamara remain in a perpetual state of espionage, never to return to Russia. For these Soviet agents, being on the move removes them from any generic satisfaction, either romance or sexual plotting.

Along with exile, at the heart of Ambler's revisionary narrative is a sustained critique of the xenophobia he disparages in prototypical heroes. An essentialising suspicion of threatening alterity victimises so many of his male characters but also empowers his villains. Antagonists are frequently mercenaries with no national identity, interests or loyalty, but unlike many of their victims, this is a choice. Mailler, in *Background to Danger*, is a former Black and Tan officer who we can assume finely tuned his sadism while brutalising Irish rebels, innocent women and children during the Troubles, but has no singular political allegiance. Saridza, his handler, is a stranger everywhere, serving the interests of the highest bidder. Their mastermind, Balterghen, thought to be of Bulgarian origin, is corporate chief of an oil cartel based in London, who expands his resources by creating geo-political destabilisation. The masculinity of these villains is defined with one characteristic: portable brutality.

Marukakis, the Marxist journalist in *The Mask of Dimitrios*, interprets this brutality as emanating from the ideology and machinations of a ruthless Darwinian economics, materialising in Expressionist form as the villain Dimitrios:

> For him there is no other nexus between man and man than naked self-interest. He believes in the survival of the fittest and the gospel of tooth and claw because he makes money by seeing that the weak die before they can become strong and that the law of the jungle remains the governing force in the affairs of the world. And he is all about us. Every city in the world knows him. He exists because big business, his master, needs him. International big business may conduct its operations with scraps of paper, but the ink it uses is human *blood!* (81)

As a weapon of choice, *blood* also suggests a resemblance between Dimitrios, the elusive menace who leaves his lethal mark everywhere and on everyone he encounters, and Dracula, the predatory vampire of Gothic lore. No futurist fantasy, this use of Gothic Expressionist tropes constructs a dystopian vision of the present political reality. If, as Andrew Smith argues, the Gothic 'substantively refer[s] to a world of horror', Ambler visualises it as his political analysis ('Rethinking',

84). Ambler's vampire represents the horrific embodiment of a parasitic, fascistic drive in the inter-war period that sucks the blood of nations, threatening them with infectious addictions to destructive power.[12] Relentlessly on the move, seeking new blood for his own survival, the vampire is also a creature in perennial and boundless exile while insinuating himself everywhere. His Transylvanian origins, in a claustrophobic, isolated Gothic castle, are out of time and place, lacking affiliation with community or national culture or interest in the authority they might endow. In Ambler's interpretation, this site represents the Fascist force exploding the internecine conflicts of Central Europe. The vampire is the logical heir to Central Europe's legacy and promise of unbounded violence.

A stateless being, like Dimitrios, the vampire embodies the dominant perception of the refugee or stranger as an ominous, omnivorous invader, an alien wherever he appears. But Ambler's vampire is not a victim of xenophobia; he is its Fascist incarnation. His indeterminacy also extends to the gendered nature of his being. Because his targeted sources of regenerative blood are women, and because men are supposed to be women's protectors, Dracula's defeat of men emasculates them. With this sexualised domination of men and women, the vampire's powers defy heteronormative distinctions and boundaries.[13] And yet because displacement is a state of deprivation, without nurture or support, it is also enervating – life denying. Despite the vampire's blood transfusions, despite the threat he represents, he remains in an unmanned, unearthly stasis; he is the ungendered undead. And so the last we see of Dimitrios resides in shadows, his last resort before he and his nemesis destroy each other and fascist capitalism implodes.

Ambler challenges the tradition that individual action can confront and destroy the Fascist nemesis. With the exception of the parodied superhero, Conway Carruthers in *The Dark Frontier*, there are no heroes in Ambler's fiction. His protagonists are amateur agents who through errors of judgment or fatal curiosity find that their intelligence is a primitive tool when confronted with Machiavellian enterprise and their alien own status within and beyond Britain. Their resourcefulness grows as plots thicken, but never approaches superhuman strength or even political agency. As with Graham Greene's Rollo Martins in his 1950 novella *The Third Man* or Charlie in John le Carré's 1983 novel *The Little Drummer Girl*, theirs is not a mythical journey into knowledge, wisdom or maturity. Instead, they confront the challenges of developing political knowledge or, as with Latimer in *The Mask of Dimitrios*, their masculinity is mocked for retreating into apolitical fantasy. Although some protagonists are British, they do not represent a unified or assertive face of Britain but rather critically constructed facets of prototypical British superspies and strands of political debate and confusion. That this confusion reflects a crisis of national purpose, stability and control is apparent in the absence of the British government, including its security sectors. In the only case among Ambler's novels of the 1930s where a British location appears, it is Wolverhampton in *Cause for Alarm*, a Midlands industrial city whose Spartacus Machine Tool Company supplies the Italian Fascist government with machinery that assembles munitions. Instead of signalling economic success or the rebellious heroism suggested by its name, it is figured as 'a dingy, sprawling collection of buildings at the end of a long and very muddy road' (*CA*, 19). Given the lack of interference from British authorities, this abject appearance does not signify guilt or shame about the company's opportunistic collaboration with Mussolini's Italy. Indeed, the aptly named Spartacus Company is not the least bit interested in freeing itself from self-serving enslavement with fascist capitalism. Nonetheless, the overall impression of Britain's economic politics in this novel is one of depression, especially since Marlow, the engineer protagonist, is introduced as indistinguishable from the hordes of unemployed. Britain in these novels signifies a dystopian warning about using Fascism as an economic aid while waiting passively, in a state of political suspension, for Europe to implode.

With a hybrid identity and gambling habit, Desmond d'Esterre Kenton, the protagonist in *Background to Danger*, mocks the notion of a stable homogeneous Britain standing resolute against feckless Europe. Whatever their origins, all of Ambler's protagonists find themselves caught in the oppressive circumstances of threatening European places that render them undesirables. In all cases, their interventions produce or exacerbate the very danger they seek to escape or eradicate. Ambler's amateur agents find that their escapes and searches for knowledge energise the vampiric undead which lie, only seemingly inert, in wait for them. Conversely, the pursuit of knowledge and solutions takes the agent all too close to a state of complicity so that whether by design, in ignorance or innocence, the protagonist's quest is responsible for revitalising the villain's evil, as in Latimer's search for Dimitrios or Barstow's search for atomic plans. The epistemology of Ambler's thriller is therefore neither objective nor empirical; nor does it reveal any truths or solutions. It is an impassioned warning about the British writer's responsibility for the investigative and persuasive work of the imagination in a decade riddled with political and economic crisis.

Dark Parody

Ambler identified his first novel of the 1930s, *The Dark Frontier*, as a parody of all he deplored about pot-boiler spy plots, villains and heroes: 'I had set out to upgrade the thriller genre [. . .] by doing a parody of secret agents who never fail. But I got swept up in it' (qtd in Wolfe, 32). A sure sign of the novel's parody is the identity of the alter-ego of the physicist protagonist Prof. Henry Barstow: superspy Conway Carruthers, star of Erskine Childers' 1903 novel, *The Riddle of the Sands*. Typical of the genre, in *The Dark Frontier*, the world's fate is threatened by a mastermind villain in league with an autocratic ruler and corporate greed. Based on his engineering background, Ambler imagines the key weapon of mass destruction as an atomic bomb being developed by a mad physicist in the seemingly inconsequential Balkan state of Ixania which he parodies by referring to it as 'Ruritania', the Transylvanian home of Dracula, werewolves and the chocolate soldier (*Here Lies*, 121).[14] The triple dose of instability characterised by the monomaniacal scientist and Ixania's potential for global economic blackmail and physical destruction suggests the explosive union of Fascism, rogue capitalism and the disintegration of Central Europe. Ambler later recalled that 'In 1935 [. . .] my solemn nightmare of Fascist plotters in a Balkan state using atomic blackmail to dominate the world was flawed by my ignorance. If I had known a little more I might have written a science fiction novel of some consequence' (*Here Lies*, 121). Despite Ambler's self-mockery, this is a novel of 'some consequence', using parody to explore how conventions of spy fiction and German Expressionist film can be adapted to express a political warning.

The plot is propelled by a car accident in which mild-mannered Professor Barstow suffers a concussion, the effect of which we are led to assume produces the onset of amnesia from which emerges his transformation into the swashbuckling Carruthers. Parodying scientific verification of this mental jolt, the novel's Epilogue presents a case study of 'dual personality' from the papers of C. G. Jung, thus explaining this metamorphosis as a psychological phenomenon (*DF*, 253). In his autobiography, Ambler mocks his inclusion of this treatise by admitting that using Jung as his 'psychiatric authority [and] play[ing] dual-personality games with the hero [. . .] was plain cheating. The "Carruthers" half of the personality was a parody hero [. . .] making fun both of him and of the early E. Phillips Oppenheim kind of thriller [. . .]' (*Here Lies*, 121). Indeed, both Barstow and Carruthers are caricatures of hyper-masculine heroes. Carruthers mocks the superhero while Barstow is the quintessential ivory tower professor, a prototypical figure of fun in Leslie Howard's 1941 espionage film *Pimpernel Smith*.

Unlike the protagonists' divided psychologies or oppositions between protagonists and antagonists in earlier spy thrillers, Carruthers/Barstow does not signal duality, for each of these twinned protagonists embraces qualities of the other. The narrator tells us that after reading a Carruthers novel, 'Barstow the mathematician had no use for Barstow the romantic. Yet, in some men the romantic vision never fades' (*DF*, 28). Likewise, Carruthers is both the 'paragon' of pragmatic 'competence' and an idealist (*DF*, 28). As Peter Wolfe observes, these characters blend into each other by orchestrating 'the action after suffering concussions', a narrative design that includes repeating the characters' initials in the name of the arms dealer firm, Cator and Bliss (Wolfe, 34–5). As complicated as it may be to dissect these transmuted polarities, this depiction is no tribute to the characters' binary complexity. Instead, Ambler's portrayal of Barstow/Carruthers suggests a narrative fluidity in which each man's dualities absorb the other's, obfuscating definitive or caricatured masculine typologies. The narrative effect paradoxically renders Barstow and Carruthers as both indeterminate and iconic parodies of themselves and each other. Since each of them subsumes the other's character, there is no individual to examine or understand through psychological models. There is only a representation of one character's transposition into another, owing no debt to mimetic characterisation in any social or psychological sense.

In addition to the mirroring images of Barstow/Carruthers, the novel multiplies the narrative meanings of doubling by featuring photographic imagery as a method through which to explore literary and historical indeterminacy in the form of political warning.[15] The very first page of *The Dark Frontier* conflates narrative and image to raise questions about their epistemological relationship. Barstow recounts the following retrospectively:

> The events in this book comprise, I am told, an account of my life during the period April 17th to May 26th of last year.
> This I am unable either to confirm or to deny. I have been shown a photograph, taken by a press photographer and forwarded by the British Consul in Ixania, in which a person resembling myself can be seen alighting from a large car [. . .] in Zovgorod. Unfortunately, a portion of the face is obscured by the body of a soldier who had moved across the lens of the camera. In any case, my features are cast in a mould too commonplace for me to accept the photograph as proof of my presence in that picturesque city. (*DF*, 1)

That Barstow's voice represents himself as a serious, self-conscious critic of representation is confirmed by the page heading, an endorsement of his narrative's integrity and gravitas: 'Statement of Professor H.J. Barstow, F.R.S., Physicist of Imperial College, University of London'. Purveying his sceptical, empirical approach, the physicist proffers the uncertainty produced by narration. All of the material and human subjects in this passage are destabilised by being refracted through the lens of the camera, which in turn is mediated by the photographer's chosen or accidental perspective. The 'obscured' photographic image that reduces Barstow's individuality to a generic 'face' and that flattens it into an abstract image leaves us uncertain about Barstow's/Carruthers' appearance and whether it becomes indefinable as a result of their fused characters. In tandem with this representational ambiguity, photography is also used as a disguise in this novel. Carruthers decides that pretending to be an 'amateur photographer' armed with a camera, he could spy on the suspicious agent of Cator and Bliss – Groom (*DF*, 81).

Bernd Hüppauf argues 'that while they do not lie, photographs do not tell the truth either. Rather, they have to be seen as elements of a highly complex process into which both photographic techniques and the concept of reality have been dissolved' (95). Susan Sontag observes that even captions cannot authenticate photographs:

> Captions do tend to override the evidence of our eyes; but no caption can permanently restrict or secure a picture's meaning [. . .] The caption is the missing voice, and it is expected to speak for truth. But even an entirely accurate caption is only one interpretation, necessarily a limiting one, of the photograph to which it is attached. And the caption-glove slips on and off so easily. (108–9)

Because photographs cannot narrate themselves, they require intervention to lead the viewer. Any guide, however, can be equally misleading: 'Photographs, which cannot themselves explain anything, are inexhaustible invitations to deduction, speculation, and fantasy [. . .]' (Sontag, 23). Throughout Ambler's 1930s novels, photographs signify the suspicious nature of intelligence gathering. In *Cause for Alarm*, a passport photo of General Vagas, a Fascist agent, turns out to be 'a photostat of a photograph taken some years before', an image of an image that in its dual temporality, represents the conundrum of deciphering his multiple identities and allegiances and thereby the shifting, duplicitous alliances of Fascist Europe (*CA*, 121). Just as Vagas exploits his usefulness to both Germany and Italy, so the two nations 'swore eternal friendship [and] agreed to present a united front to the Western powers' while manoeuvring against each other (*CA*, 123). After first viewing the photograph, the protagonist Marlow dreams he is being smothered 'with huge stacks of photographs' (*CA*, 65). As Sontag remarks, 'Strictly speaking, one never understands anything from a photograph [. . .] Only that which narrates can make us understand' (23). Because the photographs in Ambler's novels are represented as written narratives, not as graphic images, it is as though they become their own captions and therefore question the heuristic value of both image and interpretation.

The critical implications of the photograph and Barstow's description in *The Dark Frontier* recall another physicist's theory – Heisenberg's Theory of Uncertainty. All of the novel's events, objects and characters are constantly in motion and subject to a variety of definitions, descriptions and interpretation as rendered by the various perspectives of viewers and participants. In combination, the constitution and value of these narrative elements shift according to who is describing or presenting it and with what purpose for the character and plot. For example, the perspective and voice in the novel's latter sections shift to the journalist Casey's narrative which, Barstow ingenuously confides, 'has, I feel, a ring of truth about it; but I would warn the reader, as I warned myself, that journalists are inclined to let imagination run to self-deception' (*DF*, 4). Whatever we think of the self-proclaimed ideal of the objective journalist, Barstow intervenes critically. Performing his own imaginative construction as well as that of Carruthers, he instructs us to read this novel as structured like a hall of mirrors, where self-reflections recede into successions of infinitely fused, undifferentiated and dissolving images. In Casey's assessment of Carruthers as 'the ham lead of a third-rate stock company playing the Englishman in a bum crook melodrama', verisimilitude regresses into self-reflecting parody (*DF*, 177). Casey's slang is telling. In addition to the double dose of mockery in his assessment of the Carruthers cartoon, his voice parodies American pulp fiction, reminding us of both genres' self-parody of tough masculinity.

The novel's indeterminate representation of photography also reflects Ambler's deployment of German Expressionist film, where surreal set designs represent the fantasies that transform oppressive social and political ideologies into experiences of terror. *The Dark Frontier* deploys the excesses of an adventure plot not only for entertainment value but also to show the multiple dangers of fantasy. Fantasy can refer to the ideological goals of political extremism when they are translated into policy and practice, as in the myths of Nazism's masculinist, militaristic Master Race. The formal elements of fantasy as a genre also serve propaganda purposes, as in the hyper-muscular monuments built to celebrate Italian Fascism. The depiction of the laboratory in *The Dark Frontier*, where an atomic weapon is being developed, encapsulates the dangers of political fantasy when it evolves into political reality. The scene is narrated by the journalist, Casey, whose otherwise steely nerves are frayed by not knowing what to expect, an uncertainty intensified by the blinding darkness in which he and Barstow/Carruthers move. Entering the building, the journalist finds that there are no objective correlatives to guide his understanding of what he sees:

> I had never before seen the interior of a high-voltage laboratory. To my unscientific eye it looked very like a shot from an early German film about 'the future'. Suspended from the roof on a ganglion of long corrugated-glass insulators were two large copper globes. There appeared to be an arrangement for raising and lowering them. Two gleaming copper tubes descended vertically from the globes to another pair of insulators embedded in the concrete floor and thence passed to where row upon row of tall metal containers paraded against one wall. (*DF*, 201)

The description continues with even more of this elaborate detail, as though by accretion, it will become a template for deciphering a fantastic environment and translate it into political and experiential reality. But the reference to 'early German film about "the future"' is Ambler's revisionary guide.

Figure 1.1   Fritz Lang's 1927 Expressionist film *Metropolis*

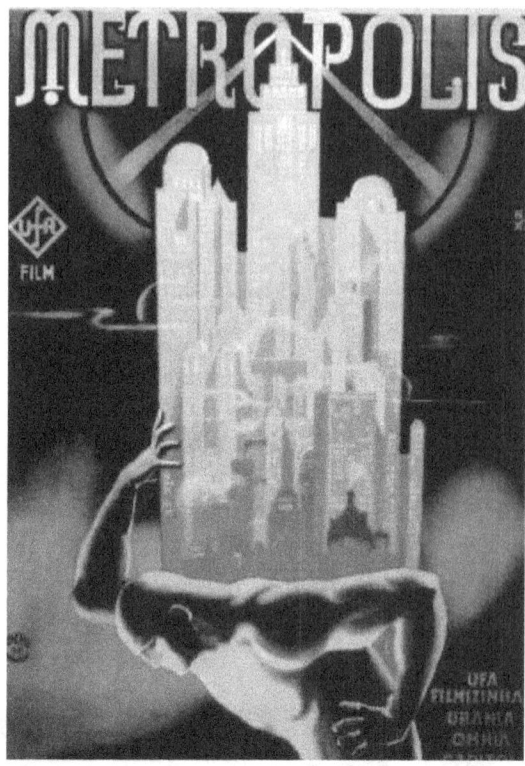

Figure 1.2　Poster for Fritz Lang's *Metropolis*

The source is Fritz Lang's 1927 science fiction Expressionist film *Metropolis*. Like *The Dark Frontier*, the film is a dystopian warning about the oppressive merger of autocracy and fascist capitalism. The film depicts two antithetical cities: monstrous tower blocks house despotic industrialists whose oppressed workers occupy claustrophobic underground tunnels, exiled from the dominant culture. Like *The Dark Frontier*, the film features a protagonist who suffers hallucinations from exhaustion, a scientist working for a fascist capitalist regime and a worker's rebellion. In Ambler's novel the peasants of Ixania overthrow the capitalist dictatorship. His point about the setting is that 'The general effect was highly decorative. Far from decorative, however, was the scene for which it provided so dramatic a setting' (*DF*, 201). Like scenes in Helen MacInnes' and John le Carré's spy fictions, Ambler dramatises his anti-fascist polemic as 'a rubber truncheon, the *totschläger* or "beater-to-death", of Nazi Germany, the persuasive element in many a Third Degree' (*DF*, 201).

The novel's parody of heroes, villains and narrative causality is tempered by political analysis and warning that become a defining feature of Ambler's next novels. In a narrative space between Barstow's opening statement and the start of Carruthers' adventures, the physicist reflects seriously in response to an invitation to become an agent of Cator and Bliss in their atomic weapons project:

> What else could you expect while war was still regarded as a feasible means of settling international disputes? [. . .] What else could you expect from a balance of power adjusted in terms of land, of arms, of man-power and of materials; in terms, in other words, of money? The actual outbreaks of wars might be heralded by [. . .] expressions of hatred and defensive mobilisations, but the real wars were made by those who [. . .] in satisfying their private ends, created the economic and social conditions that bred war. (*DF*, 25)

As though already planning the change in his narrative form from parody to dystopia, this passage from the novel's opening is the first of the anti-Fascist urgent pleas he issues in the 1930s.

That these pleas extend to his American readers is evident in his American journalist narrator, William Casey. Aware of recalcitrant American isolationism in the late 1930s, Ambler creates Casey as a witness to European Fascism and voice of intervention. To entice his readers, Casey narrates and interprets the adventure story of Barstow and Carruthers as political analysis in the guise of entertainment. As in Helen MacInnes' World War II espionage novels *Above Suspicion* and *Assignment in Brittany,* American journalists appear spontaneously, as though the product of wishful thinking, to assume activist anti-Nazi roles in occupied Europe. Embedded in counterespionage plots, they need to survive, not to celebrate America's heroism or that of a fictional prototype, but to write persuasive stories that would counter the political disorientation deriving from the clash between searing memories of the Great War's losses and Europe's dystopian present.

An Accidental Propagandist

> Spies were always sneaking foreigners. (Introduction, *To Catch a Spy*, 13)

In response to the consolidation of Fascist power in Central Europe in the mid-1930s, Ambler's 1937 novel *Background to Danger* questions the continuing British policy of appeasement by creating an off-stage position of weak-willed bystander. With the passage of Germany's Nuremberg Laws in 1935, enforcing Nazi racialist ideology, stripping its Jewish undesirables of citizenship, and closing escape routes, the oppressively shadowy spaces of Gothic Expressionism intensify in this novel to depict Central Europe as a prison and a warning to its readers that Nazism cannot be assuaged. Caught in transit within the region and transition between innocent bystander and political activist, the novel's protagonist, Desmond Kenton, is a phlegmatically intelligent freelance journalist and gambler, whose luck and resolve are as fleeting as the clarity of his identity which includes 'at least six pseudonyms' (*BD*, 87). For example, in addition to being identified as speaking European languages 'with an un-English accent', Desmond d'Esterre Kenton looks 'more like an American than an Englishman' but is 'actually neither', with an Irish father and Breton mother (*BD*, 14, 13, 14). In its tangled web of hybrid, politicised and negated identities, in his cluelessness and impulsiveness, Kenton's character encapsulates a tangled web of international relations: Eire's professed neutrality, Northern Ireland's British allegiance, Brittany's separatist sentiments, and Britain's and America's disjunctive relations with European nations in the 1930s. Metonymically, this hybridity suggests the ominously shifting political borders of the continent and its contested identities. Kenton's persistent but thwarted searches for escape from danger, his 'feeling of panic-stricken helplessness' when faced with 'absolute darkness', drive the discontinuities that create the novel's suspense and political analysis (*BD*, 111). All told, his unsettled character as wandering and perplexed outsider can be understood as a hybrid state of political and 'psychic exile', which internalises the transnational upheavals in which he is thrust (Hoffman, 57). In effect, Kenton's character attests to the novel's efforts to juggle and interrogate the ambiguous ethical and narrative implications of the premonitory dread produced by political and economic uncertainties in the mid-1930s.

The travels of Desmond Kenton into the underworld of fascist capitalism correspond to Marek Haltof's delineation of the 'physical and psychological levels [. . .] of the journey into unknown territory characteristic of Gothic novels and Expressionist films' (447). Kenton's journey exposes Fascist power as the silhouetted presence of Joseph Balterghen. A former arms dealer and now chairman of the global cartel, Pan-Eurasian Petroleum, Balterghen authorises brutality from within the 'highly respectable' boardrooms of British corporate finance (*BD*, 3). Barely visible, the chairman is a 'very small man', mention of whose appearance occurs only once, in the novel's Prologue (*BD*, 3). In this condensation of a prototypical villain and as his 'Rolls-Royce oozed silently' through the City of London, he is marked as a sinister alien (*BD*, 3). His name suggests a meld of Baltic and Balkan origins while his fascistic imperialism is mocked by his effete Second Empire and

Orientalist office décor and by his Hitleresque 'black tooth-brush moustache that sprouted surrealistically' (*BD*, 3, 4). Rather than an object of fear, however, he is an exemplary immigrant, acquiring legitimacy through his naturalised British citizenship and his London base of operations. Solidifying his entrenched position, his multi-national company enjoys British complicity with its ominous designs, finding unambiguous support among Britain's home grown 'capitalist exploiters' (*BD*, 9).

For example, a knighted member of Pan-Eurasian's board of directors and a strike breaking mine owner, Lord Welterfield, is only too eager to be seduced by the promise of rogue profits and to help the oil cartel meddle with the 'destinies' of Italy and Romania (*BD*, 9). Turning a blind eye to Balterghen's hired assassin, Saridza, and his human weapon, Mailler, Welterfield's support of Balterghen's plans suggests the fantasy of some upper-class Britons that they would retain their economic power and positions under Fascist domination.[16] Despite his 'dissimulation and disguise', key features of Gothic Expressionist characters, Balterghen's lethal forms of capitalism lead to 'nations arming as fast as they could' (Elsaessar, 96; *BD*, 59). Ambler here uses historical evidence to show the spreading danger of fascist capitalism benefiting from British passivity as well as the manipulation of Romania's conflict with the Soviet Union over the oil fields of Bessarabia, a former Soviet satellite taken by Romania in 1918. The link between Welterfield, the London-based Pan-Eurasian conglomerate and fascist capitalism is prescient, suggestive of Nazi Germany's use of its nation's industrialists, I.B. Farben, Krupp and Thyssen. By 1939, when Ambler's novel *Cause for Alarm* is published, fascist capitalism is transnational. As its agent, General Vagas, puts it, 'Business is business and so logical. It has no frontiers. Supply and demand, credit and debit' (*CA*, 43). In turn, the ominous and border crossing machinations of 'capitalist intrigue' extend the generic features of the spy thriller to debates about Britain's economic and political interests in the 1930s (*BD*, 8).

Unlike the uncertainties of the modernists of the period, however, these do not represent an epistemological rebellion against cultural or aesthetic stability. Instead, Ambler's thrillers challenge the cultural and political instability exacerbated by the West's uncertain response to the metamorphosis of Fascism into Nazi racialist laws and practices. As Robert L. Snyder observes of Ambler, 'the author [. . .] is acknowledging how problematic detection is in the real world, especially one beset by all the political duplicity practiced throughout Europe in the anxiety-ridden thirties' (238).[17] Ambler describes the major source of this anxiety in his epigraph to *Background to Danger*: 'with Europe assuming the appearance of an armed camp in which an incident, unimportant in itself, would be sufficient to ignite a conflagration that would consume Europe and perhaps spread to other quarters of the globe' (*BD*, np).

Although Desmond Kenton never encounters Joseph Balterghen, the journalist's travels into Central Europe take him to Balterghen's lair, the source of the potential conflagration and emblem of political and ethical displacement. With its ominous sense of descending into an atavistic polity of ungovernable violence, Kenton's travels recall Jonathan Harker's sojourn to Transylvania in Bram Stoker's *Dracula*. Marek Haltof directs our attention to this part of Europe that has become 'the Heart of Darkness', an 'oneiric landscape' of nightmarish political ruthlessness' (448). When Kenton finally returns to 'the diurnal world', he has become 'stronger, experienced, and more mature' (Haltof, 448). Entering and escaping the nightmare has destroyed his innocence, but with the help of allies, he has learned not just 'to live in an adult world' but that its lack of political courage has helped create the alien world of Central Europe (Haltof, 448).

Kenton's odyssey begins on the Orient Express from Nuremberg to Linz. In search of ready cash to repay his gambling debts, he encounters a seedy, 'small and very dark' fellow traveller who calls himself Hans Sachs and who identifies himself as a German Jew on the run from the Nazis (*BD*, 17). Ticking off all the details that mark Sachs' tale as suspect, but driven by self-pity and recklessness, Kenton accepts three hundred marks to smuggle Sachs' bank securities across the border. But the fugitive's identity and motives are confirmed as dubious when he is accused of being a Russian spy and traitor named Borovansky, and the bank securities he entrusts to Kenton turn out to be photographs of Russian mobilisation instructions. No wonder Kenton feels that Sachs' 'talk of securities, Jewish suspects and Nazi spies was sheer nonsense', even 'offensively melodramatic' (*BD*, 38, 24). But if Kenton is spy fiction's quintessential amateur, unwilling agent and captive of foreign intrigue, his confusion also signals the novel's foray into a snarled weave of geo-political and narrative interpretation. The genre's melodramatic plot turns merge with Gothic Expressionist settings, gendered characterisations and self-reflexive experimentation, encapsulated in the object of the chase, a photograph.

That Kenton is a journalist, like Casey in *The Dark Frontier*, warns us that Ambler positions his narrator and readers as investigating stories whose value and truths, like that of photographs, will remain unstable: 'But it was one thing to interpret a story correctly when you knew a little more than you should; it was quite another matter when you knew nothing at all about the story-teller or his probable motives. The whole business was very puzzling' (*BD*, 38). This pointedly self-conscious statement is one of the more stable clues in a novel about the dislocations of geo-political interests and their offspring, espionage. In effect, the statement interrogates the competing, ambiguous and duplicitous political perspectives necessary to a spy thriller plotting Britain's ambivalent relationship with Europe in 1937. If the novel's version of Romania seems more like Ruritania, the comic opera site mocked in *The Dark Frontier*, documented history reflects the novel's rude awakening for Kenton and readers. The record of Soviet plans to protect Romanian oil fields from a German takeover are not merely fictionalised as Sachs/Borovansky's photographs are. For even if the photographs turn out to represent nothing more than a false clue or are empty of meaning, their misleading, unstable information depicts the political anxieties emanating from the probability of Europe's explosion.

Like its characters, the plot is always on the move, and deceptively so. The novel's twists and multifaceted goals are established as a self-questioning political argument once Kenton travels to meet Sachs/Borovansky, only to discover his corpse in the decrepit Linz Hotel Josef. A metonym for links between Central Europe's politically discontinuous spaces and the novel's unsettling questions, the hotel is described as 'a maze of small corridors in which doors were set at unexpected angles and culs-de-sac abounded' and where 'pitch darkness' is lacerated by 'a single naked lamp' (*BD*, 45). The hotel's disorienting architecture recalls the Expressionist settings of stories by Edgar Allan Poe and the film *The Cabinet of Dr Caligari*, where walls and houses inexplicably crush and entomb characters as though this has been decreed by an ineffable evil force. The nightmarish claustrophobia suggested by the fusion of exterior and interior space defies the narrative logic of social or psychological realism but registers the anxiety that neither sensory experience, nor analytical acumen, nor artistry produces usable knowledge. The resemblance of Ambler's spyscapes to a 'manipulation of space and spatial coherence' is perceptible in Anton Kaes' description of German Expressionist film: 'harsh lighting that produces deep shadows cutting across a scene, rooms and objects that register both their own two dimensional artificiality and the characters' confused feelings, mute signs that signify what cannot be put into words' (84). Thomas Elsaesser's analysis of Expressionist space as representing unstable knowledge applies to Ambler's graphic descriptions of ominous physical space illuminating false or deceptive clues and the abnormal, the combination of which signifies the new norm of strangulating fascist capitalism.[18]

The Hotel Josef is fabricated with misleading and claustrophobic spaces. Originally a house, its carved up spaces are clearly unintended for hotel purposes. It occupies a weird and oppressive setting in an area of 'narrow and squalid' streets where the exterior and interior seem to incarcerate each other and anyone who enters (*BD*, 43). With a name that recalls the Emperor Franz Josef, the Hotel Josef suggests an impacted inter-war Central Europe. Like the demise of the Austro-Hungarian Empire and the decaying Allied victory since 1918, the hotel has disintegrated and now represents a memorial to elusive and yet dangerous political stability. The Central European romance of palace balls, merry widows and effete chocolate soldiers is now noir. Just as there was no escape for Sachs/Borovansky, the building seems to wall Kenton in as he attempts to make his way to and from the 'grotesque' and deadly room 25 (*BD*, 47). Like German Expressionist film, the architectural opaqueness in *Background to Danger* signifies the Kafkaesque terror of being engulfed by political oppression with no discernible source of power or help. Kenton may hold a British passport and be on the lookout for a good story, but his entrapment aligns him with Sachs' story and the stateless, helpless condition of the besieged refugee. Because the details of Kenton's entanglement here and throughout the novel defy any semblance of realism, they lead only to partial, generalised or mythic explanations that denote further mystification. Reality emerges in Ambler's Expressionist details as they also suggest a pervasive distrust that infects the very idea of ally or safe harbour.

Distrust and insecurity pervade Kenton's relationship with his only allies, Andreas and Tamar Zaleshoff, sympathetically portrayed Soviet agents. In fact Kenton's escape from Saridza and his henchmen is made possible only by the Zaleshoffs. Identifying himself as a 'fellow-traveller' in the mid-1930s, 'sympathetic' to the Communist Party's expressed causes, Ambler notes that the Zalesoffs represent one of the novel's 'few novelties: Soviet agents who were on the side of the angels [. . .]' (*Here Lies*, 123–4).[19] The novel's only committed and active combatants against Fascism, the Russian siblings represent the difficulty of using fiction to declare political alliances, but this plotting also finds a narrative solution in self-questioning. Like the ambiguities of Kenton's background and voice, Andreas' Russian identity is confounded by his American accent. When this inspires Kenton's inductive talent, we discover that Zaleshoff was 'deported from the United States for Communist agitation' in 1925 (*BD*, 120). Rather than establishing explanatory certainty, the Zaleshoffs' identity rivals Kenton's in its fluidity. As Tamara recounts,

> Our father was killed secretly by the Ochrana in nineteen hundred and ten. Our mother escaped from Baku with us to America, through Mexico, where I was born. But she never took out the proper papers and when Andreas

got into trouble with the police for his propaganda they found out about us and we were deported. Our mother was dead; we spoke Russian better than English, so we claimed Soviet citizenship. It is quite simple. (*BD*, 121)

Not so simple. While the novel portrays the Zaleshoffs as anti-Fascist protectors, they are not heroes. Despite his long experience as an agent, Andreas is no match for the wily Saridza who anticipates and stops the Russian's incursion into a Fascist compound. The novel also unsettles Andreas' good intentions by embedding a critical perspective on his defence of the 1936 Soviet show trials and cynicism about justice. The novel's association of renegade capitalism with obdurate fascistic power may very well be driven by Ambler's leftist politics, situating 'capitalist exploiters' at centre stage, just as with 'the Eurasian Credit Trust' in his 1939 novel, *A Coffin for Dimitrios*, and with the Rome–Berlin Axis in his other 1939 novel, *Cause for Alarm*.[20] But in a move that establishes both narrative coherence and discontinuity, fascistic capitalism in *Background to Danger* creates a catalysing force that will underwrite Europe's destabilisation, its enforced unification by the Third Reich and the persecution of its undesirables. In effect, this novel constitutes a warning of impending catastrophe that will not wait for Britain's political debates to be resolved. Like other writers mentioned earlier, Ambler argues that to confirm its own moral coherence and political power, Britain must intervene on behalf of European national sovereignties and ethnic identities and cultures.

Background to Danger dramatises this argument in an episode that exploits and satirises the spy thriller's penchant for omnipresent danger and red herrings. Kenton's inept attempt at disguise reaches a climax of suspenseful chills as he tries to elude capture by travelling to the border on a tour bus and then crossing the Czech–Austrian frontier on foot. Sporting a moustache that 'made him look extremely bad-tempered', 'peek[ing] right and left like [. . .] a villain in the pictures', and wearing an oversized overcoat adorned with 'a stain the size of Lake Geneva', Kenton is spotted by a British travelling salesman, Mr Hodgkin (*BD*, 151, 167, 168). The momentary parody of the Englishman abroad turns serious, however, when instead of exposing Kenton, Hodgkin enlists as his ally by targeting the villainous escalation of Fascist violence:

I was in sunny Italy when the Fascisti went for the freemasons in twenty-five. Florence it was. Night after night of it with shooting and beating and screams, till you felt like vomiting. I was in Vienna in thirty-four when they turned the guns on the municipal flats with the women and children inside them. A lot of the men they strung up afterwards had to be lifted on to the gallows because of their wounds. I saw the Paris riots with the *garde mobile* shooting down the crowd like flies [. . .] I saw the Nazis in Frankfurt kick a man to death in his front garden [. . .] (*BD*, 170)[21]

Hodgkin's self-appointed role as a British witness to European Fascism addresses Kenton's political position and that of Ambler's readers in 1937. Because Hodgkin's speech is so fraught with political passion about Europe, it questions the political and ethical viability of Britain maintaining its role as neutral or conflicted bystander. As Hodgkin's character and travels attest, his roles as travelling salesman of British textiles and witness to European tensions are enmeshed with Britain's economic self-interest. While Kenton's identity is border crossing and his political affiliations appear to be reticent and unclear, his entanglement with this steadfast Briton in Central Europe as well as with so many European characters and plots suggest a political involvement that challenges both appeasement politics and the ahistorical politics of more conventional spy fiction.

Ambler's critique and warning are unified politically and narratively in ways that defy the stock conclusions of most spy thrillers. For however we choose to resolve the ambiguous identity of Sachs/Borovansky and the photographs he carries, we will not find textual support. The photographs, which may be forgeries and which Kenton burns at the end, could very well turn out to be nothing more than what Alfred Hitchcock would call 'a MacGuffin' – the hunted treasure as empty signifier.[22] The explanations or captions supplied by the narrator and by Zaleshoff cannot illuminate an image whose textual grounding is as elusive as its explanations and which as the novel proceeds, seems to evaporate into an interpretive neverland. And yet the very elusiveness of the photograph's concreteness has political meaning, analogous to the timorous nature of alliances and borders throughout Central Europe.

By contrast, the narrative and political meanings embodied by Sachs/Borovansky are overdetermined if insistently disjunctive. Ambler's choice of the name Hans Sachs is enmeshed with German and German Jewish history. It resounds with that of the renowned sixteenth-century German *Meistersinger*, inspiration for Wagner's opera based on the rebel storyteller whose religious adherence to Luther made him an outcast and a secret agent. The spelling 'Hanns Sachs' also refers to one of Freud's assistants who with another colleague, Karl Abraham, collaborated with German Expressionist filmmaker G. W. Pabst on the 1926 'dream-work' film *Secrets of a Soul* (Haltof, 447). As Haltof explains, the film is constructed with 'unreal, distorted, dreamy-like images' that show how 'fragmented dreams' are cured by psychoanalytic treatment

(447). Of course in films like *The Cabinet of Dr Caligari* or *Nosferatu*, the psychoanalytic import is that the unconscious reigns deeply, darkly and supreme, representing a drive and force that are impervious to treatment. Viewed through the constellation of this cloudy psychoanalytic lens and a Gothic Expressionist style, the Jewish story carried by Hans Sachs in *Background to Danger* is a nightmare that cannot be cured. Instead, it is ensnared by the political unconscious of Fascism and its forms of expression. With its rejection of psychoanalysis as an effete Jewish science, Fascism in its Nazi guise will interpret its own dreams of a Master Race as a coherent masculinist reality.[23] One result will be that the Jewish story, like its storytellers, must be erased before it contaminates the Reich's body politic and its self-affirming narrative. By the time Ambler writes this novel, it is four years since the beginning of Hitler's book burning, consisting of 'huge bonfires of books by such Jewish authors as Albert Einstein [. . .] communist and left wing authors like Bertolt Brecht and Heinrich Mann', an event dramatised in Leslie Howard's 1942 film *49th Parallel* (Bergen, 66). That dissident storytelling had to be suppressed highlights the dangers of Kenton's roles as witness to political oppressions and as reporter/storyteller.

In Ambler's novel, although Sachs/Borovansky is murdered early on and therefore silenced, his disappearance from the text does not erase either the story he carries or its historical meanings. He may have exploited the story of Jewish persecution for his own ends, but its content carries the historically validated and stable weight of truth about Nazi policies and practices. Bernard Wasserstein reports:

> The Jewish refugee, long a familiar figure in Europe, mutated in the 1930s into a major social and political problem and a human catastrophe. Jewish homelessness assumed a sharper edge than ever before. Instead of the 'portable homeland' of which Heine had written a century earlier, more and more European Jews found they had no homeland at all. (361)[24]

A corollary to this history, Kenton recalls a Jewish instrument maker named Rosen, who might lend him some money in gratitude for the journalist's help to escape Munich in 1934. Extending the story of Jewish persecution to reflect the Nuremberg Laws of 1935, Sachs tells Kenton that although his father was a Gentile, he is persecuted because his mother was Jewish and is prevented from leaving Germany with any money. If caught, he is certain to be transported to a concentration camp. On the other hand, Kenton lists details of Sachs' story that could easily refute it and after he is murdered, all the characters refer to him as Borovansky, not that this is trustworthy evidence. Concurrently, the Jewish story also draws attention to the consolidation of antisemitism into state policy wherever Fascism is to be found. According to Nazi antisemitic policy, carrying a Jewish story as well as trying to escape it warrants suspicion, if not persecution. The message and its messenger blur the divide between witness and victim. Like the Jewish refugee, the Jewish story travels or wanders across Europe, suspect and unwanted.

The Jewish story resonates with that of the Wandering Jew which, as Carol Davison observes, served as an antisemitic icon from nineteenth-century British Gothic literature through to Nazi propaganda films which 'fostered a new and terrifying stage in the development of the vampiric Wandering Jew: he blurred yet another boundary by purportedly wandering into "reality" where he was deliberately manipulated to intend harm. As the immediate audience reactions to these films and the establishment of the death camps attest, these nightmarish projections were hugely successful in their aims' (160). Judith Halberstam notes connections between the quintessential wandering monster, Dracula's characteristics and antisemitic tropes prevalent in Victorian and early twentieth-century culture: 'In the Jew, then, Gothic fiction finds a monster versatile enough to represent fears about race, nation, and sexuality, a monster who combines in one body fears of the foreign and the perverse' (14). The spectre of the Jew 'unites and therefore produces the threats of capital and revolution, criminality and impotence, sexual power and gender ambiguity, money and mind' (20, 95).

Reflecting this perceived threat as a narrative challenge to a conventional genre, *Background to Danger* will neither integrate nor rescue the teller or the tale. Instead, Ambler unsettles the relationship between Sachs/Borovansky as a character, as a fictional story and as historically resonant. These disjunctive textual and contextual elements are reflected in the novel's discursive method. Rather than narrate the historically documented story of Jewish persecution in a linear realist style, Ambler's oblique encoding of gritty details both discloses and questions the story as it is told by a narrator with a dubious identity and credentials. With the possibility that even in its haunting presence, the story is a lie, a fiction within fiction, the novel bears witness to the doubts and indifference that marked the actual reception to the Jewish story of persecution in the years following the 1935 Nuremberg Laws.[25] Ambler testifies:

> But certainly *to* anyone who came to maturity during the Fascist years the importance of papers became overwhelming. People are denied passports – that means now the right to travel freely – for often, it seems to me, illogical reasons. If you don't like someone, the best thing is to give him a passport and tell him to go, isn't it? The Russians found that out. Or don't give him a

passport and tell him to go; but get him out. It's a question of control to deny him freedom of movement. I knew so many people during the Hitler era for whom papers were life or death. (qtd in Hopkins, 290)

Perhaps this is why Sachs/Borovansky's exiled state, from Central Europe and the novel, concludes as violent death, and the only thing that matters about his corpse is its effect on Kenton's political consciousness and roles as witness and reporter. An observation by Smith and Wallace about the use of the body in Gothic and modernist iconography is especially pertinent here:

> The body can seem to promise authentic personal identity, yet is ghosted by a sense of something potentially alien and strange. Anxieties about the physical health of the collective body – human species, race, nation-state, culture – become anxieties about the idea of the self. (3)

In effect, as it travels across Central Europe, the unsettling Jewish story not only drives the entire plot, but its political analysis. More broadly, including the Jewish story calls attention not only to official reticence but also to the antisemitism shared by the British public and esteemed writers.[26] As the end draws near, Kenton and Zaleshoff confront the antisemitic ideology that drives Nazi propaganda power in a comment by the director of the German newspaper *Prager Morgenblatt*. Identified only as 'the German', he proclaims the enemy to be 'the reality of the Jew-Communist menace', an iconic identification of a mythic cabal that justifies Nazi Germany's will to conquer (*BD*, 258). The proclamation also haunts the novel beyond the ending to support its irresolution. For at the end, although Kenton has a chance to shoot Saridza, he lets him go. The novel prepares us for Kenton's reasons when he responds to his first experience of the assassin's brutality:

> The Nazi concentration camps and the Italian penal islands are full of men who have refused to compromise with violence. To compare my present attitude with their amazing courage is absurd, but I find now that I have an inkling of their point of view. I used to wonder how they could suffer so much for the sake of such transitory things as political principles. I realize now that there's more in it than that. It's not just a struggle between Fascism and Communism, or between any other '-isms'. It's between the free human spirit and the stupid, fumbling, brutish forces of the primeval swamp – and that, Colonel, means you and your kind. (*BD*, 90)

While this speech is easily viewed as a set piece of melodramatic hyperbole, the novel's specific but unstable historical moment and Jewish story reveal the limits of a classic liberal humanistic stance and its outward bound implications. Dramatising documented history also subverts the thriller's conventional conclusion that 'justice eventually triumphs through evil's self-cancellation' (Snyder, 249). For based on Saridza's intractable character, Kenton's decision will not lead to the end of the assassin's career or Fascist sadism. In fact we can assume that from 1937 onwards, the highest bidder will make Saridza an instrument of their brutal designs.

In turn, if we view Kenton's combined identities as representing the Allies and neutral Ireland, then his decision to release the freewheeling sadist highlights the dangers of isolationism and appeasement in ignoring the signs of Germany's expansionist movements. On his initial train ride Kenton entertains a fantasy that 'Perhaps Hitler would be on the Linz train on his way to meet the leader of the Austrian Social Democrats' (*BD*, 16–17). With all its indeterminacy, the novel ends on a note of certainty. The story Kenton carries on the Berlin train taking him back to Britain via Prague is neither generic nor fantasy. Instead, in its political prescience, Kenton's story shows how the Fascist threat and its imminent war of conquest and persecution necessitate a literary travel itinerary that countermands narrative and political stasis.

Agent of Exile: *Epitaph for a Spy*

> What makes exile the pernicious thing is not really the state of being away, as much as the impossibility of ever *not* being away – not just being absent, but never being able to redeem this absence. (André Aciman, 10)

In his 'Footnote' to *Epitaph for a Spy*, Ambler notes that he wrote the novel 'in 1937 and it was a mild attempt at realism. The central character is a stateless person (fairly unusual then), there are no professional devils, and the only Britisher in the story is anything but stalwart. I still like bits of it' (*ES*, np). His autobiography *Here Lies* notes that 'In March 1938 when *Epitaph for a Spy* was being subscribed, Hitler invaded and annexed Austria. In those circumstances a thriller with a refugee as its protagonist was bound to lose some of its appeal' (131). Despite these historically specific references, the novel has been read as an espionage version of the 'English country house tradition' in which a group of guests 'all have something to hide, and thus all are suspect' (Wolfe, 4). While the setting of the Hotel de la Réserve on the Côte d'Azur may seem apposite to Agatha Christie's bucolic English country houses, instead of her usual suspects, the landed gentry and upwardly mobile poseurs, the pedigrees of the French hotel guests are stamped with exile rather than political or social belonging. In English country house mysteries, disguised identity is the hallmark of villains, but the solution inevitably exposes their deeply rooted connection to the local social culture. No strangers allowed. By contrast, *Epitaph*'s social culture has dissipated, with anxieties about political invasion and both protagonists and antagonists are strangers everywhere.

In this novel the idea of the stranger as a refugee is focalised through the voice of the protagonist, Josef Vadassy, a stateless Hungarian who holds a delegitimised Yugoslav passport and tremulous hopes for a permanent French work visa, and whose father and brother were killed by the Yugoslav police for being social democrats. Listing possible safe harbours, he concludes that he 'would be merely another undesirable alien [. . .] Officially he did not exist; he was an abstraction, a ghost' (*ES*, 22). As a stateless exile, his identity has no material or experiential reality; it bears no connection to any sense of a birthright. The shifting borders after World War I have dislocated identities associated with the nations of Central and Eastern Europe. In turn, national identity is unsettled by the refugees who yearn for safe haven in nations clinging to their own sovereignty and threatened by porous borders.

Vadassy's first person narrative, which typically creates suspenseful unreliability, carries political urgency. The uncertainty, dislocation and anxiety that underwrite a thriller's plot trajectory derive from Vadassy's condition as a refugee. If in 1937 Kenton's fecklessness can be bound to mercurial circumstances, by 1938 the threat to Vadassy is politically fateful, not a function of his individual subjectivity. He becomes trapped in a counter-espionage plot because without protection from any political source, he must comply: 'What right had Beghin [French Naval Intelligence officer] to place me in such a despicable position? If I had been an ordinary person with a consul to defend my rights he would not have dared' (*ES*, 158). To refuse means incarceration by either the French or the Nazis. To agree does not mean self-discovery or heroic agency; his fate will depend on the grinding utility of his investigation. He is an agent without agency.

The displaced condition of the refugee also determines the characters and actions of the hotel's guests – all of them political or social outliers: Mary and Skelton, American cousins 'living in sin'; Duclos, a lowly clerk posing as an entrepreneur; Emil Schimler/Paul Czissar/Heinberger, a concentration camp fugitive;[27] the Vogels, disguised Nazi agents; Roux, a French army deserter with family ties to Mussolini's Fascist Italy and his mistress; and the proprietors, Albert and Suzanne Köche, German exiles and anti-Nazi resistors. Each of them lives a secret story that translates into puzzling narrative shards they recount while rousing suspicion in each other. This would include the only British character in the novel, Major Clandon-Hartley, wounded in World War I and on the run from an Italian revenge farce. After a fist fight on the beach with a 'shrieking' Italian, the Major ingenuously enacts a caricature of masculinist British exceptionalism, confiding to Vadassy, '"I know," he said, "that it's damned bad form unloading one's private affairs on strangers [...]"' and then, imputing the craven connivances of '"these damned foreigners [...]"', he appropriates the moral high ground: '"I knew nothing about business [...] Give me some men and guns and a job to do with them and I'll do it"' (*ES*, 98, 121, 126). This is Ambler's British representative in Europe, a wounded veteran of World War I, deeply attracted to Europe's sunny promises yet repelled by its crude internecine cruelties. His unsuspecting role in a *commedia famiglia* mocks Britain's relationship with Europe in 1938. Implicated in and disdainful of the continent's encrusted intrigues, he becomes trapped by his ambivalence.

Although Vadassy's identity consists of multiple national strands, unlike the others, his character is transparent and unitary. He is neither in disguise nor on the run. Rather, he is stuck in his unstable identity, related only to an entrapping place. The plot turns on his stateless condition and lost camera, the combination of which is used by Michel Beghin, the French Naval investigator, to coerce Vadassy into uncovering a spy for Mussolini who is filming secret French naval installations on an island near Marseilles. The spy took Vadassy's camera either accidentally because the two cameras are identical, or as a subterfuge. Threatened with deportation, Vadassy is imperilled even though he was only photographing lizards (the association with slimy slipperiness is telling). As Ambrosetti reminds us, lizards are noteworthy as inescapable icons of 'camouflage, *chiaroscuro* [...] and the motif of the "serpent in the Garden of Eden" prefigures the imminent danger and fall of the natural, stateless man' (41). With political and historical contingency as determining factors in this novel, as a 'stateless man', Vadassy's character and narrative of displacement seems to question the very idea of 'the natural' man. He has no access to the knowledge that would precipitate his fall and expulsion; his condition is preternaturally and politically fallen. He is in exile even before his story begins.

The garden in which he lands, the hotel's sunny environs, is quickly polluted by 'an ugly tension in the atmosphere' (*ES*, 153). Rather than idyllic, Hotel de la Réserve's beach setting is claustrophobic as the serpents, aka the Axis powers, widen their net and the bright open spaces of the Mediterranean coast become imprisoning. Light here is the reverse side of the Expressionist sign of danger, suggesting the peril of being blindsided by the coast's deceptive openness. Issuing a warning about the setting's treacherous beauty, Vadassy introduces it as sharply angled, like an Expressionist set, bounded by 'a sheer drop of about fifteen meters' with 'gashes of red rock' surrounded by 'tortured branches [. . .] as if you were watching a magic-lantern show with highly colored slides and an impatient operator' (*ES*, 4, 3). The sense of apprehension in this passage intensifies with links between the hazardous landscape and the threatening powers of light and photography to expose secrets. No longer do archetypal associations of light with nurture and revelation obtain. Instead, light in these atmospherics is equivalent to meanings of darkness as ominously ensnaring, an exploding exposure. No wonder all of the hotel guests are often shown with cameras in hand, as though the photographed image will somehow reveal a pathway to escape and safety. As mechanisms that use both light and darkness to create images, the twin cameras that entrap Vadassy capture these compressed oppositions. The refugee's innocent hobby is overcome by the treachery of the enemy spy's camera. In fact, the actual hazards of camera work accentuate this metaphorical rout: when an aperture opens too widely, it produces an overexposed image, too dark to discern. But such lack of definition serves Ambler's revisionary epistemology as it signifies the illusory, treacherous relationship in all spy thrillers between representation, investigation and ratiocination. Bernd Hüppauf's analysis applies here as photography captures only an '[i]mage frozen in time, a fabrication, a fiction, spun into a narrative that can divorce itself from context or be understood in relation to its context' (6).

As in *The Dark Frontier* and *Background to Danger*, Hüppauf's interpretation informs the centrality of photography in *Epitaph for a Spy* where, depending on the 'angle', the intended image can be 'wholly obscured' or made ambiguous by shadows or uncertain contexts (*ES*, 20). The camera's penetration of human reality cannot exceed its two-dimensional reach. As Vadassy understands in his search for the spy, cameras can't capture mind:

> A man's account of his own actions was, like the look he habitually wore on his face, no more than the expression, the statement of an attitude. You could never get at the whole man any more than you could see four faces of a cube. The mind was a figure with an infinite number of dimensions, a fluid in ceaseless movement, unfathomable, unaccountable. (*ES*, 209)

Conversely, from his first-person perspective, Vadassy's unitary character is obscured by Beghin's lens or angle, which constructs the refugee's indisputable innocence as ambiguous and uncertain and therefore malleable and available for manipulation. For Beghin, Vadassy's humanity has no inherent significance or dignity; like his camera, his character must be instrumentalised to acquire value. Vadassy and his camera are one – weapons of espionage. Only halfway through the novel, but long after his entrapping circumstances, Vadassy understands that his reality at the Hotel Réserve had been filtered through lenses signifying the perspectives of conflicting and manipulative interests. His own perspective is distorted by attempting to adopt those which manipulate him:

> Looking back on those next twenty-four hours is, I find, like looking at a stage through the wrong end of a pair of opera-glasses. The people on it are moving, but their faces are too small to see. I must try to turn the glasses the right way round. And yet, when I try to do that the figures are blurred at the edges and distorted. It is only by, so to speak, looking at one portion of the stage at a time that I can see things clearly. (*ES*, 118)

Of course 'one portion' cannot represent or help explain the whole. Indeed, the stateless refugee has no point of reference that will shed light on the machinations that govern him. He has no template to guide him to construct a coherent narrative. Ambler's narrative will manipulate the genre's conventions to show how they can only blur distinctions between victimising manipulation and the necessities of French national defence. Beghin may represent an imperilled French democracy, but the role he imposes on Vadassy is not merely a performance. It is ruthless exploitation of a refugee's powerlessness.[28]

Assuming at first that photographic experiment is simply an aesthetic enterprise, Vadassy ignores the medium's dangerous implications. At a time when totalitarian oppression is overtaking Europe, photography assumes political import that cannot be distinguished from aesthetics. In fact, as in other Ambler novels of the period, photography can be a dangerous weapon, capturing 'elevation angles of guns [. . .] details of fortifications, positions of ammunition stores, disposition of key factories, landmarks for bombers' (*ES*, 59–60). Because these sightings suggest concrete certainty, the inherent ambiguities of images either floating free of context or framed in a chosen context invite interpretations that can be construed as documentary evidence of guilt. Such is the fate of the refugee, Vadassy. For above all, photography in this novel warns that 'The world was getting ready to go to war' (*ES*, 60). As a stateless refugee with no promise of asylum, Vadassy represents the war's first victims.

This novel, like Ambler's others of the 1930s and MacInnes' images of 1939 Nuremberg, represents a dystopian warning of the Nazis' mandate for a war on democracy, human rights and its Others. Emil Schimler/Paul Czissar/Heinberger, another of Ambler's besieged exiles, testifies:

> It begins in 1933. I was editor of a social-democrat newspaper in Berlin, the *Telegrafblatt* [. . .] 'It is no longer in existence [. . .] The trouble with postwar German social-democracy was that it supported with one hand what it was trying to fight with the other [. . .] Its great illusion was its belief in the limitless possibilities of compromise. It thought that it could build Utopia within the constitution of Weimar [. . .] Worst of all, it thought that you could meet force with good will, that the way to deal with a mad dog was to stroke it. In 1933 German social-democracy was bitten and died in agony. (*ES*, 173)

As Schimler's narrative continues, it illuminates a primary weapon of Nazi Germany's war against humanity:

> 'I dare say you've heard a lot about concentration camps [. . .] To hear some talk you would imagine that the entire day was spent in knocking the prisoners' teeth out with rubber truncheons [. . .] and breaking their fingers with rifle butts [. . .] Nazi brutality is much less human. It's the mind they get at. If you'd ever seen a man come out of a fortnight's solitary confinement in a pitch-dark cell you'd know what I mean [. . .] The discipline is fantastic. They give you work to do – shoveling piles of stones from one spot to another and then back again – and if you stop working, even to straighten your back for an instant – you get a flogging [. . .] They never relax for a moment. They change the guards constantly so that they don't get tired of watching [. . .] If you let them see that your mind is still working like a human being's instead of a beast's, you're done for.' (*ES*, 174–5)[29]

That Schimler is a journalist and anti-Nazi fugitive signals an important shift from the incidental role of the journalist in *Background to Danger*. Although Kenton's character develops from lackadaisical self-interest to political consciousness, we never learn if he writes the story of Fascist oppression. Like the rescued dissident journalist in Leslie Howard's 1941 film *Pimpernel Smith*, Schimler cannot escape the story of Nazi persecution because he and his family embody its threat. If he cannot write and dispatch it, his narrative represents the consequences of escalating Nazi horror. If identifying and capturing the Nazi spy drives the plot of the novel, Schimler's exiled testimony is its rallying point, a dystopian recognition that it may very well be too late to stop Nazi Germany's lethal hunt for all those it deemed degenerate.[30] Ambler's novel, like Phyllis Bottome's 1937 fiction *The Mortal Storm*, presents the testimony of Nazism's targeted victims and survivors. With the potential of filling both roles, Vadassy testifies: 'I can see the scene now, clearly. There are no blurred edges. Here nothing is out of focus. It is as if I were looking through a stereoscope at a perfect colored reproduction [. . .]' (*ES*, 208).[31]

An Espionage Narrative in Exile: *The Mask of Dimitrios*

Ambler's last novel of the decade, *The Mask of Dimitrios* (1939), can be read as a summation of his self-questioning Expressionist treatment of fascist capitalism as its dangers spread from the beginning of the decade across Europe and threatened Britain. Brett Woods describes the novel as

> an imaginative history of the decisive years between the World War I and the rise of Hitler, when Britain, France, the United States and the other powers position themselves for influence and power while the situation in Eastern Europe, Russia, the Balkans, the Mediterranean and the Middle and Far East deteriorated, making World War II all but inevitable. (13)

Recalling the context that constitutes the subject of this novel, Ambler expresses anxieties that he felt were becoming increasingly urgent as the 1930s drew to a close: 'Meanwhile, Hitler had torn up the Munich Agreement and invaded Czechoslovakia. I went back to Paris where it was easier to read, without losing one's temper, about British guarantees of Polish territorial integrity' (*Here Lies*, 150).

As dramatised in *Cause for Alarm* (1938), which immediately preceded *Dimitrios*, Ambler's angry suspicion that Britain would cling to its exceptionalism and appeasement also tightened his ambivalence about the Soviet Union as an anti-Nazi ally. *Cause for Alarm* resurrects Andreas and Tamara Zaleshoff from *Background to Danger*, but the intrepid Soviet spies are now subject to interrogation by Marlow, a more self-contained and reflective British protagonist than Kenton. Andreas Zaleshoff's attacks on Britain's indifference to fascist capitalism are now met with a Briton's refusal to accept that the Soviets are 'on the side of the angels [. . .] the people who can resist the forces that have beaten the people of Italy and Germany to their knees' (*CA*, 177). Marlow understands that despite Zaleshoff's zealous hatred of 'Fascism, of stateworship', he would sacrifice his British friend and ally 'negligently to [his] fate' before abrogating his role as 'a Soviet agent' (*CA*, 207, 212). Yet at their final parting, Marlow thinks, 'No, you could not help liking Zaleshoff' (*CA*, 278). *Cause for Alarm* debates the hopes and suspicions about whether the Soviet Union would fulfil its anti-Fascist promises. Marlow's affection for his ally vies with his thoughts that align 'Lenin and Stalin [. . .] of the Lubianka prison' with Germany's 'goose-stepping men with steel helmets, of concentration camps' (*CA*, 213). The juxtaposed images of state terror suggest that Ambler was reconsidering his politics as totalitarian oppression was erasing the differences between

Nazism and Soviet Communism. By August 1939, he was asking, 'Who were going to be the allies against Hitler?' (*The Story So Far*, 8). In recognition that 'the pang of fear' had overcome doubt and disenchantment, Ambler recalled the time when he had considered himself

> a man of the Popular Front,[32] that short-lived coalition of the European Left against the spread of Axis Fascism that was jumping the frontiers of Versailles Treaty Europe with the remorseless ease of a medieval plague. I believed, with many others, that the Munich Agreement of the year before had been a humiliating disaster, but I had also believed, also with others, that the Soviet Union would in the end join with the French and British democracies to confront and contain the common enemy. Now, suddenly there was light on the stage and the hero could be seen climbing into bed with the villain. We did not know then, of course, that the pact signed by Molotov and Ribbentrop had, as well as giving the Nazis a free hand to take anything they wanted of the pre-1914 German territories, secretly partitioned Poland and ceded the Baltic States [...] to the Soviet Union; but the fact that Stalin and Hitler had done a deal of any sort was enough. The war, for long inevitable, would now certainly be total. (*Story So Far*, 8–9)

The anxiety Ambler expresses about the certainty of war coincides with British public opinion in 1938–9. As Mass-Observation reported, while there was 'resistance to the idea that war is coming', there was also 'bewilderment' at 'official secrecy and newspaper contradictions'; and finally a 'sense of helplessness' (qtd in Jo Fox, 17).

Ambler's intensifying concerns about Britain's responsibility to Europe's fate as Fascism and Nazism spread are encapsulated in *The Mask of Dimitrios* in two characters: the fascist capitalist mercenary Dimitrios and British writer, Charles Latimer, who sojourns to Turkey and then backtracks through Europe in search of inspiration. Like a culmination of his other self-questioning fictions of the decade, *The Mask of Dimitrios* dramatises the ethical quandary of the writer who exploits stories of Fascist economic manipulation to revise the novel of escapist intrigue while wanting to escape its political implications. In effect, Ambler's decision to embed his own impassioned political analysis and warnings reflects critically on his writer protagonist. Instead of escapist intrigue, Ambler creates the thriller as anti-Fascist propaganda. Despite Latimer's efforts to maintain a non-aligned stance as he investigates the villainous character of Dimitrios, the narrator's interventions mirror Ambler's disdain for neutrality. As with all of Ambler's protagonists in the thirties, Latimer ultimately learns that fear is the logical response when confronting Fascist danger face to face. What to do with that fear is Ambler's confrontational question for his British and American readers as another world war looms.

Unlike Ambler's earlier accidental and fated spies, Latimer designs his own adventure into criminal and political intrigue. A 'lecturer in political economy at a minor English university', Latimer turns to writing pot-boiler detective fiction as an antidote to the depressing experience of having worked on 'the philosophy of National Socialism and its prophet, Dr Rosenberg' *(A Coffin,* 18, 3, 4). A list of Latimer's successful titles parodies the genre's escapism: *A Bloody Shovel, 'I,' said the Fly* and *Murder's Arms.* Like his creator, who revised the conventions of spy thrillers, Latimer decides to abandon the confining conformity of his undemanding genre and seek a muse beyond the cardboard country villages where detective work is a genteel profession.[33] Mocking his similar career trajectory, Ambler told an interviewer that despite their status as classics, his own first five novels

> were cartoons for later books. What happened was simply *having failed* at playwriting, *having failed* as a songwriter, *failed* as an engineer, I looked around for something I could change and decided it was the thrillerspy [sic] story. I would do something different. The detective story ha[d] been worked over and worked over, but no one had looked at the thriller. It was still a dirty word. So I decided to intellectualize it, insofar as I was able [. . .] I changed the genre and couldn't write the books fast enough. (qtd in J. Hopkins, 286)

As Robert Snyder affirms, to create a more intellectual spy fiction, Ambler 'introduced "seriousness" [. . .] by incorporating a dimension of skeptical critique' in the form of a 'set-piece on warmongering, a maneuver that reveals his authorial struggle against the modernist imperative of "impersonal" narration' (230). Exploiting modernist conventions, *The Mask of Dimitrios* jostles between impassioned, cynical, unctuous and angry narrators' fragments, none of which can be trusted as anything more than misguided, misleading and self-serving, a problem that over the course of the novel extends to Latimer himself. It's therefore no wonder that these duplicitous approaches fail to discover any truth. We can extend this statement to include Ambler's investigation of the political ethics and limits of the spy thriller.

Ambler expands his geo-political topography in this novel by transporting his protagonist narrator to the exotic eastern end of the Mediterranean where he searches for a new form of investigation. Writing thrillers as open inquiry will release Latimer from conventional frames of political and cultural reference. Peter Lewis reminds us that 'With Nazism in the ascendant, it is possible to interpret Latimer's change of direction as an instance of *la trahison des clercs,* the intellectual "treachery" with which members of the intelligentsia were often charged during the rapid growth of fascism' (65). Despite his detached self-presentation, Latimer becomes increasingly frantic, unsure of his itinerary from Athens to Istanbul to Smyrna, Sofia,

Geneva and Paris. During the first leg of his journey, inspiration seems to blossom in Istanbul when he meets Colonel Zia Haki, chief of the Turkish State Police, who takes him to the city morgue for a glimpse at the gritty realism of actual police procedure. The scene does not, however, represent either a confrontation with political reality or an introduction to writing realist investigative crime fiction. Instead it registers the first of the novel's many suspicions about the thriller's verisimilitude and the writer's intentions and methods by revealing the Colonel's preference for entertaining 'trick' solutions (*A Coffin*, 8). The novel's parodic intertextuality, comparing its self-questioning to the genre's self-affirming formula, escalates when Haki enlists Latimer's advice for writing his own thriller, *The Clue of the Bloodstained Will*, a '*roman policier*', so 'much more sympathetic' and 'artistic' than 'a real' murder case (*A Coffin*, 9, 11). The *roman*'s title and murder plot, including the usual country house suspects, may be all for fun, but it also signals Ambler's critique of the thriller's diversion from more self-reflective narratives, represented by his own titles, *The Mask of Dimitrios* and *A Coffin for Dimitrios* (the latter for the US publication). For it turns out that the corpse on the slab is not Dimitrios and that claims for gritty realism and open inquiry fall well short of substantiation. For Ambler, to accept realism as self-evident is tantamount to self-deception.

Representing the search for character and plot, Dimitrios becomes Latimer's muse. The corpse, however, resists discovery of its history and identity, remaining so ambiguous as to be ultimately unknowable, complete only as a dead end, finalised as a corpse. If the introduction of Dimitrios presages his end, as his own corpse, nothing definitive or resolved emerges about either his character or fate. As the novel's titles suggest, his only materiality emerges either in inscrutable, indeterminate forms or as a corpse, ripe for burial. Dimitrios' villainy may be indisputable, but any information about him remains, as Latimer muses, 'mysterious [...] like being faced by an algebraic problem containing many unknown quantities and having only one biquadratic equation with which to solve it. If he *were* to solve it [...]' (*A Coffin*, 75). Dimitrios Makropoulos or Talat may be a Greek survivor of the Armenian 'holocaust' or the Turkish imposter, Taladis; Mark Mazower suggests he might even be a Jew (*A Coffin*, 20; Mazower, vii) He also assumes the fake identities of a German, von Kiessling; a Frenchman, Rougement; and the non-specific C. K. A summary of his background offers little in the way of stable information: '"Born eighteen eighty-nine in Larissa, Greece. Found abandoned. Parents unknown. Mother believed Rumanian. Registered as Greek subject and adopted by Greek family. Criminal record with Greek authorities. Details unobtainable"' (*A Coffin*, 12).

Paradoxically, a unifying thread among these impersonations are the inherently unstable status and persona of the political or racialised refugee and frequently unverifiable position that informs so many characters in Ambler's other novels of the decade. As Ambler asserted in his introduction to *Waiting for Orders*, his short story collection, 'to belong noticeably to the times we were living in [the master detective] must be a refugee' (5). Interestingly, in its non-specific designation, in awarding refugee status to his 'master' detectives, Ambler's statement would include those who are British. But contrary to conventional British thrillers of the period, British subjectivity in Ambler's novels guarantees neither moral certainty nor protection, and as grouped with non-British refugees, reminds us of their tenuous political and narrative positions when placed in Europe or beyond. Exerting historical pressure on British political and ethical agency, as well as on modernist detachment, Ambler's British subjects represent narrative opportunities to question their nation's responses to the victims of Fascist nationalism. Stateless characters may set narrative and political plots in motion, but their position prevents them from benefiting from or even surviving this narrative agency. The unsubstantiated character of Dimitrios complicates the narrative condition of statelessness as both features serve his villainy and its political significance.

Latimer's search for Dimitrios as a muse for a new genre and forms of character and plot, produces an investigative spy thriller shaped by problems and questions with dubious answers. In fact, the only responses available take the form of ellipses and fragments. The novel elides both a linear plot and resolution as the villain's tale becomes increasingly entangled in the various narrators' fragmented and nebulous stories. Their selective memories and tales of betrayal can only produce bias in extremis. That the characters of these narrators are as disjointed as their stories is apparent from Latimer's first interview with Colonel Haki, who is identified as a patchwork of unverifiable rumours, just like Dimitrios. But with even more narrative dissonance, what we learn of Dimitrios is hearsay. Lacking any self-presentation, even when he finally makes his appearance, the story of Dimitrios can only be a compilation of his dastardly deeds, with unbridled greed the only motivation that coheres. With no perspective of his own, Dimitrios is less a fictional character than a proposition about the construction of the character of the villain at the end of the 1930s. The 1939 British edition of the novel includes a passage in Chapter 5, 'Nineteen Twenty-three', omitted in the American editions, that offers Latimer's reflection on the problem of representing Dimitrios:

As for the description, it might, like most other tabulated descriptions, have fitted tens of thousands of men. With most persons, recognition, even of an intimate, was based on the perception of vague, half-observed quantities which together formed a caricature significant more in its relation to the observer than to the observed. A short man, conscious of his lack of height, would describe a man of medium height as tall [. . .] But he, Latimer, needed more. He needed a portrait of Dimitrios, a portrait by an artist, an arrangement of accented lines infused by some alchemy with the spirit of the sitter. And if that were not available he must make his own portrait of Dimitrios from what crude daubs he could find in police dossiers, superimposing them on one another in the hope that two dimensions might eventually become three. (76–7)[34]

The result of Latimer's quest to understand the villain in any coherent terms is, in Marek Haltof's terms, a Gothic Expressionist construct of 'reality which is haunted by fantasies, emotions, memory, dreams and the tension between the subject and the object' (443). Or, as the sum of his crimes, 'It would be as if a waxwork in a chamber of horrors had come to life' (*A Coffin*, 139). But this is life in a static figure who is always either a corpse or a facsimile of petrified humanity. His character never develops; despite his frenetic travels, encounters and crimes, it remains a lifeless list of infamies, as Latimer's charts reveal. Dimitrios' character is empty of feeling. As with all his contacts, his betrayed lover, Mme Preveza, represents Dimitrios as passionate only about money, his one sexual charge and the sum and substance of his masculinity. The combination of Dimitrios' haunting absences and presence, his innumerable escapes, splintered but circular fate, and the novel's two titles, *Mask of . . .* and *A Coffin for . . .* imply that these narrative shards defy assumptions about creating coherent villains. Instead, Dimitrios' character questions whether classic or revisionary detective or spy fictions can create mimetically recognisable human villains or track them through ratiocinative logic. Whether Dimitrios is ultimately unknowable or the object of vengeance, his character is suspended, a fictional choice, residing and materialising in an Expressionist space endowed with more material reality than his character – Ambler's political dystopia.

Latimer's travels westward to Geneva where he interviews Grodek, a master spy and another writer, produce only another narrative chip which confirms that knowledge of Dimitrios remains shadowy and unsubstantiated. Although the list of the villain's infamies expands, it does not endow him with subjectivity. It is as though his character has been set on automatic pilot, without consciousness or will, driven by his two authors' desire to dislodge him from conventional fictional templates. Whatever lucidity Latimer anticipates as his story of Dimitrios moves through Europe, ends darkly in Paris. The Gothic Expressionist depiction of the city of light is represented as though the tools of gritty realism have lost their revelatory edge. Instead, realism is transformed into a grotesque montage of a decaying and monstrous cityscape, a suitable atmosphere for the materialisation and dematerialisation of Dimitrios, whose Fascist villainy is both expected and elusive:

> a panorama of low, black clouds moving quickly in the chill, dusty wind. The long façade of the houses on the Quai de Corse were still and secretive. It was as if each window concealed a watcher [. . .] Paris, in that late autumn afternoon, had the macabre formality of a steel engraving. (*A Coffin*, 98)

Reminiscent of medieval engravings of dystopian cityscapes, far removed from realism, this menacing Paris matches the building where Latimer first meets Dimitrios: shuttered and empty, built of a 'sightless expanse of cement' with 'drainpipes [that] writhed like snakes' (*A Coffin*, 98). The materiality of villainy suggests that Paris is already politically infected by the presence of the Fascist opportunist, recalling Expressionist cityscapes that connote 'moral chaos and conflict, malicious cruelty, greed, and the anxiety and disorientation elicited by these' (Tirohl, 142).

As though the atmosphere of the city, the building's exterior and its interior were co-ordinated by a Gothic Expressionist set designer, the room where Dimitrios first appears also parodies an orientalist nightmare of a den of iniquity. Ambler's jabs at Fascist Europe include a gendered mockery of its 'effete imperialism' or the 'baroque-Gothic' home of General Vagas, the Fascist agent in *Cause for Alarm*, as well as his rouged cheeks and love of ballet (*CA*, 132, 86). Dimitrios' backdrop indicates the counterfeit promises and unstable gender of masterful masculinity disguised and embedded in brutal economic politics. Set off by a curtain 'of imitation cloth of gold', Dimitrios is only partially visible in the room where 'the walls and ceiling were distempered an angry blue and bespattered with gold five-pointed stars' (*A Coffin*, 105). Intensifying the room's Expressionist aura, after Mr Peters and Dimitrios kill each other, Latimer imagines that their bodies 'might lie there for weeks in that ghastly room [. . .] while the blood congealed and hardened and collected dust and the flesh began to rot' (*A Coffin*, 164). With feverish apprehension about Dimitrios' appearance, Latimer imagines that 'the silence in the room' is 'almost tangible; a dark grey fluid that oozed from the corners of the room' (*A Coffin*, 146). As though already decomposed, the viscous presence of fascist capitalism slithers into the room as a disembodied, silhouetted form in smoky shadows, proclaiming his undying threat, 'I *shall* come back for more' (*A Coffin*, 160).

Allusive questions at the beginning of Latimer's quest for Dimitrios reverberate in this indeterminate appearance: 'By what route had he travelled to his appointment with Nemesis?' (*A Coffin*, 18). Relying on Ambler's reading of Jung, Nietzsche, Darwin and Spengler, Ambrosetti identifies this route as leading to a mythical shadowland, a hell where Nemesis is identified as 'the "free spirit"' of 'the Dionysiac Dimitrios' who represents 'the primeval depths of the collective unconscious' where the 'will to power' runs free (53, 57). Snyder notes that 'the signifier "Dimitrios Makropoulos" is always already a [. . .] spectral trace that exists [. . .] only under erasure'. Dimitrios haunts Latimer as an insoluble enigma because having passed '"beyond good and evil", he defined himself by moral vacancy and incommensurate alterity' (247). Latimer's attempt to construct Dimitrios as a character reminds us of how this *doppelgänger* both eludes and is trapped by all allegorical attempts to define and contain him. Mythic allegories create equivalent narrative planes that contain Dimitrios in a symmetrical explanation, but his elusiveness defies this certainty. He does not represent the content of a story but rather an assortment of narrative styles and allusions emptied of mythic, psychological or philosophical content. For example, the construction of Dimitrios also recalls Mary Shelley's Dr Frankenstein and its Gothic Expressionist film adaptations where the doctor stitches the corpse into a life form that runs amok in the darkened daylight world of reason.

Like the Doctor's monster and like Dracula or Nosferatu, Dimitrios is one of the stalking undead: he materialises only as a corpse; his spectral presence which even in its almost limitless suggestiveness cannot be contained in a generic story of terror. As Barbara Creed defines the corpse in horror films,

> it represents the body at its most abject. It is a body evacuated by the self – but worse still, it is a body which has become a waste [. . .] The existence of the abject points always to the subject's precarious hold on what it means to be human. For the abject [. . .] beckons from the boundaries, seeking to upset the already unstable nature of subjectivity, waiting to claim victory over the 'human'. (146, 150)

The troubling place of Dimitrios' humanity is parsed in a long passage in the 1939 British edition analysing the chemical formulation of heroin, Dimitrios' drug of choice for trafficking and habit. A journalist calling himself '*Veilleur*' depicts 'thousands of Frenchmen – yes, *and* Frenchwomen! – suffering the tortures of the damned through this diabolical traffic which was sapping the virility of the nation' (*MD*, 157). Redolent with anxieties about a plague of alien infestation, figured as 'alley rats', the passage recalls racist denunciations of East

European immigrants to the West, encapsulated in Dracula's travel from Transylvania to Britain (*MD*, 158). Dimitrios is the quintessential outsider to definitions of the human, a suspicious alien wherever he goes, complete with multiple identities. In this sense he embodies racialist dehumanisation of the alien but with a critical distinction. The novel judges him, not as an abject victim but as linked to the spread of a Fascist 'plague'; he is a perpetrator of dehumanisation. His own migrancy leads not to empathy for other stateless refugees but to his exploitation of them in his transnational sex trafficking in which gender and racial abuse conflate. For Dimitrios there is no difference between 'a white girl from a Bucharest slum' and 'a negro girl from Dakar or a Chinese girl from Harbin' (*A Coffin*, 110). Dimitrios applies his inside knowledge of statelessness to provide these sex slaves with 'fake birth, marriage and death certificates' and 'several identities' (*A Coffin*, 110). But unlike their victimiser, these women are damaged so indelibly by their objectifying abuse, they have neither individuality nor access to the amorphous character that can break out of exploitation.

As the novel cites repeatedly, the story of Dimitrios' serial infamies is historically bounded, from 1922 to 1936. He may belong nowhere and appear everywhere, but where and when he appears, his activities manipulate political conflicts of the past. With no barriers to stop him, his machinations bleed into national and transnational social and political insecurities and instability in the present of the novel. He is the instrument, manipulator and beneficiary of fascist capitalism. His robberies and trafficking may seem paltry crimes besides Fascist or Nazi oppression, but combined with political assassinations and inciting internecine violence, his infamy symbolises Fascist exploitation and functions on its behalf. Peter Lewis identifies 'parallels between Dimitrios and Hitler', but not as Ambler's conscious efforts (73). And yet the accretion of corroborating evidence throughout Ambler's writing of the 1930s indicates that the parallel represents an aesthetic and political choice, fusing dystopian warning with Dimitrios' Gothic Expressionist form. As in Ambler's other novels of the decade, the escalating danger emanates from perpetrators of fascist capitalism like Cator and Bliss, the armaments cartel in *The Dark Frontier*; the Eurasian Credit Trust in *Dimitrios*, responsible for a Bulgarian coup and organising two assassinations; or in *Background to Danger*, Pan Eurasion Petroleum. The Marxist investigative journalist Marukakis analyses the connection between Dimitrios and fascist capitalism: 'Can one explain Dimitrios or must one turn away disgusted and defeated? [. . .] All I do know is that while might is right, while chaos and anarchy masquerade as order and enlightenment, those conditions [that create] the special sort or criminal that he typified [...] will obtain' (*A Coffin*, 167). Despite the narration of Dimitrios' death as a certainty, despite Latimer's testimony, this may not be 'the end of an Odyssey' (*A Coffin*, 18). Instead, the undead Fascist menace lives on to threaten Europe another day.

Ronald Ambrosetti succinctly observes that 'the notions that civilization should reach such a final period of corruption and that a man such as Dimitrios should embody the very spirit of the age are equally as logical and consistent in their grotesqueness. Hitler and Dimitrios had won out over Beethoven and Einstein' (52). Linking the Nietzschean concept of the will to power to Jungian psychology and Darwinian struggle, Ambrosetti argues that the novel invokes 'a turbulent, and sometimes demonic, dynamism that constitutes the shadow-side of a human being' (57). If we link this observation to Ambler's historicist analysis, a key point is that Nietzsche's Superman materialises as central to Hitler's racialist ideology of the Master Race and its policies and practices. We can see Ambler invoking this Hitlerian spectre in his Gothic Expressionist character of Dimitrios. The 1939 British edition prefigures the troubling awe inspired by a charismatic leader when Mr Peters, Dimitrios' comrade in crime, proffers that all the wisdom and stimulation he has sought in reading 'philosophy and the arts' has only led him to 'just wait until the Great One summons us' (*A Coffin*, 167).

Latimer's quest reveals only displaced knowledge and meanings. Nothing in his study of political economy has prepared him for the fascist capitalism Dimitrios represents. The depression that drove him to escape 'the philosophy of National Socialism and its prophet, Dr Rosenberg' is prescient, but there is no escape from their crimes, as manifest in those of Dimitrios. But instead of Colonal Haki's claim that gritty realism is the nature of true crime, the many masks of Dimitrios, including 'a devil mask', challenge the mimetic value of realist detail, linear chronology, empirical investigation and the genre's powers of representation (*A Coffin*, 147). The only identifiable theme that coheres throughout the partial narratives of Dimitrios is that of rogue economics: Dimitrios' robberies in Athens and Smyrna; his fees for helping to assassinate the Bulgarian Prime Minister and spying for France; the unpaid debt owed to his lover Madame Preveza; the blackmail price for procuring strategic maritime charts; and profits from sex slave and drug trafficking. His career reaches its zenith when he becomes an officer at the Eurasian Credit Trust, signifying the equally opaque corporate body responsible for such nefarious enterprises as 'the clandestine manufacture of heroin in Bulgaria for illicit export' (*A Coffin*, 45).

Yet no matter how many dossiers summarise his biography or how meticulously Latimer reads police reports and newspaper articles and charts the chronology of Dimitrios' movements and actions, these documents reveal little complexity about the man, none of the logical progressions of the detective or spy thriller and no philosophical or psychological insights, as Latimer concludes:

> But it was useless to try to explain him in terms of Good and Evil. They were no more than baroque abstractions. Good Business and Bad Business were the elements of the new theology. Dimitrios was not evil. He was logical and consistent; as logical and consistent in the European jungle as the poison gas called Lewisite and the shattered bodies of children killed in the bombardment of an open town. The logic of Michael Angelo's *David*, Beethoven's quartets and Einstein's physics had been replaced by that of the *Stock Exchange Year Book* and Hitler's *Mein Kampf*. (*A Coffin*, 136)

Haltof explains that 'In both the Gothic novels and Expressionist films, the struggle between good and evil is usually projected into the external self – the double which Expressionist films represent as a shadow living its own life' or some kind of 'monster' (*A Coffin*, 451). In psychoanalytic theory, which became a prominent epistemology during the same period as the flowering of Expressionist films, the double would represent 'a 'return of the repressed' (*A Coffin*, 450). The political psychology of Ambler's thrillers would externalise the repressed as the fear of confronting the dangers of Fascism and Nazism. Dimitrios would be the face of Fascism.[35] In his shadowy form, he reflects back on those who would appease rather than confront the Fascist and Nazi threat.

As a writer of escapist detective pastorals, Latimer ultimately tries to escape the dystopian story and state of Europe and the Mediterranean to which his muse, the character Dimitrios, leads him. In the 1939 British edition, the narrator instructs Latimer and readers:

> The worlds of escape, the fantasies you created for your own comfort were well enough if you could live within them. But split the membrane that divided you from the real world and the fantasies perished. You were free and alive; but in a world of frustration [. . .] In any case, the detective story-writer has no business with reality except in so far as it concerns the technicalities of such things as ballistics, medicine, the laws of evidence and police procedure. Let that be quite clear. (*A Coffin*, 120)

At the end of the novel, Latimer contemplates writing 'worlds of escape' far from the turbulence of Europe and responsibility for interpreting its story. As the 1939 British edition explains, he would escape 'The story of Dimitrios [that] had no proper ending' (*A Coffin*, 239). Instead, he would be writing a detective story with a beginning, a middle and an end; a corpse, a piece of detection and a scaffold. He would be demonstrating that 'justice triumphed in the end [and] Dimitrios and the

Eurasian Credit Trust would be forgotten. It had all been a great waste of time' (*A Coffin*, 1939, 239). In his aesthetic and political practice, Latimer would return to the more comforting climes protected by the ratiocination of the mildly interventionist Miss Marple:

> There was plenty of fun to be got out of an English country village, wasn't there? The time? Summer; with cricket matches on the village green, garden parties at the vicarage, the clink of tea-cups and the sweet smell of grass [. . .] That was the sort of thing people liked to hear about. It was the sort of thing that he himself would like to hear about. (*A Coffin*, 168)

Miss Marple can solve every murder that comes the way of her St Mary Mead because the human geography of the village is already mapped and she only needs to persevere, knitting her way to the patterned solution. As the last line of Ambler's novel indicates, however, writing fun fiction is not this writer's goal. When we're told that 'The train ran into a tunnel', we can surmise that Ambler's narrative of a transnational dystopian threat will blindside Latimer's refined fiction of country fête mayhem. Peter Lewis interprets this last sentence as showing Latimer's 'tunnel vision [. . .] Ambler's bitter comment on the naïveté and blindness of the English intelligentsia in the face of the fascist threat' (67). The perpetrator of many crimes may finally be killed, but as Latimer learns, he is only 'a unity in a disintegrating social system' (*A Coffin*, 46). This comment is important because it denotes the power of fascist capitalism that Dimitrios represents and which lives on as the product of dehumanising self-interest. Rationalised or even utilised by appeasers and isolationists, the fascist capitalism that transmogrifies into Nazism is a foregone conclusion. As discussed in the next chapter, Pamela Frankau's 1939 novel *The Devil We Know* and Helen MacInnes' and Ann Bridge's wartime novels show that there is no escape from the political philosophy of National Socialism and its stranglehold on Europe's political economy. As in all of Ambler's novels of the 1930s, these writers dramatise critical commentaries on the writer's political responsibility. Ambler's response was to develop a mode of non-realist fiction that would replace homogenised villainy, heroics and romanticised solutions with the irresolution that expressed anxiety about confronting totalitarian and British *realpolitik*. Anxiety would serve as muse for writing his Gothic Expressionist thrillers.

Although Ambler wrote film scripts for British army agencies during World War II, he only wrote one novel, *Journey into Fear*, published in 1940. Like *A Coffin for Dimitrios*, it begins in Istanbul, but narrates a different journey home to Britain from Latimer's. Instead of escape into the romance of a timeless England, *Journey* charts a voyage home to confront the war. Graham, the protagonist, is a British armaments engineer carrying blueprints for a Turkish defence system that can be interpreted metaphorically as plans for the creation of an allied system to defeat the Axis powers. That system is translated into human terms in the wartime fictions of Helen MacInnes and Ann Bridge, which imagine a united anti-Nazi front as a joint American and British mission.

Notes

1. Ernst Toller, a Prussian Jew, began his career as a leader of the Bavarian Soviet Republic and was acclaimed for his plays, *Transformations*, *Masses Man*, *The Machine Breakers*, *Hinkemann, the German* and many poems. Stripped of his German citizenship by the Third Reich in 1933, he emigrated to the US, joining other German writers, such as Klaus Mann, but depression engulfed him upon learning that his sister and brother were deported to concentration camps and he committed suicide in 1939.
2. For Ambler's concerns about political instability in 1930s Central and Southeastern Europe, see Robert L. Snyder, Chris Hopkins, Brett Woods, Ronald Ambrosetti, Peter Lewis and Peter Wolfe. Michael Denning argues that Ambler's anti-fascism is more aesthetic than a reflection of 'his politics, which remain relatively unfocused', p. 65. I maintain that Ambler's aesthetic is political.
3. Ambler also assessed Buchan's spy fiction as achieving 'a higher level of reality than those of Oppenheim' but his 'spy-heroes [. . .] who went about their work with a solemn, manly innocence [. . .] could lapse into stupidity. They were also emotionally unstable', 'Introduction', *To Catch a Spy*, pp. 16–17.
4. Between 1940 and 1951, Ambler gave up writing novels to become Assistant Director of Army Cinematography in the British War Office; while producing propaganda films, he co-wrote the screenplay for Carol Reed's *The Way Ahead* (1944) with Peter Ustinov. After the war, he collaborated with director David Lean on *Passionate Friends* (1949), and in 1952 with Ronald Neame on *The Card*, based on Arnold Bennett's novel. His later writing for film and television includes *The Cruel Sea* (1953), *The Purple Plain* (1954), *A Night to Remember* (1958), *Checkmate* (1960–2), and *Topkapi* (1964).
5. Given Ambler's unequivocal indictment of Fascism and Nazism, I disagree with Brett Woods' claim that 'Ambler struck a note of neutralism in his spy novels [. . .] enlightening the reader that, in the pursuit of espionage, one side was really as bad as the other' (np).
6. Wesley Britton notes that 'until the rise of Adolf Hitler [. . .] national defense was more a matter of the imagination and romance and not a reflection of cultural and ideological fears beyond the racism and anti-Semitism that dominated the period', p. 19.
7. Le Queux and Oppenheim were best-selling authors between 1900 and 1914, producing hundreds of spy thrillers between them. Although John

Buchan's World War I novels are far more complex and accomplished, with contemporary resonance, he universalises political conflict.
8. Like other critics, Peter Lewis finds that Ambler's novels of this period realistically depict Europe's political crises, p. 38. Woods refers to Ambler's style as 'sinister realism' but in my reading, 'sinister' realities become so extreme as to require a different aesthetic.
9. Thomas Elsaesser discusses the films of Fritz Lang and other Weimar filmmakers as detective fictions.
10. Tony Kushner shows that in response to the Nuremberg Laws, while 'the persecution of the Jews, however much disapproved, was not seen as a problem for the democracies [. . .] Indeed many were content to accept that such matters were the internal affair of another sovereign state' (*LIH*, 43). Arthur Marwick observes that 'in the light of the contemporary belief that Germany had been harshly treated at Versailles', Germany's reoccupation of the Rhineland 'was a particularly unattractive issue on which to rattle the sabre', and was rationalised further as the region 'after all [being] a part of Germany' (252).
11. In Ambler's 1930s novels, threats to the spy's masculinity or to the power of the nation do not include femmes fatales. The sole possibility is Irana Preveza, the prostitute mistress of Dimitrios. Since, however, she is already a brutalised victim when she makes her appearance, she never has a chance to show her skills at seduction. Ambler's typical female characters are either sidelined by male bonding and antipathy or absent wives and fiancées and fleeting romantic interests. The exception is Claire, the fiancée of Marlow, the protagonist in *Cause for Alarm*, who has no intention of sacrificing her career for housework. Otherwise, women are incidental in Ambler's plots.
12. Roger Luckhurst argues that Gothic tropes should reflect their historical time and place: 'the ghosts of London are different from those of Paris, or those of California', p. 542.
13. See Rachel Carroll's study of fictional representations of heteronormativity.
14. Ambler admits 'underestimate[ing] the economic and industrial resources needed to develop the bomb', *Here Lies*, p. 121. For literary uses and abuses of the Balkans, see Vesna Goldsworthy.
15. In his study of John le Carré's novels, James M. Buzard argues that photography plays 'a central element in all espionage activity', p. 159.
16. Peter Neville discusses how Lord Astor, host of the Cliveden set, owned the *Times* and the *Observer*, whose editors agreed that even though the Nazi regime 'was essentially brutal and ruthless [. . .] Hitler had restored German honour and given the country stability' (22). Debates about the affinity of the Duke and Duchess of Windsor with Hitler continue. Neville's view is that, like others of his class, the Duke 'found the order and community spirit brought by Nazism attractive' (28).
17. Snyder observes that in Ambler's first novel 'seriousness disrupts its mimetic framework' with a 'set-piece on warmongering' that 'reveals his authorial struggle against the modernist imperative of "impersonal" narration', pp. 230–1.
18. Carol Diethe explains that Expressionist films use exterior scenes to produce plot distortions that reflect the 'lack of anything resembling normal family life', creating 'a curious vacuum', p. 60.

19. Ambler wryly notes that Communist speakers at literary meetings were 'in special need of dialectical assistance and straight-from-the-shoulder Marxist common sense', *Here Lies*, p. 125.
20. The variety of critics' interpretations of Ambler's leftist politics echoes debates of the 1930s: Ambrosetti interprets Ambler's Marxist references as conveying 'a very un-Marxian feeling of personal helplessness', p. 38. Snyder notes that Ambler's 'embedded [socialist] critique' characterises many '"serious" thrillers during the 1930s', p. 248. Chris Hopkins explores contradictory responses of 1930s leftist critics to the spy thriller and shows how Ambler distinguishes the thriller's escapism and 'truth of the contemporary world', p.157.
21. This quotation and others in Ambler's fiction opposes Homberger's claim that 'No "serious" novel of the 1930s registered the true nature of Hitlerian aggression', p. 88.
22. See Deutelbaum and Poague, p. 114.
23. Sander Gilman offers different perspectives on Nazi constructions of Jewish men and women as sexual predators and the interdiction against *Rassenschande* or race defilement.
24. With incisive historical analysis, Katarzyna Marciniak critiques theories of transnationalism that assert a 'somewhat salutary tone of mobility'. Instead, 'it is important to acknowledge that for many exiles such crossings are extremely problematic, risky, or sometimes not possible at all', p. xiv.
25. In his study *The Holocaust and the Liberal Imagination*, Tony Kushner examines British and American responses in the late 1930s, including the 1939 British White Paper that documented German atrocities but 'was unhappy using stories involving Jews' out of 'reluctance to identify in any direct way with the Jewish plight or to somehow connect the British war effort with the protection of the Jews', p. 123.
26. For example, see the articles on Virginia Woolf in the volume *Philosemitism and Antisemitism* and the essay 'A Tale of Two Cities' (2008).
27. Peter Lewis reports that Paul Czissar was the name of a prominent Czech anti-Nazi newspaper editor who Ambler knew 'in London, using his name for the central character of a cluster of detective stories with the overall title, *The Intrusions of Dr Czissar*', p. 50. In Ambler's story 'The Army of Shadows' Czissar lives in Switzerland where he produces anti-Nazi propaganda.
28. Wolfe points out that because Beghin uses the same tactics as Fascism, they are 'so pernicious and important to defeat', p. 51.
29. Peter Lewis notes, 'Schimler's conversion from social democracy to communism' questions 'which enemy – Nazi or Communist – is interested in the coastal fortifications of the Fr Navy?' For Ambler, the world of 1938 was one committed to more than one course of self-destruction, p. 42.
30. In addition to the Jews as the Nazis' primary target, other threatened groups included the Roma and Sinti, Jehovah's Witnesses, homosexuals, the physically and mentally handicapped, Communists, and political dissidents. See the United States Holocaust Memorial Museum website: 'Mosaic of Victims'. That 1938 was already too late is confirmed by the international conference at Evian-les-Bains on 6 July organised by President Franklin Roosevelt in which no nation in attendance agreed to take in any

Jews. As Bernard Wasserstein reports, 'On the night of October 28, 1938, German police abruptly arrested eighteen thousand Jews of Polish citizenship in cities throughout the Reich' (*On the Eve*, p. 372).
31. Suggesting unwelcome news, Wolfe cites the novel's publication in the US fourteen years after its British appearance, p. 53.
32. The Popular Front was a response to the Fascist threat to Spain's Republicanism and included Socialists, Communists, the Marxist POUM and two bourgeois parties. The coalition fell apart over contesting visions of a Communist or bourgeois future. When the Communists won control, persecution of other factions ensued. See Fyrth for Britain's role.
33. Robert Snyder reports that scholars who take Ambler seriously 'concur that, as World War II approached, he intentionally set out to transform the conventional thriller', p. 23.
34. Peter Lewis notes that Knopf's cuts in the American edition were intended 'to speed up the action, but the removal of [...] description, character analysis, introspection, and even dialogue' represents a loss of 'depth and amplitude', p. 63.
35. Lewis finds biographical parallels between Dimitrios and Hitler, including dates of their involvement in political coups and interference in other nations in the later 1930s, p. 73.

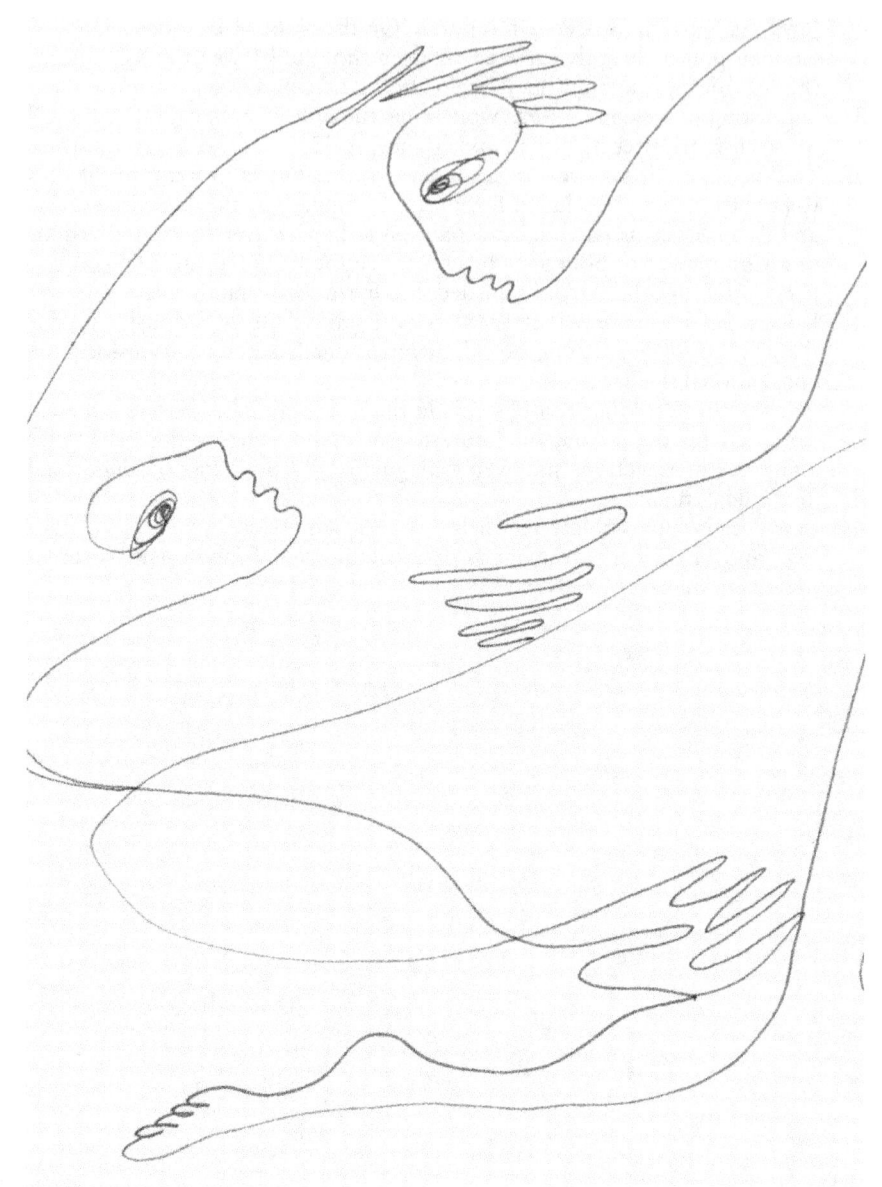

Chapter 2

Double Agency: Women Writers of Espionage Fiction

While critical attention to women writers of detective fiction only continues to proliferate, those who wrote espionage fiction are still neglected. Studies of 'golden age' writers of detective fiction such as Agatha Christie, Dorothy Sayers and Margery Allingham abound, while mention of Helen MacInnes and Ann Bridge produces mostly blank stares.[1] This disparity is especially surprising since plots in both genres are based on similar templates: suspicion, assassination, investigation, deception and betrayal. While it is also true that spy fiction is most often a man's game and of political import beyond the social order of country houses and picturesque villages, this is not so different from the key players and subjects of detective fiction. Christie's Hercule Poirot, Sayers' Lord Peter Wimsey and Allingham's Albert Campion are frequently called upon to save the nation from internal plotters and international agents. Indeed, despite different narrative constructions of suspense and investigation, both genres are often classified as thrillers.[2] Of course the neglect of espionage fiction by women writers is also a matter of the marketplace: having been out of print for decades, their novels have been invisible.[3]

If, however, one considers this phenomenon a case of gendered neglect, then voluminous questions arise, including women writers' narrative relationship to the conventions of spy fiction. As with studies of middlebrow fiction, reading women's spy thrillers reveals their keen insights into narrative and political relationships.[4] As Janet Montefiore demonstrates, these insights are based on viewing 'women as historic subjects' and as voices of political conviction and activism (20). Interestingly varied in narrative techniques and insights, such writers as Helen MacInnes, Ann Bridge and Pamela Frankau also share thematic ground with other writers in this book. Like Eric Ambler and Leslie Howard, MacInnes, Bridge and Frankau dramatise ethical and political concerns about the viability of a second world war. Like those by John le

Carré, women's novels of the Cold War are compelled by reassessments of victory over Nazism in World War II. This chapter will examine how women writers' representations of pre-war tensions, wartime espionage and Cold War memories of World War II trouble and revise the genre's gendered conventions and perhaps even readers' expectations.

One significant difference between the men and women writers I study is that spy protagonists created by women writers are often women.[5] Like Ambler's spies, they are amateurs, but rather than stumbling into the Secret World, these women agents make deliberate choices to become secret operatives based on political convictions, not unlike Leslie Howard's Horatio Smith, discussed in the following chapter. Instead, however, of situating conflict within male dominated spheres of power and creating suspense by deploying thrilling chases, Pamela Frankau, Helen MacInnes and Ann Bridge reconfigure suspense as the development of individual agency. Neither heroes nor anti-heroes, neither femmes fatales nor matinee idols, their men and women spies occupy a challenging narrative space that questions and revises distinctions between home front and battleground, and between exile and espionage as action, state of being and gendered identity. These women writers show that when female protagonists become secret agents, they infiltrate the male domain of espionage, but not in the roles of sidekick or handmaiden.[6] Instead, as they activate their missions, they also critique and revise official and conventional political convictions. In the process, women spies exile themselves from the domestic sphere and their private roles. The result is a revisionist double agency.

This chapter will consider how Pamela Frankau, Helen MacInnes and Ann Bridge narrate various political crises of the twentieth century as producing the conditions and experiences of deracination and exile. Choosing espionage isolates their women protagonists from the social and political spheres with which they and their gender roles have traditionally been identified. Whether or not they return home, this estrangement unsettles the genre's construction of masculinity and femininity. Such reigning features as double agents and double crosses are complicated and replaced by cross-dressing, gender doubling and the emergence and activation of women's and men's political consciousness. Overall, they mobilise different definitions of spying to question what it means to be human at a moment of historical crisis when humanity is under siege. Helen MacInnes' 1941 novel, *Above Suspicion*, dramatises the genre's reliance on violent action as insubstantial compared to a woman's political polemic. In Ann Bridge's 1953 novel, *A Place to Stand* the social and domestic stability and constraints of women's lives are shattered as women assume resistance roles, for which their prior experiences offer no preparation.

Pamela Frankau's Unlikely Spy

> If I were capable of cataloguing my preference among people I should head the list with writers and Jews. The hero-worshipping public [...] has not much use for writers (or indeed for Jews)'. (*I Find Four People*, 277)

> I do not believe that there is a single person alive in Europe at this moment who is not afraid. (*The Devil We Know*, 468)

I begin this chapter with a novel that might seem an anomaly in this book. Although it engages a time of intense international intrigue, Pamela Frankau's 1939 *The Devil We Know* would certainly not be found on any canonical list of spy fiction. I chose it because it is a woman writer's prelude to ongoing concerns of the genre about citizenship and displacement and the narrative relation of these legal and political terms to the gendered characterisation of racialised difference. Frankau published over thirty novels in addition to short stories, an autobiography, journalism, and stage and radio plays. Although her writing was critically acclaimed and popular in her time, engaging subjects that remain compelling today, she has yet to generate the scholarly interest her writing deserves.[7] Recalling Eric Ambler's depiction of statelessness in the 1930s, *The Devil We Know* portrays the refugee's indelible mark of exile as producing both cultural and gendered disorientation. For Philip Meyer, Frankau's Jewish protagonist, this unsettling combination produces the impetus for espionage. In its temporal progress from January 1931 to September 1937, Frankau's novel dramatises how the character of a spy is created out of Jewish exile in Britain's social culture and as a prime target in Europe's emerging catastrophe.[8] From its opening scene through to its epilogue, the novel traces Meyer's moral and psychological awakening from being a self-loathing refugee to becoming a secret agent on a rescue mission. Meyer's mission, to rescue his disabled brother from Germany in 1937, could be read as an act of redemptive transformation, and if it were to follow the annals of the genre, as on its way to being a heroic success, much like the efforts of Leslie Howard's Horatio Smith. Instead, the novel enters fully charted but unstable narrative and historical territory where tragic failure looms. In 1938–9 when Frankau writes this novel, she knows that what awaits the brothers is the probability of a dead end – two of the Nazi programs to kill designated undesirables were already in place: the *Aktion T4* for the disabled and concentration camps for all others – life unworthy of life (*Lebensunwertes Leben*).⁹ While he acts as an individual, on his own initiative, and therefore suggests self-determination, history will stonewall and more than likely devour him.

Although he resembles Ambler's Desmond Kenton in lacking a plan of action, Philip Meyer is not an accidental agent. His spy story is determined by and forms a critical history of Anglo-Jewish immigration when Meyer reveals that at the age of six, he was sent from Germany to Britain in 1913, 'a nasty yellow little boy' (*Devil*, 7). Although this is Meyer's retrospective voice, it ventriloquises social and political attitudes that prevent his character and plot from following the narrative trajectory of the *Bildungsroman*. Instead of learning from his mistakes in a world of moral complexity, he internalises and embodies a modern history of race hatred that disallows participation in stories of confronting and overcoming adversity.¹⁰ Atypical of the *Bildungsroman*, Meyer will not integrate into any community. From beginning to end of the novel, the stain of antisemitism drives the narrative and the ambiguity of Meyer's gendered character as outsider, outlier and spy. The novel's round trip but circular itinerary, from exile to exile, promises no end to dystopian foreboding, especially since the novel ends with his return to Germany in 1937.¹¹ Like a double agent, Meyer identifies all locations as enemy territory; even among friends and colleagues, he acts as though he is behind the lines, urgently gathering secret information and trusting no one. Since he has no nation he calls his own, his intelligence work is on behalf of his obsessive suspicions and quest to determine if there is rescue anywhere for the wandering Jew. The novel's suspense is churned by the question of whether his quest will reinforce or heal his position as outsider. Will his suspicions turn against him or will they produce redemptive truths? Like a spy, will his suspicions replicate his distrustful character and will his vulnerability become a self-fulfilling fate?

Sociologist Zygmunt Bauman theorises that 'strangers' and those who occupy 'ambivalent' positions in a national or local social culture can only hope to integrate if they erase their differences and adopt social and cultural codes to become 'indistinguishable from the hosts, and by the same token guarantee their reclassification as insiders, entitled to the treatment that friends routinely receive' (71).¹² The biological and social connotations of the word 'hosts' apply easily to Frankau's construction of Meyer. Biologically, 'host' is the body supplying the necessary nourishment for the life dependent on it, typically, according to the *OED*, 'living in or upon it' (vol. 1, 1336). Socially, 'host' refers to someone who supplies home or commercial hospitality. Both meanings have political resonance insofar as a 'host' nation takes in those who immigrate for acceptable reasons, such as political or economic oppression. In light of each other, these meanings also reflect the status of the immigrant who regardless of resources or sponsorship can be viewed in racialist terms as an alien being and as a parasite on the national body. The *OED* notes an ancient meaning of 'host' as 'stranger or enemy' (1336).

Despite affirmation for his work as a screenwriter and a circle of warm friendships, Meyer never overcomes his Jewish refugee status.[13] Instead he internalises and recreates the negative stereotypes that mark Jews, particularly Jewish men, as unassimilable to mainstream British culture: 'Outward persecution was less always than the persecution in his own mind, the fear of giving offence, the fear of losing money, the fear of failure' (*Devil*, 21).[14] Whereas fictional spies typically combat fear in order to serve their nations and allies, for financial gain or to discover and stabilise their identities as authentic men, Frankau's repetition of 'fear' suggests perpetual victimisation and exile, not only politically but in gendered terms as well.[15] Like a repetition compulsion, 'fear' here is an imprisoning response to omnipresent danger: 'Jews always think that things are not safe. They are scared stiff of illness and doctors and microbes' (*Devil*, 209). All 'things' in this novel are weapons of destruction, disguised as ordinary objects; there are no benign 'microbes'. It is as though the Jews have absorbed their historical status as strangers and the condition of persecution so that these have become features of their DNA, following a Lamarckian trajectory – history as the source of biology, psychology and narrative: 'He had translated his sufferings into a world allegory. He saw his sickness reflected on the face of all things' (*Devil*, 368). Fear in *The Devil We Know* forms the essential constitution of the Jews' exiled and gendered Jewish double bind. Fear makes them suspicious and suspect, consolidated as spies.

No matter how long they have resided in Britain (since their readmission from expulsion in 1656) or served the nation as citizens, the Jews in Frankau's novel reflect a pervasive anxiety. As their individual, sometimes conflicting responses, form a collective pattern of defensiveness, they cohere as a nation of troubled difference and mutual suspicion. The Jews appear to occupy a compressed, claustrophobic spatial and temporal structure within the nation they and its citizens imagine as unified. In the novel's imagined social reality, however, the Jews occupy an exiled position defined by the differences that make them an uncanny presence. Whether they have allies is a moot point in Philip Meyer's Britain. The quotidian for Jewish characters is to be suspected of dual, sometimes conflicting loyalties, and therefore they occupy a liminal status that rarely heals or undoes misunderstanding and mistrust.[16] Featuring several Jewish male characters, *The Devil We Know* argues that self-determination and self-affirmation for Jewish men as individuals, as community leaders and as integral to British economic and cultural production, depend on deciphering, understanding and accommodating British social and cultural expectations. All this while not abandoning their chosen differences. Both wishing to assimilate and to retain their Jewish difference, Jewish men function like double agents, whether in disguise as English bourgeoisie or as eternal refugees. The result of choosing ambivalence means accepting their status as social and gendered intruders, reflected in Philip Meyer's response to an antisemitic slur:

> My race doesn't fight: it has got what it wanted by a policy of acceptance tempered with denial for two thousand years. It excels at turning the other cheek. Which, when you come to consider its profile, is a deliberate instance of self-depreciation. (*Devil*, 280)

In this jab at conventional models of masculine militarism and at allegations of insidious Jewish passivity, Meyer asserts a gendered Jewish identity as deliberately unsettled.

In this novel, featuring the Jewish film industry, commercial success depends on producing stories that win popular approval by subordinating aesthetic concerns to perceived consumer desires.[17] Of course this surrender only demonstrates the film producers' contested position between accommodating and creating British cultural values. Reflecting age-old accusations of usurping and corrupting national cultures, not to mention dominating the film industry, the Jewish film mogul Jacob Lowenstal considers upward cultural mobility as a way out of his industry's cultural bind. He would like to inject 'taste' into his studio's potboiler, 'The Savage Saint', by 'bringing Bloomsbury in' (*Devil*, 130). Whether high modernist culture will rescue Jewish shlock from its crass commercialism remains an edgy and unresolved joke. The endeavour, which requires the Jewish moguls to perform as double agents, is doomed to fail. Attempting to pass as artists only exposes their hucksterism, the result of which is external and internalised antisemitic scorn. Accused of 'seldom mention[ing] anything but money', Jewish men are both admired and disparaged for their financial acumen which is assumed, in Philip Meyer's estimate, to originate in venality and to produce 'well-tailored' and 'bullying Jews [. . .] The rich ones are the worst' (*Devil*, 102, 214, 61). Jewish men may be accused of 'own[ing] Mayfair', but invitations to its drawing rooms and boardrooms elude them (*Devil*, 47). Marginal in so many ways, Jewish men in this novel also suffer a gendered double bind. Too aggressive, they are also perceived as effeminate. Like women, they are not expected to act on their own behalf but when they do, they are perceived as pushy. Because Frankau's depiction of Meyer's Jewish self-loathing knows no narrative bounds, determining the constitution of all events, references and interactions, she takes an enormous risk.[18] The danger that his introjection, perceptions and projections, that his monological expressions could be taken for hers and therefore accord with prevailing antisemitic stereotypes, might have been acceptable in the 1930s but remains problematic today.[19] The audacious critical thrust of the entire novel suggests that Frankau dramatises these stereotypes in order to subvert them. However, the story of Philip Meyer's odyssey across London, yearning for both affirmation and rejection, does not end there.

Meyer conducts each of his interactions and relationships as surveillance, an investigation into personal and political loyalty. Like a spy, he suspects deception and treachery everywhere and from everyone – friends, lover, employers and colleagues. Perceiving everyone as a stranger constructs the world as an alien place into which he, the perennial stranger, cannot be integrated. Akin to the self-cancelling character of double agents, he is a double negative. Projecting romantic wish-fulfilment fantasies onto his love relationship fulfils his suspicions rather than his desires. His love affair with a society dressmaker, Victoria Lloyd, appears to be chosen in part because its reality tests his self-doubts and misgivings as a Jewish man, the result of which is a fated betrayal. As her name indicates, Victoria represents the romanticised, unalloyed, unattainable British identity of which he cannot partake. Yet as Margaret Stetz observes, the name Lloyd may very well be Welsh.[20] There is a kind of dissonance between the two parts of her name, suggesting that she, too, is a hustler, trying to break into the mainstream. Like Meyer, she is an outsider, but as a working woman, doubly marginalised in upper-class British society. Their reciprocal sexual attraction is fraught with the tension of mutual suspicion and on her part, fear that he could destroy her ambitions to be an insider. His attraction to her is treacherous to both, a constant reminder of each being an interloper. The mirror in her apartment reveals the threat each represents to the other – the unbridgeable differences between them as multivalent: ontological as well as a projection of his and her suspicions and those of others:

> The glass gave him his own head, the lacquered hair and [. . .] smooth, honey-coloured, Jew-boy's face with the interruption of the white teeth, the large dark hollows for the eyes. His hands moved upward into the reflection and he was ashamed, letting them drop quickly to rest upon his knees. In the glass he saw Victoria turn slowly until the full view made her pale and compassionate as the Madonna. (*Devil*, 308)

Like Alice's looking glass, this mirror reflects the realities and fantasies of the viewer's experience of his world. Through his self-effacing consciousness, its image interlaces multifaceted connections between Meyer as a real and imagined outsider and his search for both confirmation and denial. Both designated and performed, his hunt for authenticity and acceptance questions the gendered and racialised character of the Jewish man by positioning him as a double agent. Meyers' double image functions like a camera's double exposure. As in Ambler's *Epitaph for a Spy*, two images combine as a result of being photographed without advancing the film. In this case, the double image is both accurate and distorted, reflecting a narrative that cannot move forward.

Although the mirror reflects two different people, Meyer's perspective constructs them both as refracted through his racialised and gendered self-perception. His perception idealises Victoria, but Meyer's self-portrait is self-incriminating. He depicts himself as a double traitor, acting on behalf of two opposing sides: his desire for her and his desire that she remain unattainable. His vision betrays both desires. Meyer sees Victoria turn 'to full view', but instead of this reflecting her volition and complexity, she remains a stagnant projection of his imprisoning self-rejection. His construction of their double portrait exposes their romance as a self-inflicted conflict exacerbated by transgressing an ideology of racial purity and gendered high definition. The language of 'honey-coloured' Jew-boy and the 'pale [. . .] Madonna' spotlights racial and gendered incompatibility. Certainly, by 1939, when the novel is published, Nazi ideology would identify the couple as committing *Rassenschande* or race defilement. That Meyer is both aggressive and defensive in this coupling is apparent even in a family friend's affectionate assessment: 'His neatness, his beauty, were overdone and obvious' (*Devil*, 487). This ascription of inherent and adopted excess suggests that the Jewish man is born into exile from British definitions of masculinity, an incurable condition. Meyer's physical appearance and transparent attempts to integrate defy British reserve and, like a blown cover, expose him as a poseur. A relationship with the beautiful, upwardly mobile non-Jewish woman can therefore only occupy enemy territory. His desire to marry her is an impossible mission – it would represent cross breeding in his acquiescence to Britain as a racial culture. Despite her protestations, Meyer is correct in telling her, '"I was just a temporary adventure"' (*Devil*, 312).

Whether or not Victoria really loves him matters less than his obsession with her. Not only does he desire to learn everything about her, as though she embodies secret intelligence about British identity, but he does this to the point of possessing or absorbing her racial and gendered difference into his sense of self. Like a self-fulfilling prophesy, his disproportionate desire signals his uncertain gender. As in Frankau's 1960 novel, *Colonel Blessington*, heterosexual identity and desire implode from the pressure of wanting to absorb the other. Although Meyer breaks off his relationship with Victoria and she moves on to one more compatible with her ambitions, he begins to stalk her, to spy on her, lurking in her hallway, lying in wait at 'the Café Royal where their story began' (*Devil*, 314). Whatever intelligence he gathers about her, they each remain 'a stranger' and a double agent to the other (*Devil*, 313).

The Jew as Historical Subject

Instead, however, of providing an explanatory backstory or psychological profile to explain Meyer's self-abnegating desire, Frankau is insistent about his historical and political position. If his suspicions become self-fulfilling prophesies, it is because of Frankau's 1939 political perspective, when the plight of European Jewish refugees seemed to replicate an ongoing history of betrayal. In that same year, Dorothy Thompson testified:

> There have been anti-Semitic movements in the world before. Polish and Russian pogroms are alive in the memories of many. But the Jewish persecution of our era is peculiar. It is not directed against the ghetto Jew alone, but against the Jewish race as such – against the Jew who has retained his religion and against the Jew who has discarded it. (382–3)

As though Meyer embodies this history, he distrusts his fellow Jews as much as he assumes the hostility of Gentiles. He never enters a room without 'scan[ning] the faces [to] identify the members of his own race, a practice which he indulged punctually and instinctively' (*Devil*, 37). Each of Meyer's encounters and relationships must withstand his only mode of conversation – interrogation – the end result of which confirms his suspicions. Despite the sympathetic and stalwart understanding of his cousin Sally and best friend, Jennifer Nash, there are no allies in Meyer's world view. Although Jennifer Nash offers political perspective, including reminders of the perils facing Meyer's brother, there is no cultural or social framework or institution that can dispel his sense of isolation and the exile from which there is no escape or respite. His self-loathing reveals distrust of his own character, isolating him from the sense that his life holds any possibility for reconciliation either with his yearning for connection or individual achievement. Although Meyer is the focalising consciousness of the novel through which Frankau represents the other characters, whether their responses are affectionate, questioning, barbed, supportive or deceitful, their differences collapse into unified proof of his suspicions.

The novel leaps from 1931 to May 1936, leaving a temporal gap that coincides with Meyer's disappearance and return to London where he appears as author of self-flagellating treatises against the 'damned fate' of the Jews: '*I have the honesty to admit, where others dare not, that no single man in this world could say now with absolute truth: "I am glad to be a Jew"*' (Frankau's italics, *Devil*, 353). As though reciting the Nazi racialist ideology he may have heard while in Vienna, he conflates antisemitic myths of the wandering, perfidious and indelibly marked Jew with the blood libel: '*And remember that this is a race without a country, living scattered* [. . .] *Dilute the blood with Christian blood and still the child of one Jewish parent is unquestionably a Jew*' (*Devil*, 353). For Meyer there is no self-determination for the Jew, no alternative destiny to '*persecutions*' and their lesson, '*that I deserved them*' (*Devil*, 354). Although physically absent when this polemic is read, Meyer's confrontational voice dominates the pages on which it appears, and in its relentless diatribe, resembles interrogation as psychological torture. His writing makes it nearly impossible for the reader on the page or of the page to look away. His interlocutors can lament what appears to them as a 'piece of atrocity' or 'lunacy' but neither they nor the narrative averts their attention from Meyer's text (*Devil*, 355). If we wish to continue reading, we yield to his hammering repetitions. At the same time, however, his writing calls attention to his worst fear: he is indeed a troublemaker, an intruder. There are no rhetorical or metaphorical signs that his writing is a plea for understanding, support or comfort. It is as though a key function of Meyer's writing is to exact the truth from his accusations while recognising, as spies do, that whatever the truth, it is duplicitous. He will nonetheless ensnare his British readers with their willingness to suspend disbelief in the process of enjoying their cultural heritage: '*the deprecating shrug of the Jew, caricatured along the ages. From Shylock to the music-hall comedian, you know the gesture*' (*Devil*, 354). We know the gesture and its encoded and troubled place in British cultural history. Our remit is to read on to the end.

The last 136 pages chart Meyer's return to London to be discovered by his friends living hand to mouth, unemployed except for occasional paid writing. Caught up in sympathy for Meyer's state, his friends debate whether antisemitism is a product of Meyer's 'mania' about history or politics, or exposes 'the devil who is no stranger. The devil who is a part of ourselves' (*Devil*, 358). Engaging a theological icon, the novel then rejects it as a model of analysis when Meyer essentialises his self-loathing as a 'taint' but then subjects this to history, to 'this moment when there is no escape'(*Devil*, 367). It is at 'this moment,' 1936–7, that *The Devil We Know* joins rhetorical forces with Eric Ambler's polemical espionage novels of the same period. Both writers, and as we shall see, others as well, find the conventions and metaphors of spy fiction productive for the dissemination of intelligence about the persecution of Europe's Others. As though creating his own historical document, Meyer states his intention to write a study of antisemitism, but predicts that whether Europe is controlled by Communism or Nazism, another Dark Ages would emerge in which such a book would be outlawed (*Devil*, 401). The only place for the Jews and their cultural production in either totalitarian system would be elimination.

The novel's Epilogue marks the final stage in Meyer's evolution as a secret agent and a self-determining Jewish man, returning to Germany to rescue his incapacitated brother from Nazi obliteration. On the boat, he muses:

> His own attitude, his own body, his own thoughts had become unfamiliar; he might have been saying good-bye to himself [. . .] There was some identity here. Not his own identity. That was gone; in a series of faded little snapshots showing an ordinary man who thought that he was hated because he was a Jew; who had forced his whole world into the frame of his hatred and seen it made flesh and blood again. (*Devil*, 494)

Meyer is no ordinary man like the amateur spies of Eric Ambler and Leslie Howard, vaulted into foreign intrigue and returned home to Britain safe and sound as valued citizens to join the good fight. Philip Meyer may be an amateur, but his double identity and agency remain foreign and at risk from beginning to end. Featured in 'faded little snapshots', as though the estranged meanings of Ambler's photos are receding further into dissolution, Meyers' identity is about to be consigned to a memory trace. Nonetheless, his new beginning is an act of self-rescue whereby he recognises his identity, not as a self-punishing victim, but as identifying with his Jewish humanity. Regardless of the risk or outcome, he is on a voyage to save his imperilled brother and by extension, to rescue Jewish identity from its historical alterity and antisemitic mythology.

Frankau's 1939 construction of Philip Meyer and his precarious fate returning to Germany in 1936 serves as a historical and narrative bridge to the 1939 and 1941 settings of Nuremberg in *Above Suspicion* by Helen MacInnes and Budapest in *A Place to Stand* by Ann Bridge. In 1938 Dorothy Thompson reported from Central Europe:

As I write this article the news from Europe is distressing in the extreme. Hitler is in Vienna. Central Europe is in turmoil, as every small state of the Danubian Basin feels the increasing pressure of Nazidom. Great Britain, and, following their leadership, France, are considering whether – and if so how – to protect Czechoslovakia, and whether – and if so how – to save even a modified League of Nations. The Soviet system seems in a state of serious disintegration. The war in Spain continues, what final dénouement we cannot yet foresee. But one thing is certain: these chaotic situations cannot fail to add to a problem which is already a world headache – the problem of dispossessed social and political minorities. (375)

Spies of Their Own

Like Philip Meyer, the protagonists of Helen MacInnes' and Ann Bridge's novels of espionage must confront the threat of Nazi conquest and occupation. But like the spies of Ambler and Howard, they possess the assurance and confidence their British or American citizenship promises. That their missions involve life-threatening risks and that their courage will be expressed as anti-Nazi arguments there is no doubt, especially as MacInnes expressed this as her goal. As Christine Bold reports, MacInnes and her husband Gilbert Highet moved to the United States in 1937 to stimulate 'international resistance', and while Highet wrote 'psychological profiles of Nazi leaders', MacInnes' thrillers of the 1940s exposed the psychological and ethical dangers of collaboration and passivity (31). Over a forty-year career, MacInnes published nineteen espionage novels, two in other genres and a play. Ann Bridge, the nom de plume of Mary Dolling (Sanders) Lady O'Malley, wrote fourteen novels, a collection of short fiction and autobiographies, as she accompanied her husband, a career diplomat, to posts in Budapest, Lisbon and China, where she set her breakthrough novel, *Peking Spring*, published in 1932.

Helen MacInnes, Ann Bridge and Pamela Frankau respond critically to the way conventional spy thrillers draw heroes and villains as caricatures of hyperactive good and evil while women characters serve their male masters as either disposable attractions or damsels in distress. In contrast to glamorous, indomitable James Bond and his swooning Bond 'girls', both men and women spies in the works of women writers almost always develop from vulnerable naïveté into politically self-conscious activism. My hesitation reflects the historical contingencies that curtail the assurance of heroic victory over Fascism in these wartime fictions. Gender analysis also reveals critical interactions between masculinist assumptions about political and physical power and women's intervening voices. In this light, it is no wonder that women writers depict women secret agents as amateurs, outsiders to male dominated espionage agencies and plots. Unlike the amateur spies but professional men in Ambler's and Howard's fictions, the women in the novels of MacInnes and Bridge enter the practice of espionage as a journey from insular privilege and protection to worlds of political danger. Although these women writers share the historical, ethical and political concerns of their male colleagues, their representations interrogate women's domestic and political relationships to the meanings of citizenship and activism.

Queen of Spies

> I'm against totalitarians in general – national or religious, extremists of the right or left. (Helen MacInnes qtd in Mitgang, 22)

> If Agatha Christie is justly dubbed 'Mistress of Mystery' Helen MacInnes deserves the title of 'Mistress of Mesmerism'. (Alice Dixon Bond, np)

Helen MacInnes' reputation as 'Queen of International Espionage Fiction' was established with the publication of her first novel, *Above Suspicion* (1941), and confirmed by US sales of 23 million copies of her twenty-one books ('Miss Helen MacInnes', 12). As her *Times* obituary notes, 'In a field in which men tended to predominate she produced novels noted for their literate qualities, the authenticity of their settings and the acuity of their perceptions about current affairs' ('Miss HM', 12). That MacInnes would be subject to the genre's gendering is clear in her 1942 interview with *New York Times* writer, Robert van Gelder, following the publication of her second novel. Van Gelder notes suspicions that her husband might have helped write *Assignment in Brittany* since it lacked the 'rather feminine tone in some of [the] rough action sequences' of *Above Suspicion* (BR2).[21] MacInnes rejected the charge, adding, '"If the second book is less feminine – well, it is a man's story, with no woman tagging along through everything that happens. I didn't want to repeat, anyway"' (van Gelder, BR2).

Enlisting a Woman's Voice

> It was strange, she thought, how people seemed to change in a foreign train. More than half in this coach were English, but already they seemed so different. (*Above Suspicion*, 37)

Above Suspicion features a married couple, Oxford don Richard Myles and his artist wife Frances, who in the summer of 1939 accept an espionage mission to travel to Germany to discover the fate of a missing British agent. To a point, the characterisation of the couple conforms to the genre's 'innocent abroad' and 'most elementary kind of flight-and-pursuit narrative' (Denning, 67; Wallace, 5). Michael Denning qualifies this view; Richard Myles is 'not the sort of enthusiastic and willing amateur' but rather an 'incompetent and inexperienced amateur in a world of professionals' (67). The assessment of Richard Myles is accurate but neglects the significant role of Frances, who is also an amateur, but does a lot more than 'tagging along'. Although Christine Bold's analysis of the Myles' marriage as teamwork is persuasive, as the novel charts the couple's movements from Oxford to Germany, Frances' reactions to their surroundings and encounters play a politically assertive and acute role. It is she who, from the very beginning, expresses the fear that compelled MacInnes to tell 'every one I met of how dangerous Hitler was' and then to fill a journal 'with prophecies of what the Nazis were likely to do' (van Gelder, 18). Frances joins forces with the narrator to respond to the Nazi threat by persistently interrogating its ideology, policies and practices.

From the opening scenes, Frances is no angel of the hearth. Although she is well protected as a privileged member of Britain's intellectual aristocracy, her political responses are undomesticated. As with Sheila Matthews in MacInnes' 1944 novel *While Still We Live* and Hope Kirkland in Ann Bridge's novel *A Place to Stand*, the transformation of women's social and economic security into political consciousness also criticises privileged isolationism. Engaged with the world beyond Oxford's gated greens, Frances' views highlight the dangers of intellectual, artistic and political insularity. In expression and effect, her voice only gathers force the more vulnerable the couple becomes, as they venture beyond their Oxford sanctuary into Nazi territory. A large share of the novel's trajectory charts her journey into questioning the kind of abstract knowledge that invites rationalisation, culminating in her final peroration:

> But knowing evil could be worse than guessing. When you guessed, you could always hope that evil things might not be so bad as your worst fears. But when you knew, then there was no hope left. Then you knew this and this, and the evil of it drove away all hope. (*AS*, 332)

Regardless of whether the narrative registers her unspoken thoughts or voice, from beginning to end, her responses consistently reality-test her assiduous knowledge of Nazi political ideology and practices. Only with direct experience, spotlighted by her assertive position in the novel's ongoing adventures and resulting abandonment of wishful thinking, can her knowledge of 'evil' become a persuasive tool of the novel's impact.[22] Refracted through her own convictions, her knowledge at the beginning of her journey is affirmed by news reports. The combination challenges the genre's stereotypical assumption that critical analysis and leadership are a man's domain. Enacting her intellectual acuity, Frances contests the politics of their former Oxford friend and now devoted Nazi representative, Sigurd von Aschenhausen:

> 'You believe you have not changed. And yet, under the leadership which you praise so much, you may only read certain books, listen to certain music, look at certain pictures, make friends with certain people. Isn't that limiting yourself?'
> 'Oh well, limiting oneself to the good, eliminating the bad – all that is better in the end [. . .] I suppose you will now lecture me gravely on the wickedness of Germany's claims to natural *Lebensraum*. It is easy to talk when you have a large Empire.'
> 'On the contrary, Herr von Aschenhausen, I like to think of all people having their *Lebensraum*, whether they are Germans or Jews or Czechs or Poles.' (*AS*, 22–3)

Taunting Frances in response, von Aschenhausen reminds her that there is no need to fear war in the summer of 1939 since 'You are all good pacifists, here' (*AS*, 24).

The combined accusation of British imperialism and appeasement only moments before Germany invades Poland presents an opportunity for a woman's construction of World War II history.[23] Like Storm Jameson's argument on behalf of cultural independence in her 1942 novel *Then We Shall Hear Singing*, Frances' continuing observations test her universalist convictions. Both women's writing grants the epistemological perspective to a woman's empirical and inductive talents and challenges the boundaries between the genre's assigned role for women as follower. The timing is propitious. Published in the insecure year of 1941–2, when Allied victory remained in doubt, Frances' ripostes perform the novel's critically questioning consciousness. Her barbed responses to the Nazi remind British readers that the war for which so much sacrifice is being demanded is not about saving their Empire. In the lexicon of universal sovereign rights and peoplehood, with documented historical evidence, she argues instead for the right of national self-determination, for the war being about saving Britain and other nations from the Reich's planned conquests. Whereas Ambler's and Howard's male characters rally the call to arms, here the woman's voice performs the work of political analysis and critical propaganda. Frances may share narrative space with her husband, but her position in the social culture of espionage is liminal. While the banter of male characters reveals their clubby rapport, her voice persists as that of a critical outsider. And if the men are required for her rescue, she is the focalising consciousness through which the novel's political and historical perspective will be analysed. By subjecting her to the mission's greatest risk, capture by Nazi agents, the novel examines what difference her voice and performance make to its investigation of the war's moral force, to Britain's responsibility to the Continent and to the role of women in modern espionage fiction.

In order to perform successfully as a British secret agent in Germany, Frances disguises her plucky intelligence so that she's recognisable only as a 'dim wife' (AS, 24). Donning a dirndl, she attempts to blend in to the traditional culture of the Tyrol where women assume their customary roles in charge of *kinder, kirche, küchen*. Privately and among friends, however, Frances never fails to override her husband's flippant political assessments, as when she reminds him that rather than dismissing the 'uncivilised' Germans as unworthy of a second thought, 'if a nation allows concentration camps', it will also kill 'a lot of the civilised [. . .] Ignoring doesn't abolish them [. . .]' (AS, 28). Although the 1941 perspective from which this novel is written allows Frances to be portrayed as politically prescient, her logic brings critical attention to the concentration camps already in operation and proliferating in 1939. In its condensed form, her statement exposes the purpose and effects of the camps, designed for no other reason than to rid the Reich of its designated undesirables, such as Philip Meyer and his brother in *The Devil We Know*. Referring to the victims as 'civilised' countermands the Nazis' racialist category of *untermenschen* or subhumans, those who would be targeted for brutalising labour, starvation or disease. Assembly line gassing would begin after the January 1942 Wannsee Conference authorised the Final Solution.[24]

Frances disputes the pacifist position that casts Britain as 'just another of those belligerent countries', not acting in self-defence or in order to protect others (AS, 32). Threaded throughout the novel, her acute dissections of British appeasement and US isolationism remind readers that by 1938, when Germany annexed the Sudetenland, peace with Germany was revealed to be an illusion, to which MacInnes responded with relief: 'we've come out of the ether [. . .]' (AS, 93). While Frances' declaration appears confident, it also betrays apprehension. Her inclusive address, 'we', celebrates a transformation of individual conscience, assumed to be the strength of liberal thought, into collective recognition of the perils of non-intervention. Her insistent, unquestioning declaration in the summer of 1939 registers a hopeful response to the ambivalence of Britain's government and popular opinion about intervening in escalating German hostilities.[25] Even by 1941, in the context of MacInnes' writing during the Blitz and as the war front became global, Frances' faith in Britons' unified support of the war would need to be tested.[26] Her insistent defensiveness may therefore embed MacInnes' apprehension that her propaganda pleas would be criticised and even rejected. Tethering her political agenda to her fiction left MacInnes vulnerable to the charge, reported in her obituary, that 'There were some, even among her staunchest admirers who feared that her politics – staunchly anti-totalitarian as she admitted – were occasionally in danger of triumphing over her creative impulses' ('Miss HM', 12). MacInnes asserted that her anti-totalitarianism shared political ground with George Orwell and Rebecca West whom MacInnes identified as her 'mentor – she's a very courageous woman' (qtd in Mitgang, 181). One can hear echoes of West's ironic assessment of non-intervention in her 1941 tome *Black Lamb, Grey Falcon*, which MacInnes could very well have read. While MacInnes asserted that she designed her novels to offer 'a thoroughly good time', her propaganda methods do not betray a lack of self-questioning (van Gelder, 2). The novel's interweave of 1939 and 1941 creates a narrative experiment in dual historical perspectives, a method that Ann Bridge would also adopt in *A Place to Stand*.

Although described subjectively in non-realistic images, the city of Nuremberg becomes one of Frances' reality tests. Her depressed reactions to the city are expressed in language that combines the visual lexicons of German Expressionist film and, as she puts it, the 'Gothic [. . .] as if Gibbon's idea of the Middle Ages had interpreted itself here in the tortuous streets, the thick walls, the narrow crowding houses. A triumph of religion and barbarism' (*AS*, 73). Endowing the cityscape with critical faculty, Frances depicts its architecture as signifying the claustrophobic, entrapping ideology and practices of Nazi Germany. Her description metonymically represents the achievements of Nazi conquests as spaces resembling the ghettos where enemies of the Reich would be tortuously crowded. Likewise for one of the city's treasures, the castle Dutzendteich, a museum of torture instruments that functions as exegetical commentary on the sanctity Nazi Germany awarded to its medieval modernism.[27] With intertextual insight, she represents the city as a tomb ready to be filled with Nazism's victims, but her sardonic reference to 'triumph' also registers the wish that Nazism would entomb itself (*AS*, 90). Focalised through Frances' historical narrative and in her dreams, this portrait of Nuremberg and the 'hidden threat' of its blank-faced storm troopers express her understanding of the long-range effects of Nazi education in consolidating a nation's ideological conformity. As though corroborating Frances' impressions of the city, a Nuremberg newspaper editorial offers a lesson in racialist mythology by vilifying 'the inhuman Poles and the wicked Jews [who] were behaving with abominable, not-to-be-tolerated cruelty to the Germans who were living in Poland' (*AS*, 85).

Umberto Eco characterises the mythological drama underwriting Fascist and Nazi ideology:

> [E]ven though Nazism was proud of its industrial achievements, its praise of modernism was only the surface of an ideology based upon Blood and Earth (*Blut und Boden*). The rejection of the modern world was disguised as a rebuttal of the capitalistic way of life, but it mainly concerned the rejection of the Spirit of 1789 (and of 1776, of course). The Enlightenment, the Age of Reason, is seen as the beginning of modern depravity. ('Ur-Fascism', 14)

Zygmunt Bauman explains how this revisionary ideology took hold:

> Modernity meant [. . .] a new role for ideas – because of the state relying for its functional efficiency on ideological mobilization, because of pronounced tendency to uniformity (manifested most spectacularly in the practices of cultural crusades), because of its 'civilizing' mission and sharp proselytizing edge, and because of the attempt to bring previously peripheral classes and localities into an intimate spiritual contact with the idea-generating centre of the body politic. (*Modernity and Ambivalence*, 44)

Reading Eco's analysis alongside Bauman's shows how Nazism's ideological contradiction between the rejection and embrace of modernity could produce a rhetoric that promised the synthesis of a past and future paved with glory that would be fulfilled by totalitarian rigour.[28]

MacInnes witnessed how this synthesis appealed to the 'tendency to uniformity' when she was in Munich in 1932 as 'the *effect* that [Hitler] had on his audience – he got them. There couldn't be any doubt about it – you could feel them respond. Then he won [election] not much later [. . .]' (van Gelder, 2). The consolidation of Nazi ideology into a 'cultural crusade' is programmed in the passage of the Nuremberg Laws of 1935, which affirmed German Aryan culture as the apex of civilisation by legalising the violent oppression of Jews and Hitler's other targeted victims.

> There is more antisemitism in England than we care to admit [. . .] It does not at present lead to open persecution, but it has the effect of making people callous to the sufferings of Jews in other countries. (George Owell, 'Antisemitism in Britain', 87)

Above Suspicion positions the Myleses and their American acquaintance, Van Cortlandt, a journalist, as key witnesses to a representative incident in the Nazis' brutal treatment of the Jews. The scene also records the voice of the victim as an ethical intervention in British World War II fiction. In Nuremberg, 'From the quiet blackness of the little alley to the left of them came a bitter cry, the high, self-strangling cry of fear or pain, or both' (AS, 107). A Nazi storm trooper explains dismissively: 'It is only a Jews' Alley' (AS, 107). Materialising as corroboration for Frances' earlier response to the self-entombing city, the 'Jews' Alley' also occupies an opaque narrative space, like the Jew himself. Never present as a character or consciousness, the Jew appears only obliquely, a figure of dissolution representing historical abandonment and a rupture in both the adventure plot and canonical modernist fiction, where references are the only representation and ambiguous at best. Invisible to the Allies and to readers, the Jew has already been beaten out of Germany, dislocated into nowhere. The alley that bears his vilified identity is a passageway that marks a schism, alienated from the cultural and social life of the city. By implication, the alley also affirms the Jew's isolation from the genre's melodramatic template that typically creates a sympathetic relationship between reader and victim. His 'strangling cry' audibly signals the deadly silencing that afflicts the Jews but also draws attention to their stateless plight while it is being ignored or dismissed in Britain and the United States.[29]

Ian Baruma inveighs against the consequences of statelessness at this time: 'One of the horrors of homelessness and the total loss of rights is that others are given the license to do anything they wish with you' (157). If Jewish persecution captures the political imagination of Helen MacInnes and the Jew's cry continues to haunt Frances' consciousness and shape the construction of her historical narrative, this attention remains exceptional. As Tony Kushner observes, 'although there was widespread revulsion at the violence associated with Nazi anti-Semitism, few in Britain appreciated the enormity of the Jewish plight' ('Beyond the Pale', 156). Extending this point further, the inability of the novel's British and American witnesses to intervene raises questions about the war's goals. To defeat Nazism and Fascism was of necessity paramount, but whether it could have included rescue of the Jewish victims remains contentious.[30] Nonetheless, the Jew's stateless condition in MacInnes' novel, with no national identity he can claim and no official or authorised protection, offers a historical gloss in the form of a sharp contrast with the Allied characters.

Even under siege by German agents and isolated from any support, MacInnes' protagonists, like those of Leslie Howard and Ambler, are guaranteed rescue by the genre. In this case, British amateur agents must return home to rally their nation. In MacInnes' propaganda initiative, the woman spy is the keynote speaker and speaks on behalf of Hitler's victims. Howard's and Ambler's anti-Nazi messages are delivered by men as the primary witnesses. Despite their differences, however, these spy fictions lead protagonists and readers to epistemological victory, and they remain safe as they learn through witnessing and reading, to decode the threat of Nazi power. That such anti-Nazi warnings became a compelling theme and narrative armature across genres is evident in the intermodern writing of other women. Propagating similar messages, Katharine Burdekin's and Storm Jameson's dystopian fictions of the period wrenched their protagonists and readers from the probability of escape by depicting the Nazis' destruction of home and homeland. In their fiction, lethal knowledge needs no decoding because it is embodied by protagonists who are tortured, caged, lobotomised and otherwise murdered by conquering Nazi armies. Nazi brutality in these dystopias is so extreme that even as protagonist-victims elicit sympathy, they also distance audiences emotionally and politically through their unprecedented representation of abjectness.[31] Characters who serve as models of resistance are either captured or signify hope in unresolved open endings, inviting audiences to consider conclusions that reflect a teleology of democratic progress and an ideal of humane rationality. In contrast, the World War II narratives of MacInnes and other writers in this study encourage their audiences to identify with protagonists who like themselves gain political consciousness as a pathway to resistance. If the endings of these thrillers remain open, they also represent the power of resolve. For MacInnes, an apocalyptic scenario would contravene her template for ethical action. If her spy fiction imagined the Allies being destroyed in 1939, when *Above Suspicion* is set, or in 1941, when it was published, MacInnes' warnings would have failed to rally her readers to the political cause to which she committed her writing.

There is no doubt that the male protagonists, Richard Myles and Van Cortlandt, will propel the novel's prototypical espionage action, planning and implementing the defeat of the German villain and rescue of Frances. But while the men's blazing guns, 'hard punches' and acerbic retorts are defeated only by their generic predictability, Frances' consciousness and voice remain compelling today (*AS*, 311). Joining forces with the narrator, the woman agent creates a searing polemic:

> If only the methods of hate and force had been resisted at the very beginning: not by other countries (for *that* would have been called the unwarranted interference of those who wanted to keep Germany weak), but by the people of Germany, themselves. But of course, it had been more comfortable to turn a deaf ear to the cries from the concentration camps, to harden their hearts to the despair of the exiles, to soothe their conscience with praise of the Fatherland. And now, it had come to the stage where other peoples would have to do the dying, on barricades of shattered cities, to stop what should have been stopped seven years ago. (AS, 111)

There are no innocent bystanders in this prosecution of collective German indifference. In Frances' indictment, German bystanders become perpetrators. Her absolutist polemic omits any expectation or need for corroboration. Considering, however, that the case is addressed to the novel's English language readers, it also stands as a warning against unresponsiveness and a plea to share her disgust. And yet despite its one-way exhortation, it evokes other, intervening voices – 'the despair of exiles', 'unwarranted interference' and 'the cries from concentration camps'. The animating presence of such voices is explained by Mikhail Bakhtin's theory of 'dialogized heteroglossia' (273): 'the fleeting language of a day, of an epoch, of a social group, a genre, a school [...] a contradiction-ridden, tension-filled unity of two embattled tendencies in the life of language' (272). By implication, these 'heteroglot voices' represent 'specific world views, each characterised by its own objects, meanings and values', juxtaposed in contradiction and interrelationships, expressing 'the direct intention of the character who is speaking, and the refracted intention of the author. In such discourse there are two voices, two meanings and two expressions [...] as if they actually hold a conversation with each other' (*DI*, 278, 324).

Although Bakhtin situates heteroglossia within novels, I claim a place for it in dialogue between Frances' world view and the accused. Within itself the novel constructs Frances' accusations as foreclosing any response. Her verdict leaves no narrative impetus or space for ordinary, non-military Germans to acknowledge, explain or defend their alleged passive aggression. Nonetheless, the novel's doubly retrospective framework around which it creates its time-place nexus establishes a pattern of intervention through its memory work. Reading the novel as interweaving context with text produces a dialogue between MacInnes' 1941 portrayal of 1939 British espionage in Germany and Frances' 1939 diatribe against 1933 Germany. With overlapping hindsight, MacInnes and her woman spy join forces to reconstruct, interpret and judge the failure of German moral consciousness and will as Hitler was consolidating his power. Despite the univocal effect of this interchange, its combination of text and context oversteps the novel's fictional boundaries, and in so doing, acknowledges critical intervention as integral to its relationship with readers. The rhetorical result is to encourage further intercession, and if this became part of the novel's polysemous field, its critique would not stand alone. It invites other voices to join it in representing 'specific world views, each characterised by its own objects, meanings and values'. With this construction of 'heteroglot voices', we can recognise how wartime and post-war German self-criticism enters into dialogue with the novel's memory work.

Speaking at the end of the war, Thomas Mann confronts 'Germany's horrible fate, the tremendous catastrophe in which her modern history now culminates' because it 'compels our interest, even if this interest is devoid of sympathy' ('Germany and the Germans', 48). Despite having gained United States citizenship, he asserts, 'anyone who was born a German *does* have something in common with Germany destiny and German guilt' ('Germany', 48). With searing introspection and questions, writing by German intellectuals and artists who remained in Germany throughout the Nazi era or who fled into exile reveals the struggle to recount their experiences and analyse both their own efforts to resist and how the Nazis gained and retained their grip on a politically and demographically diverse population. In his memoir of the Nazi era, *Defying Hitler*, Sebastian Haffner (trans. Raimund Pretzel), an acclaimed journalist who escaped to London in 1938, contends that

> The plight of non-Nazi Germans in the summer of 1933 was [. . .] a condition in which one [was] hopelessly, utterly overwhelmed [. . .] We were in the Nazis' hands for good or ill. All lines of defence had fallen, any collective resistance had become impossible. Individual resistance was only a form of suicide [. . .] At the same time we were called upon, not to surrender, but to renege. Just a little pact with the devil – and you were no longer one of the captured quarry. Instead you were one of the victorious hunters. (155)

Haffner's juxtaposition of despair and bitter irony exposes the existence of moral and political choices despite the choke-hold of Hitler's dictatorship. As other German writers attest, protest and resistance were possible, but compared to what Haffner calls a 'collective nervous breakdown', the 'tiny groups' of resistance, 'a few in Berlin, a few in Munich, in Breslau, in Dresden, or Hamburg' had no chance of toppling the Third Reich (Haffner, 110, Andreas-Friedrich, 141). Anthony Grenville coins the term 'inner emigration' to identify those writers who were opposed to Nazism but chose to stay in Germany after 1933, resisting conformity in private but never openly. Surrounded by Nazi enthusiasts as well as the fearful, passive and compliant, resisters found themselves exiled in their own nation ('Thomas Mann', np).

Ruth Andreas-Friedrich, a prominent journalist, organised a resistance group, Onkel Emil, which hid co-resisters and Jews and spread messages forecasting the self-destructiveness of the Reich's war. With too few Germans able and willing to risk resistance, and with each German victory prolonging the war, her group hoped 'for our own [German] defeat' (A-F, 181). She explains the group's decision to remain in Germany and its resistance:

They had premonitions of what was to come. They knew of all the atrocities that took place, though only through rumor. And precisely because they knew and foresaw all this, they felt it their duty to use their energies on the spot. Then at least not all the intended outrages might be carried out. (A-F, xiii)

Even as Andreas-Friedrich accounts for the will to resist, she also recognises the vise of despotism that paralyses resistance: 'But after all, where is courage to come from when it will cost you your neck to show any? [. . .] The courage of one's convictions under a dictatorship is ruled by different laws from the opposition in a democracy' (A-F, 7–8). If the reality of brutal incarceration and murder by 'Gestapo Cossacks' produces abject fear, the 'mischief, falsification of history, distortion of truth, and slanders upon art that have been pounded into people's heads through years cannot be effaced from [German] heads so easily' (A-F, 98, 54). Sebastian Haffner adds a psychological dimension to the effects of Nazi propaganda: 'the withdrawal into [. . .] the illusion' that focusing on the 'childishness' of Nazism would spare them recognition of its 'fiendishness', that instead of having adopted the 'position of complete, powerless subjugation', they were superior, unconcerned onlookers (156). For Andreas-Friedrich, the relentless erasure of questions and dissent means that 'Each one of us bears the stamp of the Third Reich somewhere' (A-F, 54).

Bernt Engelmann, a writer and journalist, was twelve years old when the Nazis began their rule, and remained in Germany with his mother when their plans to emigrate to England stalled. After serving as a Luftwaffe radio operator, he was convicted in 1944 of helping Jews, sent to Flossenburg camp and then Dachau. *In Hitler's Germany* combines memoir and the testimony of others to offer a range of responses to the possibilities for resistance. Aligning himself with other Germans, he admits that not being Jewish, a Social Democrat or a Communist, he 'consoled' himself, but only at first, by thinking that Nazi extremism 'must be a passing phase' (16). He also records enthusiastic responses to the birth of the Reich, including the 'thrilling' marches and singing, that celebrated the 'unity of the German people' and the 'national uprising' (27).[32] That anonymous and indirect protest of 'the Nazis' suppression of criticism' was both desirable and possible is astonishing to this witness (Engelmann, 33).

I read Sebastian Haffner's political memoir of the Nazi years, *Defying Hitler*, as a critical interchange with Frances' indictment. Haffner argues that 'the chances for mankind in Germany today [1939] need not have been quite so hopeless if the outside world had intervened' (4). Instead, appeasers within and outside Germany 'suffered from a compulsive urge to offer him everything he wanted, indefatigably and at an ever cheaper price, indeed to press it upon him' (Haffner, 86). Like Louis Fischer, writing in *The God that Failed*, Haffner faults the German Communists whose failure to confront the Nazis led other opponents to ask: 'Who would have believed that there was nothing behind the façade of raised fists?' (Haffner, 98). In 1949 Fischer, once a fellow traveller, assessed the failure of German Communists as having 'helped Hitler come to power; they thought the destruction of the democratic center would facilitate their struggle with the Nazi extreme. This is an incurable Communist miscalculation' (211). He despairs that by the time the Communists and the Democratic West recognised Nazism's global threat, it was too late.

Even at the late date of 1941, MacInnes implores her British and North American audiences to recognise their individual and collective anti-Nazi responsibility. Neither ideological nor militaristic, her plea coincides with how British and American audiences would interpret and experience the war. According to historian Tony Kushner, this would be 'through a combination of nationalism and belief in the superiority of liberal democracy to "foreign" dictatorships' (*HLI*, 120). From another perspective, the 1939 setting of MacInnes' novel and its publication two years later could not have been more timely. For unlike 'the confusion and doubt' of 'British and American society and culture [. . .] over the origins of Nazi antisemitism, and its severity and impact on the Jews of Greater Germany before the outbreak of World War II', MacInnes recognised and dramatised signs of 'the attempted genocide of European Jewry' (*HLI*, 121). As a critically animating heteroglossia, *Above Suspicion* challenges those she addresses to hear the voices of those who were silenced by the blows of Nazism. The cry of one victim reverberating from a Nuremberg alley creates a chain of signification that fills the moral void of indifference with questions that trouble not only this novel but so much literature of the 1930s and 1940s.

After publishing *Assignment in Brittany*, her fictive battle with Nazi collaboration and its exploitation of Brittany's separatist desires, MacInnes waited until 1944 and 1945 to publish two novels that respond to Frances Myles' plea. These later novels depict Poles and Austrian Tyrolese attempting to 'stop what should have been stopped seven years ago'. In her 1944 novel *While Still We Live*, at the moment Germany begins its bombardment of Poland, Sheila Matthews, a young Englishwoman, activates the responsibility MacInnes assigns to the Western democracies for taking their anti-Nazi missions to Eastern Europe. Joining romance and polemic, MacInnes creates another woman spy, whose participation in Polish resistance may be spurred by love for its handsome aristocratic leader, but who also provides an independent voice that intervenes both politically and generically. Unlike

Frances, who carries her political convictions into her mission, Sheila Matthews must be taught. Her mission is an odyssey into the political consciousness of the integrity of nation states that lies beyond the cultural and historical consciousness of the Western liberal democracies. More often split off from the West's imagination and divided by the competing powers of Germany and Russia, Poland's unified national integrity and sovereignty remain a wish fulfilment fantasy in this novel and in Ann Bridge's *A Place to Stand*. The fate of the fragmented nation lies in Sheila's developing political agency, metonymically designated as Britain's moral consciousness. Read as a chronicle of Nazi-occupied Europe, the 1939 settings of *While Still We Live* and *Above Suspicion* combine proleptic and analeptic critical perspectives: what should have been and can still be done to rescue the Nazis' victimised people and nations from the decimation already on the horizon. While the Myleses return to Britain to an open ending of possible anti-Nazi resistance, Sheila Matthews remains with the Polish resistance to defend the endangered homeland she adopts as her own. In this narrative absorption, besieged Europe and Britain fulfil MacInnes' political fantasy of exile as moral rescue.

When Poland's armies were routed by Germany's invasion in September 1939, hopes for the nation's defence fell to the Polish Free Forces. Many of its partisans had to operate in exile as illegal aliens threatened with arrest, deportation and execution by the Fascist regimes in such neighbouring countries as Hungary and Romania. With a thousand-year history of invasion and occupation by such adjacent imperial powers as Germany and Russia, the attempts of Poland to recover its sovereignty lent themselves to mythic narratives of undaunted heroism. Like Helen MacInnes' portrayal in *While Still We Live*, Ann Bridge's 1953 novel *A Place to Stand* finds anti-Fascist heroism in the commitment of Polish partisans to reclaim their homeland. Bridge fictionalised her experiences as the wife of a diplomat in Budapest in 1940–1 to portray the anguish of Polish exiles during the same period when Hungary's leader, Admiral Horthy, yielded to Nazi Germany's promises for prosperity and security and joined the Axis powers. Although it would not be taken over by Germany until March 1944, the regime exercised draconian power over the refugees streaming across the borders to escape oppression. Bridge's 1962 novel *A Tightening String* is also based on her Budapest experiences, but focuses on efforts to co-ordinate basic necessities for British prisoners of war in Germany.[33]

Ann Bridge's Double Historical Vision

Ann Bridge used her knowledge and experience of Central European politics to depict the self-serving indifference and complicity of outsiders and onlookers to the fates of Hungary and its refugees. A statement she inserts in *A Place to Stand* confronts her 1953 readers with a history that she acknowledges is out of time and place but that in effect, like her dissonant voice, will serve as a guide to reading her novel: 'In 1941 the world at large knew nothing of Buchenwald or Belsen, Katyn or Oswieczim' (*AS*, 189). The present of the novel, 1941, is so weighted down by the near future of the Final Solution and Soviet infamy, every plot move and character development will emerge in their shadows. Nothing in the novel's present, Bridge warns her readers, can be read as transparently self-evident, as solely contemporaneous. Instead, everything in her account is contingent and determined by the imminently horrific European future. Despite the heroic efforts of her imagined Polish underground, the atmosphere of 1941 Budapest portends only catastrophe. The inclusion of Katyn reminds her Cold War era readers that the Nazis were not the only perpetrators of mass annihilation, but that among their other atrocities, it was the Soviets who slew 30,000 Polish officers at Katyn. Bridge's rhetorical aside, disrupting her heroine's sole encounter with state violence, delivers a shock that also unsettles the promise of spy thrillers to comfort readers with action-filled fantasy. Instead of imagining state violence as contained within narrative conventions, this rupture connects the historical outcome of wilfully ignoring Nazi atrocities with the imagined development of an outsider's recognition.

If Hope Kirkland, the novel's focalising protagonist, is momentarily traumatised by Fascist brutality, rather than creating her as a victim, aligning her, with bathos, to Fascism's historically real victims, Bridge emphasises the necessity of psychological shock to political understanding. In her memoir *Facts and Fictions*, Bridge discloses that her nineteen-year-old daughter Kate had created the plot based on her own observations of places and refugees in Budapest, but when she burned it, Bridge completed it with 'a first-hand account of events as they happened', including 'the Germans being allowed to come through Hungary to attack Yugoslvia' (81).

Bridge's method recalls that of Martha Gellhorn's 1940 novel *A Stricken Field*, which depicts the panic-stricken Prague in 1938, moments before Germany's invasion. Like Bridge's Hope Kirkland, Gellhorn's protagonist Mary Douglas confronts the crush of refugees and becomes involved with their plight. The fact that Mary, an American journalist, is far more sophisticated than Hope Kirkland only highlights the shock of recognition for both American women. But despite the knowledge that was available at the time of writing in 1951, Bridge does not depict the atrocities either explicitly or implicitly. Instead she returns to a time when possibilities for resistance and escape depended on bystander nations' willingness to acknowledge Nazi racial persecutions, to care about potential victims and to intervene. Her novel charts a young American woman's journey to that knowledge, concern and intervention through an act of espionage.

John Kirkland, an American industrialist living in Budapest with his wife and nineteen-year-old daughter, represents American isolationism. The self-serving indifference of this close-knit family to the plight of East European refugees becomes apparent as they never notice that 'Hungary was full of Poles – 50,000 members of the Polish army had marched across the frontier' or that those refugees rushing into the city were facing brutal incarceration (*AS*, 14). As Czeslaw Milosz attests, 'This was a time of universal migration. Throngs of people fled from the East to German occupation in the West; similar throngs fled from the Germans to the East and Soviet rule. The end of the State was marked by a chaos that could occur perhaps only in the twentieth century' (143). Like Bridge's allusion to the Nazi camps, the reference to 'the end of the State' portends the twentieth century as an apocalyptic end of time, overrun by refugees who would interrupt the progressive flow of history and historical narration. Even as *A Place to Stand* individualises the humanity of its refugee characters, their chaotic status renders them, like Bridge's own disruptive voice, out of time and place, disrupting the conventional view of the century's progress as well as the typical suspense of spy fiction plotting. The novel's title, *A Place to Stand*, like the two lines from Elizabeth Barrett Browning's sonnet, can thus be read as auguring only discontinuity, indeterminacy and ambient danger:

> A place to stand and love in for a day,
> With darkness and the death-hour rounding it. (*AS*, title page)

Bridge's plotting provides a simultaneous translation of romantic angst, spy fiction's rapid pacing and imminent political menace.

Like MacInnes' Sheila Matthews, Hope Kirkland is a privileged young woman who becomes emotionally and politically involved with a family of Polish refugees, the Moranskis. Leaving her parents and the safety their American citizenship represents, Hope assumes the role of a spy who activates the liberal democratic promise of national and individual self-determination on behalf of the Poles. Her journey into dissent from her parents' norms begins when she discovers a note from journalist Sam Harrison, her American fiancé, buried under layers of fine chocolates along with forged identity papers. Whereas Kenton and Van Cortlandt, Ambler's and MacInnes' journalists, are positioned as witnesses and transmitters of Central Europe's breaking news, Harrison romances Hope into assuming that role. The juxtaposition could not be more telling. The postscript to Sam's Valentine instructs her to take the papers to the Moranskis' apartment in a part of Budapest invisible to the Kirklands and their friends. Here illegal immigrants crowd into labyrinthine spaces that both conceal and entrap them. It is also a space that confronts the young American with an invisible part of herself, producing contradictory but commingled passions. Her instantaneous attraction to the Polish exiles is incited by their passion for their homeland: 'whether politics nourished them or killed them, that was what they ate, what they lived with [. . .] And the girl recognized dimly that this also had drawn and attracted her' (AS, 180). Political passion leads Hope to fall in love with Stefan Moranski, a resistance fighter. A conventional romantic adventure to be sure, paralleling MacInnes' Sheila Matthews, who follows her Polish aristocratic lover Adam Wisniewski into the perils of resistance.

In Bridge's novel, however, the social and political boundaries between the American heiress and stateless aristocratic Poles are both blurred and reinforced when Hope's passion for them emerges as a transgressive invitation to share their desperation. Trading clothes and giving Stefan's sister Litka her American passport, Hope relinquishes her secure American identity for one that exists only as a memory trace for the stateless refugees. The women's uncanny resemblance to each other does not, therefore, suggest reliance on spy fiction's convenient contrivance. Instead, the women's transposed identities and conditions are so intensely felt and experienced that the narrative strains to dissolve the temporal and spatial distances between the American ingénue and the abject Poles. This doubling, so typical of spy fiction – double agents, double crosses, dual identities, divided consciousness – also raises a double-sided issue: whether doubling can refigure each character to fulfil the narrative promise of each one.[34] In short, whether the 'hope' represented by the American can be fulfilled when transferred to the Polish refugee or whether the transfiguration is only another irreparable breach:

> These people had come to fill her whole world, and to fill it with a richness, an intensity that was quite outside her experience. Somehow, for a few magical weeks she had as it were slid into *their* world of loss and poverty and danger and courage – and of Stefan's love. (AS, 177)

Given the historical reality that shadows this fiction, the gulf between these characters must be read as mediated by what readers in 1953 will have learned from the stories seeping through the silences of destroyed cities and ghettos, of the Soviet makeovers of Poland and Hungary into Communist satellites. This emerging intractable division between the East and West is interpolated into Bridge's narrative by a 'magical' fantasy of romantic incorporation and transposition. In turn, the novel transposes its own structure. Political wishful thinking is expressed as a fantasy of erotic fusion. Hope becomes both Stefan's beloved and his sister's double, a suggestively incestuous triangulation that announces an inextricable relationship between erotic and political desire, transgression and punishment. On the political front, Hope's punishment is to be arrested and imprisoned after being taken for her stateless double. Romantically, the love that develops between Hope and Stefan must be abandoned and forgotten. In concert, the doubling of political and erotic desire dramatises the naïve, romantic assumption that identifying with the political exile represents mutual cultural understanding, even empathy. The American heiress can only begin her journey to political consciousness with the failure of fantasy and recognition of her irrevocable split from the refugees' story, the journey and ending of which must remain beyond the conventions her own story occupies.

What Hope learns is that despite the Moranskis' gratitude, instead of a pathway to liberation, her espionage efforts are momentary and inconclusive, 'A place to stand and love in for a day'. Her name assumes critical meaning at the end of the novel. Her hope that she 'must have become to some extent European [...] to care about Europe's things for Europe's sake, and for the sake of justice and freedom' is both endorsed and undercut by the narrative (*AS*, 182). False identity papers and American couture cannot guarantee safety for Litka, who manages to escape successfully from Budapest, but with no sponsorship from the free West, must remain unprotected, somewhere in Nazi-occupied Europe. Although Hope is jailed and abused by the Hungarian Fascists, her diplomatic connections save her and she joins her family to return to America. Even as the love between Hope and Stefan must be abandoned, her espionage adventure cannot escape the romance of America as a democratic sanctuary. Writing the novel in 1951, Bridge could guarantee that America was a safe haven for the Kirklands, but the fate of the Moranskis would need to be left uncertain at best.

A Place to Stand questions the meanings of belonging and statelessness in relation to those of home and homeland by contrasting the material conditions in which the Kirklands and Moranskis live. To escape political oppression, the Moranskis have been forced to abandon their ancestral home in Poland. All that is left is a painting of their once proud manor estate where generations of their family were born and lived in all the comfort of country squires. The portrait hangs on an otherwise empty wall of their primitive Budapest apartment, where even water must be recycled and boiled for washing and drinking, as when Hope makes herself ersatz tea from the water of boiled eggs. There is no sign of home as a place of domestic ease and cultural and political security. Even the comfort of one's own native language and, as Czeslaw Milosz asserts, its ability 'to keep alive freedom of thought', is denied (viii). What is left are the few foreign words necessary to express anxiety in an alien and threatening space. A place with no future, the refugees' apartment signifies a dead end. Both bare and claustrophobic, it stifles the life of the Moranskis and their matriarch, who dies in an abject state of limbo, robbed of her ancestral identity.

The novel, however, also assigns this space expressive meaning. Its unembellished state highlights the Moranskis' yearning for their lost homeland. Exiled to a condition of permanent transience, the younger Moranskis, Litka and Stefan, must abandon their identity as heirs to a paternalistic feudal tradition.[35] The sympathetic portrait of the Moranskis and their cultural heritage is not, however, romanticised. Embedding Bridge's 1951 political vision, when Poland exists as a Soviet satellite, the manor estate can only represent a trampled dream of Polish independence and emerging political liberalism. All hope of returning home is dashed; the timelessness of its painting portends only decay or stasis, like Madame Moranska's unattended corpse. Eva Hoffman's analysis of cultural dislocation is especially pertinent here as it includes 'the entire webwork of [...] psychological codes and conceptual assumptions – a kind of symbolic system of shared meanings that structures our perceptions from early on, and that, within each culture, shapes the very form of personality, and of sensibility' (56).[36] Like Poland itself, the very idea of home and homeland exists only as a memory trace, historically determined by the imperial ambitions of the Third Reich and Soviet Union, imaginatively and politically conflated by Bridge's novel. The treaty with Britain and France, designed to protect Poland but ignored by Hitler, has produced war with the invading German forces, but no real defence. Except for a brief inter-war period, Poland has continuously been robbed of its sovereignty, with nothing to offer its citizens from 1939 onwards besides a ruptured state of displacement and oppression.

Stefan's role as a spy for the Polish underground represents the condition of statelessness. He is a 'homeless, propertyless expatriate on the run', a spy working on behalf of a nation that like its agents, is also stateless; the treaties guaranteeing its security have turned out to be a useless fantasy (*AS*, 88). With these conditions, the underground for which Stefan works signifies an entire nation that has been trod under, including 'not only the beloved home of childhood, but the homes they had hoped and planned to make, the quiet familiar useful lives they had expected to lead in a world they knew and understood' (*AS*, 135). What remains is 'Courage in exile; that was about all' *(AS,* 135). The novel's temporal and spatial tropes dramatise this axiom as the Moranskis' living lamentation for their lost homeland. Devoid of ideology, but filled with fatalistic irony, their grief is predicated on privilege, on having been landowners, a status that endowed them with the legal and social power of belonging to a nation. Czeslaw Milosz expresses the conflict between Polish nationalism and a universalist future defined by ideology: 'To renounce loyalty toward one's country and to eradicate patriotic feelings inculcated in school [. . .] this was the price of entrance upon the road of progress. Not everyone was prepared to pay this price' (141). Stefan's intrepid resistance is born of narrative allegiance to a heroic cultural tradition. His epic ordeal through unplumbed labyrinths, threatened with peril at every turn, reimagines the myth of Theseus and the Minotaur. In Bridge's construction, however, Stefan's fate guarantees no victory for the hero. Instead, the obliquely narrated action of Stefan's endangerment suggests a different sort of power – historical contingency. The possibility of individual agency exists in Stefan's every speech and act, but so does the probability of failure to vanquish the Fascist monster.

Stefan may perform national heroism but, unlike conventional male spies, his masculine prowess will not be privileged, saved for another chapter in a franchise of turbo-driven indomitability. Like his nation, the threat is not only of obliteration but of emasculation, the dead end of a nation's ability to regenerate itself. The odyssey of return to the Poles' homeland is a hope residing alongside entombment as a haunting memory kept in place underground. In 1942 Czeslaw Milosz testified:

> [W]e were living without hope, or rather on a hope we knew to be a delusion. The empire which had absorbed our country was so mighty that only an incorrigible optimist could believe in the possibility of a totally vanquished Germany. Nazi plans in regards to our nation were perfectly clear: to exterminate the educated class, to colonize, and to deport a segment of the population to the East. (106)

The monster will empty its labyrinthine empire of all those whose differences defy its self-affirming self-image of mastery over all it surveys.

In contrast to a decimated Poland, the Moranskis' abject conditions and Hungary's Fascist chokehold, the Kirklands occupy spaces of assured safety, sovereignty and security. In Budapest, their expatriate home is a luxury apartment with 'a rich-looking hall', 'warm deeply carpeted' rooms, and where their greatest worries in planning their escape are '"what about the silver?"' and 'chocolate and tinned foods for the journey' (*AS*, 1, 121, 124, 127). A temporary home to be sure, but bearing no resemblance to either voluntary or involuntary exile. Eight years of deeply cushioned surroundings and an impeccably well-connected social and business life have insulated the Kirklands from confronting danger, theirs or anyone else's. As Hope eventually realises, 'We are Americans; we shall never know what Europeans know, or suffer as they suffer [. . .] we have passports and dollars, we can go anywhere!' (*AS*, 142). This very security, however, is fraught with a different kind of danger. Surrounded by Herend porcelain and other souvenirs of a well-endowed expatriate life, the Kirkland mother and daughter are constrained by the brand and rules of domesticity that invite good business opportunities. The social roles prescribed for them have fixed boundaries – their days are circumscribed by shopping for fresh flowers, even more bibelots, café reprieves and full dress parties. While this is an old story in the upper reaches of society, depicted by Edith Wharton, Jane Austen and Tolstoy, with its 1940s political setting, *A Place to Stand* introduces a new danger for its American women.

Bridge presents the Kirklands as a high functioning unit, their family and social solidarity hampered only by the inconsequential travails of exploiting foreign intrigues to enhance the Americans' cultural and economic capital. However, until Hope descends into the underworld of espionage, she and her mother function solely as decorative trophies, co-ordinated with their tasteful apartment to celebrate the success of American enterprise in Europe. Like Mr Bertram in Austen's *Mansfield Park*, John Kirkland is so preoccupied with his overseas business, that he only notices dissent when his daughter performs a role that threatens the stability and justification for the family's well-tempered norms. In his expatriate domain, social codes reinforce American mercantile culture, where homeland is a convenient safety net for the deserving few, bounded only by expediency and fashion. The Kirklands' distance from the Moranskis is coded as cool entitlement. Expressing passion for one's country would be considered louche. Hence the novel's careful delineation of belonging as a matter of class and capital – Hungarian titles and American wealth.

At the end of the novel Hope renounces her infatuations with romantic love and altruism and returns to America with her parents and recycled American fiancé, Sam. Whether Hope's empathy for the Polish exiles will inspire her to carry home an anti-Nazi warning like Ambler's Kenton or Marlow or MacInnes' Myleses remains an open question. One reason for this is the novel's divided resolution. The possibility of political empathy and action to which Bridge committed her narrative trajectory seems to be abandoned at the end in favour of rescuing her protagonist and depositing her into a securely domesticated romance plot. And yet our plucky Hope expresses uncertainty that extends to how Bridge designs her final message. While she appears different to Sam, 'looking awful – tired, untidy, shabby – and not seeming to care', she also reminds him of Northern Italian paintings of the Madonna, a vision that doesn't coincide with his image of his own beloved (*AS*, 270). Both strange and 'tragic', this transformed Hope confesses hesitantly that 'I – I simply don't know *what* I am, anymore!' (*AS*, 271). Not knowing '*what*' she is rather than who she is correlates with the politically objectified state of the refugees. But as a critical gloss on the fate of the fictional woman spy, this disturbance marks her as occupying a state of exile from the genre's prescribed roles for women characters. Politically and narratively, it may also very well be that like the novel itself, Hope is suspended between embodying the tragic message of a lost Europe and the hope for British and American intervention against Fascist and Communist oppression. The future is indeed implanted in the present of the novel but as a commingling of uncertain hope and despairing victory.

Pamela Frankau's Mythic Exile and Espionage

The historical uncertainty and narrative and gender challenges that shaped Pamela Frankau's 1939 novel *The Devil We Know* permeate her 1968 posthumously published novel *Colonel Blessington*. Like Ann Bridge's novel, Frankau's was written during the Cold War, though its historical uncertainties emanate not from memories of Nazi Germany's conquest of Europe, but from anxieties that cast shadows over the Allies' victory. I bracket this chapter with two novels by Frankau because their oblique depictions of suspicion, surveillance and questionable political identity expand the meanings of exile to mythic origins and the gendered character of spies. In both novels, as in John le Carré's Cold War fictions, World War II is a defining but unresolved presence. Whereas *The Devil We Know* is fraught with the tensions of a nation on the brink of war, World War II is present as a haunting memory in *Colonel Blessington*.

Although *Colonel Blessington* is set during the Cold War, the key event that forms its narrative vortex is a World War II Allied commando raid in France. Unlike many retrospective World War II thrillers, the cat and mouse plot, that of hunter and hunted, does not feature Nazi villains and intrepid Allied agents and victims.[37] Instead, protagonist and antagonist are both former Allied commandoes and present enemies, an opposition that disturbs prototypical rallying cries and celebrations of a united war and victory over Fascism. *Colonel Blessington* represents World War II as a nightmare, with missing pieces, deception and betrayal emanating all from one source. Allied victory is threatened by a mole whose identity, like those of le Carré's traitors, is concealed by membership in the clubby echelons of Britain's ruling classes. Whether or how the truth of this treachery can be the subject and goal of investigation depends on the recovery of a witness' wartime memory and its translation into a coherent narrative. But instead of the genre's favoured encoded or hidden documents, there are only uncanny fleeting, fragmented images – 'a face blackened by the fiery light', 'sinister silence' (*CB*, 62). Instead of a narrative progression of identifying and interpreting secret intelligence, there are only stories within stories, producing an encircling, mythic tale of agonistic origins and relationships. The side of the angels is bedevilled by a kind of primordial betrayal and violence that raises questions about both romantic and realistic fictions of wartime espionage. Staged expressionistically, the material realities of battling Nazis or Communists are superseded by a thriller pitting the irrationality of battle against a mythical evil.

The Prologue, which introduces thirty-three-year-old Harvey Blessington as a war hero, intertwines fragmented images and narrative to encapsulate his abandonment of a mysterious past, including ties to an absent family and to American citizenship and adoption of Britain as his home. With cryptic, decontextualised references, the Prologue also represents the war as a sinister presence that encodes the Colonel's enigmatic character and that will shadow his new life as a British citizen. A man of meticulous habits, feeling 'safe in the anonymity of the transient', he is blindsided by an uncanny intrusion of the past (*CB*, 14). Appearing out of nowhere, an unidentified figure taunts Blessington with hints that he carries a story that belies the one the Colonel is living, '*making an old nightmare real*' and driving the Colonel to wish, '*You should be dead* [. . .]' (Frankau's italics; *CB*, 17). Mirroring his apparitional presence, the nemesis disappears without explanation. Like his absent presence, his story remains suspiciously opaque even as it becomes legible as the key to the novel's mission to uncover Blessington's covert character.

Establishing an oblique connection with the Prologue's sinister warning, Chapter 1 establishes Blessington as fully integrated into British political life, but with a position that threatens to undermine the nation's democratic liberalism. He lends his support to the 'True Tories', the party whose platform accords with his retrograde belief in aristocratic individualism and which, he hopes, will erupt in a 'Right Wing Revolution' (CB, 21, 41). Once 'the weak, the unskilled, the loutish and the lazy' are overcome, victory will belong to those whose value derives from a combination of 'blue blood' and 'property and power' (CB, 41, 30). Put into practice, this ideology of 'blood' and elimination of the *untermenschen* would reverse and therefore betray the Allies' defeat of Fascism. By questioning the Colonel's role in the commando raid – whose side was he on – his supremacist principles indicate a dystopian war and post-war setting where the enemy is a conflation of Fascist and Communist totalitarian oppression. Blessington is to be feared as covertly representing a Fascist threat in the guise of anti-Communism. In contrast to Philip Meyer, who projects his foreignness onto any space he occupies, Blessington would exile undesirable citizens from the space they called home, a position that sits comfortably with his constituency and by implication, would affirm Meyer's worst fears. With ironic import, Blessington's politics oppose the democratic principles that have allowed him to become a British citizen and which the nation fought to preserve.

The novel's intertwined war stories suggest that Blessington's absolutist blood politics articulate and may originate in a dystopian myth of origins that he narrates late in the novel but that only problematises the very notion of solution. Composed of betrayed incestuous desire and its violent expression, this narrative allegorises the insular, exclusionary world of espionage fiction whose plots derive from ideological loyalties, deception and betrayal. Because, for most of the novel, this intertwined story is hidden behind the Colonel's exalted status as a war hero, Blessington is an unknowable figure of unbounded dread, as though he embodies a mythic war leading not to victory but to continuing death and destruction. Like Expressionist figures of the undead, including Ambler's Dimitrios, the spectral indeterminacy of Blessington's character raises questions about fictional relationships between the nature of heterosexuality, masculinity and political and cultural history. In Blessington's case, the masculinity of Fascism's *übermensch* and the stability of its politics are undermined by exposing the sexual violence and sterility of Fascist ideology and practice. As Blessington's character emerges from elusiveness to illusion, it mirrors that of Fascism, with its buoyant promises of glory producing only destructive delusion.

Like *The Mask of Dimitrios* and *The Devil We Know*, *Colonel Blessington* occupies a liminal narrative space between espionage and detective genres by focusing on the investigation of a suspect's identity and humanity in order to explore issues related to belonging, disguise and exile. In this regard and others, *Colonel Blessington* also bears an illuminating resemblance to Graham Greene's 1949 film and 1950 novella, *The Third Man*, assessed by Allan Hepburn as 'fall[ing] between adventure, western, detective, and espionage genres' (111).[38] Like Greene's villain Harry Lime, Harvey Blessington exists in hiding. Sexually threatening, they both use the women who love them to validate their masculinity while withholding sexual and emotional intimacy. Like Lime, who only appears more than halfway through his tale, Blessington's disguised identity represents him as 'an illusion caused by a shadow', a post-war spectre of World War II's traumatic memories (Hepburn, 110). Both Harry Lime and Harvey Blessington are uncanny agents of violence that endanger worlds beyond war. Like the diseases produced by the decomposing corpses of war (Lime markets diluted penicillin), they carry death, infecting the cities to which they migrate with their own undead incarnations. With Lime and Blessington in residence, post-war Vienna and London materialise as dystopian sites of unfinished wars. Recalling Holly Martins, Lime's old friend and wartime comrade, Blessington's fellow commando Matthew Gilroy searches for the unknown man who haunts his nightmares, compels his present day and whom he must kill to survive and cleanse the world of his treachery.

Hepburn's intriguing point that Lime is 'rejected by nature' offers a way of interpreting Blessington's identity and villainy, both of which are tethered to unstable gender identification (110). A cross-dresser, Blessington manifests a Janus-like gender-bending. As we learn only at the novel's end, he is actually a woman, disguised as the twin brother she loved, envied and murdered. As though committing an original sin for which he must pay, the brother, the actual Harvey Blessington, loses his licence to live when he rejects his sister, abandoning their symbiotic, incestuous relationship. What he leaves behind is her unwanted identity as a woman, deprived of her masculine half, decimating any possibility of wholeness for her. The word 'disguised' is therefore inaccurate. After his sister kills Harvey, '"She took on his clothes and his accent and his life. She played his part – "' (*CB*, 234). That her first name remains mysterious attests to the total absorption of her brother's identity, recalling Philip Meyer's desire to merge with his lover and unsettle definitive gender boundaries. The threat to Victoria's identity as an autonomous subject in that novel can be read as materialising in Blessington's seizure of her sibling's gender identity and the erasure of her own. But becoming her brother is only half of half the story, for as the siblings' identities become increasingly involuted – turning inwards between them – so turns the mythic espionage plot. Even as Blessington's sister feels and acts as Harvey, she also performs as another woman, one she/he invents as a cover but who replicates the twins' fused character. Jane Rolf, whose 'specialty' is 'Escape', is spurred on 'because danger was forever delightful. You felt no fear. You would always win [...]' (CB, 96). While this audacity suggests the intrepid heroism of a mythic hero, in its abstract evasion of individuality, the entire statement can be read as disguising the Colonel's Fascist politics. Performing as Jane Rolf, as one of several Blessington permutations, grants him/her undetectable freedom to swing brazenly between respectability and treachery and amongst a dizzying array of their narrative meanings of knowledge and secret intelligence.

In metafictional terms, Blessington's tortuous gender turns can be viewed as parodying the gendered plot mazes typical of a spy thriller. Clues – really teasers – are sprinkled throughout the novel; he looks 'almost womanish', 'androgynous', but then again, 'Homosexuality and heroism were not incompatible,' as in the case of 'Lawrence of Arabia' (CB, 11, 146). As these indeterminacies suggest, no sexual or gendered hybridity will emerge from the Blessingtons' incestuous cocoon. Reframing Rachel Carroll's exposition, there will be no 'transition to [completed] adult heterosexuality and the apparent "indeterminacy"' will not be 'resolved' (120).[39] Instead, the twins' incestuous, 'androgynous' case troubles the traditionally gendered power structures of so spy many thrillers which depict conflict as male protagonists and antagonists and women as ancillary plot ornaments. Although there is no doubt of their sexual and gendered identities as male and female, although their relationship is incestuous, the Blessingtons do not figure as a couple. In romantic and sexual terms, their incest precludes their 'assumption of a culturally coded set of practices, that is, as an index of successful assimilation into the world of the "normals"' (Carroll, 142). The fusion of male and female in the Blessington incestuous murder, complicated by the sister murdering the brother, rewrites the genre's portrayal of singular masculine militarism. With yet another twist, there is never any doubt about the Colonel's appeal to women, from political groupies to his fiancée Anita Gilroy. But despite Anita's beauty, the six foot tall TV star who towers over Blessington's 'slight and graceful' build suffers from the reversal of prototypical masculine and feminine bodies (CB, 75). Between Blessington's mutable gender identities and incest and Anita's sexual neglect, this thriller will disturb the genre's narrative templates for heterosexual romance and sexual objectification for male or female.

As the novel collapses the twins' distinct gender identities, transposing the spy thriller's dichotomy between masculine violence and feminine cunning onto both brother and sister, it also extends the genre's configuration of doubling. Deceiving and betraying each other, each twin double-crosses the other. Each figuratively and literally assassinates the other. The stakes are nothing more or less than a primordial sense of wholeness and belonging, the narrative effect of which is the tenor of a mythic battle, recalling the biblical stories of Cain and Abel and the expulsion from Eden as well as allusions to Greek epic.[40] The biblical resonance also suggests a sinister response to the question raised by Frankau's *The Devil We Know*: am I my brother's keeper? Although the twins are the same age as Jesus and Alexander the Great, their name Blessington suggests a mordantly ironic gloss. The twins are neither blessed nor a blessing, especially as they conflate the dichotomy of victim and villain in their characterisation as both Cain and Abel. Like the biblical tale, sibling rivalry drives one to kill the other, but the cost of winning is exile. The hunter-warrior Blessington twins are expelled from all states of belonging into an exile of wandering with no end or homeland in sight, only the promise of never-ending betrayal and violence. They are banished from a paradise they spoiled, but not only by transgressive desire. As Blessington confesses at the end, they have enacted a narcissistic sexual knowledge that violates the boundaries of selfhood and the relationship between selfhood and collective responsibility.

The biblical story and interpretations of Cain's murder of his brother Abel resonate throughout *Colonel Blessington* as a historical and mythic war. In the novel's primal scene, depicted as an Expressionist nightmare, an Allied commando kills an innocent boy, disturbing the narrative of a necessary and just World War II, especially as it recalls the association of Hitler with Cain, the murderer of his brother. In his 1944 painting, 'Cain or Hitler in Hell', German Expressionist artist George Grosz extended the meaning of the story by portraying the Führer as killer of humankind with a pile of human skeletons climbing up his leg.[41] The story of Cain and Abel is also figured by Frankau as the Ur-war on the other who is both the rival and double of the self. According to biblical scholar John Byron, some rabbinic exegesis and Christian sources identify the siblings as twins. Other commentaries note that each had a twin sister and that in order to prevent incest at a time when no other women existed to marry, Adam ordered each brother to marry the other's sister. In this variation, the murder of Abel is attributed to Cain's incestuous passion for his twin sister that turned to fury when his brother married her (Byron, 27–8). In the first volume of his comprehensive study, *The Legends of the Jews*, Louis Ginzberg collates variations on the twins' story, including conclusions about Cain's punishment, fate and the impact of his character: 'he changed the world into cunning craftiness. Like unto Cain were all his descendants, impious and godless, wherefore God resolved to destroy them' (116). In their compressed and expanded convolutions, the multiple doublings in these legends coincide with the murderous story of the Blessington twins.

While Frankau never mentions these sources, her conversion to Catholicism in 1942 led her to write about psychological and moral conflicts 'from the Catholic angle', in particular, 'sexual sin' (*Pen to Paper*, 190, 197).[42] Sexual sin is the basis of the Blessington mythic tale of terror:

> 'There was this girl,' she said, 'a long time ago, a girl who lived in California. And the boy she loved was the other half of herself [. . .] She was as strong as he was, and as beautiful – they were beautiful kids [. . .] and not only strong: they could be ruthless, both of them; they liked power, and using power. Other people were afraid of them [. . .] They had a whole language of their own: a whole set of characters, quite secret, not known to anyone [. . .] something like the Brontës' Gondal stories [. . .] They were too close, you might say [. . .] She was his first in bed and he was hers [. . .] Anyway, the family moved in and broke it up [. . .] He grew up without his other half. She didn't. She lived by him and in him and through him all her life.' (*CB*, 150–1)

Past and present co-exist in this passage in a narrative form and voice that combine as an Expressionist myth. Its reference to the Brontës' juvenile fantasies, to the archetypal 'girl' from 'a long time ago' and extreme, 'secret' emotionality exclude the explanatory presence of historical context or mimesis. In its condensed form, the mythic memory of betrayed belonging correlates with Blessington's extremist political position and the anger with which he articulates it. The Blessington twins' incestuous relationship resembles certain primary characteristics of the Fascist ideas the Colonel expresses in the Prologue. The oneness of brother and sister suggests a self-generated genealogy based on a Fascist myth of origins and individualism that as George Mosse explains, 'meant self-fulfillment while sheltering within [. . .] a true community in which the like-minded joined together, each through his own power of will' (84).[43] That the twins' myth of origins ends in violence is no surprise. As Julia Kristeva asserts,

> The cult of origins is a hate reaction. *Hatred of those others* who do not share my origins and who affront me [. . .] I stick to an archaic, primitive, 'common denominator', the one of my frailest childhood.

A defensive hatred, the cult of origins easily backslides to a persecuting hatred. And wounded souls may be seen to turn around and fight their neighbors who are just as hurt as they are – perhaps by the same totalitarian tyrant (political or religious) – but who can easily be taken for the weak link in that chain of hatred, for the scapegoat of one's depression. (2–3)

Instead of hatred, the twins' bond springs from an essential desire for an Other who reflects and validates the primacy of the self through the purity of their identical blood and myth of origins. This desire both resembles and contrasts sharply with that of Philip Meyer, whose fantasy of merging with his lover would unsettle Fascist conceptions of race and gender. The exclusive, narcissistic self-glorification that constitutes the twins' selfhood is based on an autocratic sense of inherent superiority and power. It has no tolerance for difference. As Roger Griffin says of Fascism, it is characterised by 'heterophobia', 'fear and hatred of those felt to be "different"' (in Iordachi, 122).[44] Umberto Eco observes, 'Ur-Fascism grows up and seeks for consensus by exploiting and exacerbating the natural *fear of difference*. The first appeal of a fascist or prematurely fascist movement is an appeal against the intruders. Thus Ur-Fascism is racist by definition' (14).[45] The twins' extremist, self-defined state of being, suggesting an embodied despotic state, enacts incest as the quintessential and most destructive form of preserving racial purity.

In the Blessington myth, difference means death of the self. When difference arises between them, when one twin discovers the other's hatred and rejection, the rivalry for absolute power demands execution. As Eco declares, 'For Ur-Fascism, disagreement is treason' and '*life is permanent warfare*' (14, 15). In effect, this destructive outcome of dissolving difference originates in the wishful fantasy to contain his and her object of desire within the solipsistic boundaries of a self-enclosed domain. But as myth would have it, Blessington arises from destruction. Having been exiled from the lived fantasy of idyllic wholeness and exclusionary power, his Fascist politics would repair his fragmented self by restoring his power over others. Like an inverted psychoanalytic model, his story and politics represent an anti-family, anti-democratic anti-romance.

As a clue to the novel's search for the source of villainy, the mythic form of Blessington's story shows how Frankau's thriller experiments with one of spy fiction's most significant tropes: the suspicious identity and subjectivity of the double agent. Here the double agent as twins shows how spies are never singular selves, never the real thing, only representations of representations. Even Blessington's confession to Matthew is double-sided, suspended between a story as subterfuge and as revelation, each both reinforcing and undercutting the validity of the other. Confession here is only another fiction, mirroring the novel's enactment of the spy's character as essentially one of disguise, mendacity and dissimulation. As the narrative becomes increasingly discontinuous, Blessington's character will be located in a story that keeps doubling back on itself, further concealing its subject and resisting solution. For example, the identity of the protagonist war hero turns out to be that of the antagonist killer, as brother and sister are so identical that each enacts the essence of the other in an allegorical fantasy of erotic fusion. This is not merely performance, however; duplicity and disguise as well as an atavistic instinct for killing defines and animates their characters. In gendered and political terms Blessington remains 'a stranger' in all his and her self-revelations, from recounting their childhood and wartime past and through his and her political and business activities. Blessington's alienation from family, domestic and gender norms unsettles the very notion of fictional character as definable individuality. But unlike Frankau's Philip Meyer, whose Jewish identity rescues him into a humanitarian mission or sense of self and purpose, Blessington's only mission is to kill. Even in death, however, Blessington cannot emerge from his and her uncanny alchemised identities as anything more than a 'dummy', a 'big bruised doll', with only 'the ragged likeness of a face' (*CB*, 218, 214). Having abandoned themselves to violence, they reject the moral knowledge that traditionally provides redemption from sinfulness and expulsion. With their only stable identity that of a killer, Blessington's character devolves into disintegration, in exile from the human.

An unpublished preface to the novel by Frankau's close friend Rebecca West attests to Frankau's understanding of gender as an unsettled metaphysical category of being and ripe for political allegory:

> She knew better than most people born women what it was like to be a man, and this has its relevance to this book. The early scene, when the fortunate and confident young man goes off in the car with a mysterious and menacing driver, is good thriller stuff but with a certain unusual intensity and it is not surprising when later we seem to be looking through the wrong end of a binocular at what, if we were not forced to put up with this diminishing mode of vision, would surely appear as a tremendous drama played out by the primal figures, man and woman, and proving some point concerning human sinfulness and divine justice. This is not without precedent. The great thriller writers, Wilkie Collins, Charles Reade, Joseph Shearing (who was Marjorie Bowen) and Simenon, write with a cryptic vigour which transcends their obvious subject-matter and must spring from serious preoccupations. The oblique view of the seriousness of Pamela Frankau also has its dynamic quality. But her friends can only regret that the whole world cannot know what her seriousness was like as they knew it in its direct form: perceptive and enduring, and illuminating and kind. (9–10)

The 'wrong end of a binocular' and Frankau's 'oblique vision' identify the novel as a gendered mythic thriller that interrogates whether investigating human sinfulness and divine or human justice is even possible. For one thing, Blessington's fused genders – man and woman – reject the notion that there is an individual sinner, possessing holistic subjectivity and agency. As Rebecca West observes so astutely, the twins' portrait also reveals the mythic dichotomy of man and woman to be a negation of the dynamics of gender identity. Harvey Blessington's duplicities may fulfil readers' expectations of enigmatic double agents, but in its doubling oscillations, shifting shapes and multi-layered gender identities, his and her character stonewalls any linear progress or stable, confirmed discovery in the narrative structure. For despite killing Blessington in self-defence, the novel's primary investigator finds no solution, resolution or irresolution in tracing the villain's encoded character. It is as though in mirroring the indeterminate figure of the double agent, the novel doubles back on itself to question the stability of its own investigation and conclusion.

The novel's lone investigator is Anita Gilroy's father Matthew Gilroy, former MI5 agent, army commando and prisoner of war survivor. Acting outside the law, on his own secret mission, in a liminal timescape between the end of the post-war and the escalation of the Cold War, Gilroy represents a psychological space between the failure to reconcile victory with the ghosts of the war's destruction and the confrontation with resurgent totalitarian violence. Ghosts abound in this novel and Blessington embodies them all as an overdetermined symbol of the failure to bury the will to absolute power and its need for violence. Contributing to the suspense generated by the hunt for the real Colonel Blessington is a narrative conundrum: that the material evidence of his deeds is present only in absence: the death of his parents, disappearance of his twin and in Matthew's traumatic memory. Matthew can only deduce his knowledge of Blessington's infamy from disjointed, shadowy images of the commando raid in France: 'Hands and hurting and killing', a 'killer's voice', the blackened, disguised face of 'a stranger' who without provocation cuts the throat of an innocent French boy (CB, 51, 65). Violating the limits of wartime violence, Blessington's actions engender Matthew's 'naked edge of anger like the sharpened edge of an axe' (CB, 69). Violent feeling replaces the possibility of revenge or justice, and so as if to conjure the spirit of his anger and test the corporeality of his nemesis, Matthew invents a sinister version of the raid. Stalking Blessington in London and preparing for his appearance at his home in north Yorkshire signal the novel's construction of England as a traumatised battleground. In this novel the nation continually prepares for the invasion so feared during World War II, and when Frankau was writing, defending against what became known as the Red scare. Replicating unresolved threats to the nation, Matthew performs a ritual of counter-espionage at his home, a 'game of creeping up on the house, as if someone waited in ambush there; entering with care and silence, as he'd been taught to in war-time, long ago' (CB, 71).

Spying on his own house transforms the present into a continuous war by re-enacting the raid as a haunting Expressionist mystery, reproducing the fear and loathing that emanated from the covert agent's unwarranted attack. Like a repetition compulsion or symptom of post-traumatic stress, surveillance here illuminates a profound need to repair or work through a disabling war memory and projection by testing its foundational reality. Surveillance also reveals that home is enemy territory, subverting the certainty of Allied victory over totalitarianism. Blending into the Cold War, an unfinished World War II doubles anxieties that warfare is a continuous state, militarily, politically and existentially. With dystopian overtones, endless war coincides with Blessington's campaign for the 'True Tories' and hope for a 'Right Wing Revolution'. The resulting combination threatens the future of such exercises in liberal democracy as free and transparent elections. A place that means a state of exile, home and by extension homeland, is neither secure nor comforting. Instead, the home site is but a signpost to wandering tautologically within and ensuring the uncertainties of an unresolved story of espionage and counterespionage. As Matthew's ominous exercise reifies into ritual, replicated symbolically in his jigsaw and crossword puzzles, it suggests that espionage is a ceremonial enterprise. The rules are self-contained and productive of only more of the same inconsequential or treacherous results, no more valuable than a game. Like a draw or stalemate, Matthew's ritualised testing confirms that resolution is always deferred and so calls for replay. At the same time as it substantiates the memory, it conjures up the question of war's ethical reality, a riddle with no answers and so produces and reproduces uncanniness.

The unresolved, opaque memory of the French commando raid and its menacing actuality become fused, binding Matthew to his nemesis and rivalling the novel's most intense and meaningful relationship. Although this intensity aligns with the Blessington twins, including a violent ending, the import of doubling here suggests the fusion of opposing political passions rather than sexual desire – a homo-political relationship. This narrative pattern alters course, however, to save Matthew from being devoured by a never-ending story, a dystopian game of spy and counterspy. Matthew's murder of Blessington also reconstructs and reverses the story of Cain and Abel. Whereas Abel cannot rise from the dead to exact retribution, Matthew retaliates by using Blessington's 'old unarmed-combat stroke' that killed the French boy and is now aimed at him: 'upward, across the throat' (*CB*, 67, 182). Blessington's sinister appearance at Matthew's house, emerging from the violence of World War II into the Cold War, is amplified by transfiguring war memory into Matthew's feared reality, and by the scene's unsettling gendered unreality. For example, Blessington enters the scene as the fictional Jane Rolf, but then, while recounting the story of the twins, she unmasks herself, exposing masculine violence as a female phantom. While there is no doubt about Blessington's corporeal reality, the man who inspired Matthew's nightmarish visions and surveillance games reveals the insubstantiality of his gendered identity when his murdered body is exposed as that of a woman warrior.

More than a startling plot twist, the identity of Blessington as a villainous woman is linked to political and literary history. Part of Nazi ideology, with which the novel identifies Blessington, is the inscription of oppressively dichotomous gender identities. While Blessington's assumption of her brother's male identity might be viewed as defiance of Nazi ideology, she fulfils its repressive mandate in being equally punitive of self-determination. Moreover, the denial of her twin's right to difference destroys her individuality as well. By contrast, Helen MacInnes and Ann Bridge create espionage plots that liberate their women protagonists into political activism to confirm the authenticity of their desire and that of others for self-determination. Recalling Ambler's Dimitrios, arising from and returning to the dead, Blessington's violent yet infinitely fracturing character belongs to a mythical Fascist underworld that represents a fear of apocalyptic war. As Allan Hepburn describes the 'subterranean spaces' in *The Third Man*, they 'register the fear that no place, anywhere, is safe, either above or below ground' (128).

Such an omnipresent threat materialises in *Colonel Blessington* in the post-war replay of pitting Fascism and ruthless authoritarian societies against the purportedly liberal democracies. Blessington's embrace of anti-democratic politics in Britain creates chaos and threatens ruin in a post-war society still in the process of restoration as it evolves into a welfare state. It is as though all the efforts of the Allies' clandestine services and special military units are undone by the residual mythic power of Fascist appeal. The novel opens a prospect onto a mythical dystopian future against which the novels of Helen MacInnes and Ann Bridge represent warnings and calls to action. Together the three writers in this chapter express fears that the equalities promised by Allied victory may never be safe from the lures of anti-democratic supremacy. Their espionage parables question whether the disguised presence of Fascist power isn't the double agent, the mole deep in the myth of a victorious democracy.

Notes

1. The MLA bibliography website confirms this conclusion.
2. Allan Hepburn distinguishes detective fiction's clues from spy fiction's codes.
3. Several Helen MacInnes and Ann Bridge novels have been reprinted. I worked with earlier editions. Most studies of spy thrillers omit women writers who challenge such categories as conservative, left and right wing. See for example, Robert L. Snyder and Michael Denning. Andrew Hammond claims that 'The left-liberal tradition of thriller writing was never a dominant strain during the Cold War' and cites Ian Fleming's James Bond series as a 'right-wing thriller' without investigating MacInnes or other women writers, p. 113.
4. Scholarship that affirms the literary value and distinction from modernism includes Brown and Grover (eds), *The Space Between: Reading Sideways* and *Middlebrow Literary Cultures: The Battle of the Brows 1920–1960*.
5. Women spies as protagonists have appeared recently in William Boyd's compelling novel *Restless* and in the fiction by the first woman director of MI5, Stella Rimington, which uses the genre's conventions to avoid realism. Ian McEwan's 2012 novel *Sweet Tooth* features a woman spy but as in his novel *Atonement*, she serves the postmodern function of exposing the unreliability of narrative itself.
6. I'd like to thank Clare Hanson for encouraging me to extend this idea.
7. In a *New York Times* review of Frankau's 1958 novel *Ask Me No More*, Orville Prescott maintains, 'In an era such as ours, when inept, clumsy and pretentiously muddled novels are acclaimed, it is all the more regrettable that an accomplished novelist with a personal vision of life and love like Miss Frankau is not taken more seriously. After all, she is just as clever as Evelyn Waugh and a lot more emotionally powerful.' Reprinted by Virago, her best known novel is *The Willow Cabin*, which through an obsessive triangular relationship, explores the political crises of the 1930s and the Blitz.
8. Dan Stone reports that before 1939, 'many writers saw the persecution of the Jews [...] as only the smaller part of a broader attack on minority groups', and 'a number of commentators gave way, seemingly unwittingly, or without malice, to antisemitic stereotypes', p. 81. Although Stone explains that 'the scale of the persecution' was often 'dismissed' as 'atrocity propaganda', the rhetoric of those commentators needs examination, p. 81.
9. Aktion T4 was signed by Hitler in 1939, committing those who were medically assessed as incurably ill. Over seventy thousand people were killed until family members of the victims protested en masse. The United States Holocaust Memorial Museum catalogue, *Deadly Medicine: Creating the Master Race,* offers a history of the program: http://www.ushmm.org/information/exhibitions/traveling-exhibitions/deadly-medicine Historian Henry Friedlander traces this program to the Holocaust. Jews who were sent to

the camps were judged as either physically fit to work or as useless and so fit only to be gassed. Dachau was in operation by 1933–4 and Sachsenhausen and Buchenwald by 1937.
10. Jed Esty discusses narrative relationships between Modernism and colonialism, but ignores Fascism or Nazism as imperialist, racist empires.
11. During the war Frankau served in the ATS and according to Rebecca West's obituary, 'alien as it was from her temperament, [it was] because she loved England with what she herself pointed out was the peculiarly ardent love for England that is felt by some English Jews', 'Obituary', p. 12.
12. Tony Kushner argues that the British liberal tradition requires Jews to assimilate to its social and cultural codes whereas Todd Endelman maintains that British antisemitism is not related to liberalism but aligned with 'deeply ingrained cultural habits', Kushner, 'Beyond the Pale?', pp. 143, 145; Endelman, 'Jews, Aliens, and other Outsiders', pp. 964, 969.
13. For histories of Jews settling in Britain, see Todd Endelman, *Radical Assimilation* and David Cesarani (ed.), *The Making of Modern Anglo-Jewry*. Deborah Cohen argues that 'Jews came increasingly to be identified as a race precisely because they were difficult to differentiate from their fellow citizens [. . .] Jews became ever more invisible as they scaled the social ladder', pp. 460–84.
14. As Sander Gilman argues, medical literature at the turn of the century 'tended to show that behind Jews' supposed intellectual superiority was an inferior ability to perform measurable tasks [and] this degenerative creativity was marked by the stigmata of disease, of madness', p. 34.
15. The Bourne novels and films exemplify action packed demonstrations of fearlessness in the service of prolonging Bourne's futile search for his authentic identity.
16. For discussions of cultural and social antisemitism in twentieth-century Britain, see Bryan Cheyette and Laura Marcus, Phyllis Lassner and Lara Trubowitz.
17. On the era's Anglo-Jewish film audiences, see Gil Toffell. Andrew Spicer notes the Jewish head of the Gaumont-British Picture Corporation, Isidore Ostrer, was attacked as an 'unnaturalised alien' in the House of Commons in the late 1930s, p. 118. Gerald Krefetz shows that from the Middle Ages, the Jews' historical experience of exile and exclusion from most commercial professions motivated them to avoid censure as dependent on the state. In response, Jews developed 'entrepreneurial spirit and tradition of risk-taking that has led to [participation] in progressive industries where innovation was rewarded', pp. 11–12. Jerry Z. Muller historicises the Jews' position as a 'diasporic merchant minority' that drew them to the financial and commercial rather than the bureaucratic aspects of capitalist economies, pp. 7, 53, 77. As Geoffrey Alderman observes, the outlook of Jewish workers 'differed fundamentally from the British craft tradition; they saw themselves [. . .] as potentially upwardly mobile, not as perpetual members of the proletariat', p. 184.
18. The risk is manifold. Frankau's grandmother, Julia Frankau, wrote *Pigs in Clover* (1903), a novel that has antisemitic representations. See Todd Endelman, 'The Frankaus of London', Sarah Gracome, Michael Galchinsky and Nadia Valman.

19. For discussion of British cultural antisemitism in the 1930s, see Phyllis Lassner and Mia Spiro. Victoria Stewart's study of Gilbert Frankau shows an interesting link with *The Devil We Know*; his 1936 novel *Farewell Romance* 'attempts to turn the stereotypical characteristics of Jewish characters into virtues' and 'unusually for 1936, there are allusions to the fate of the Jews in Europe', np.
20. Many thanks to Margaret Stetz for this. Email, 15 November 2014.
21. Gina Macdonald reports that MacInnes was also criticised for 'convoluted and predictable' plots and for her limited logic despite 'being too analytical'. 'Her Nazis and her Communists blend together; they all are vicious, ruthless, manipulative, clever, and dangerous', p. 294.
22. A *New York Times* review of the 1943 reprint attests how the novel 'so completely grasped the melodramatic essence of our times and so thoroughly convinced us of its reality', Anon., BR22. MacInnes stressed that her interest in analysing international relations was always subject to wide ranging research and informed by 'a philosophical or moral argument', Mitgang, p. 181.
23. It is important to note differences between appeasers who, for various reasons, wished for a negotiated peace, and ideological pacifists like Dick Shepherd and Vera Brittain.
24. As part of their invasion of the Soviet Union, in the fall of 1941, the Nazis began experiments with poison gas as a method of mass killing Jews in sealed trucks or huts.
25. Peter Neville situates Britons' ambivalent responses to Germany's annexation of the Sudetenland in 'an historical context in which Britishers often disdained foreigners' and looked for reasons not 'to meddle in the murky waters of Central Europe and the Balkans', p. 82.
26. From his Mass Observation interviews, Tom Harrisson reports that 'The Men and women fighting in these blitz-battles were fighting to survive and continue. They were not fighting – as at Waterloo or Arnhem – to win. Simply to live on and through the blitz was a kind of victory [. . .] made up of minute personal triumphs adding up to massive, adaptative achievement, despite savage defeats upon the way', p. 233.
27. For distinctions between Fascism and Nazism's ambivalences towards modernity and medievalism, see Roger Griffin.
28. See Alon Confino's interpretation of Nazi mythmaking as constructing its identity and foundational narrative by destroying the Hebrew Bible on which Christianity depended for its revisionist formation.
29. For analysis of this neglect, see Bernard Wasserstein and Tony Kushner, *The Holocaust and the Liberal Imagination*.
30. See Richard Breitman and Allan Lichtman for analysis of the American responses to the plight of the Jews.
31. In *Swastika Night*, 700 years into the Third Reich's victory, women are caged as breeders, with crying their only acceptable form of self-expression. More recent dystopian representations of women's biological persecution include Margaret Atwood's 1985 novel *The Handmaid's Tale* and P. D. James' 1992 *The Children of Men*.
32. Engelmann notes that 800,000 Germans had joined the Nazi Party before 30 January 1933 and that by March 1936, when Reich Propaganda Minister

Josef Goebbels triumphantly announced that '"Ninety-nine percent of all Germans have voted for Adolf Hitler" [. . .] An entire nation had bowed to a system of terror', pp. 51, 105.
33. I discuss *A Tightening String* in my *British Women Writers of World War II*.
34. The agent protagonist in *Assignment in Brittany* is parachuted into France to impersonate a French collaborator who is his double in appearance but opposite in character.
35. Czeslaw Milosz reports that in Poland, 'The peasants' class hatred of the manor was not violent [. . .] so the expelled proprietors were not harmed', p. 157.
36. Hoffman emigrated from Poland in 1959 at the age of fourteen.
37. Among many examples are the World War II novels of Alan Furst, and revisionist fictions like Robert Harris' *Fatherland,* featuring a 'good' German police officer in a dystopian Nazi future.
38. Hepburn adds the point that the novella's 'classification is made more complex by virtue of its having been written for the film', p. 111. *Colonel Blessington* would make a terrific film.
39. Rachel Carroll's study of fictional representations of heteronormativity is instructive in questioning 'conventionally understood' requirements for identity 'as either male or female, either masculine or feminine and either heterosexual or homosexual', p.6.
40. Robert Doak points out that 'the tale of Cain and Abel is employed extensively in spy novels' because of its shared themes of 'violence, evil, deception, betrayal and rationality [and] complementary depiction of the Fall', p. 13.
41. See Cheldelin, Druckman and Fast for tracing modern conflicts to the foundational story of sibling rivalry in Cain and Abel as it appears in the Hebrew Bible, Christianity and Islam, pp. 59–62.
42. Writing in 1962, Frankau noted the problems for creative writers produced by what she felt was 'sex-mongering', where sins of the flesh had 'come to mean sex and sex only', *Pen to Paper*, p. 198. Among those afflicted writers were Nabokov, James Purdy, Grace Metalious and James Gould Cozzens.
43. As the collection *Modernism and Fascism* shows, Fascism was, in theory and practice, full of contradictions and 'like a scavenger [. . .] scooped up scraps of romanticism, liberalism, the new technology, and even socialism', Iordachi, p. 90.
44. Although, as Griffin and others argue, 'Fascism is also intrinsically anti-cosmopolitan, axiomatically rejecting as decadent the liberal vision of the multi-cultural, multi-religious, multi-racial society,' it does not 'necessarily lead to' racial persecution, but rather 'a campaign of propaganda and violence against their presence as "immigrants" who have abandoned their "natural" homeland', in Iordachi, p. 122.
45. Eco bases his analysis on his own experience growing up in Fascist Italy under Mussolini.

Chapter 3

Leslie Howard: Propaganda Artist

British born, of Hungarian Jewish descent, Leslie Howard became a Hollywood star during the 1930s. Celebrated for performing 'sophisticated comedy' as well as 'the tragic hero of romances' like *Of Human Bondage* (1934) and *Intermezzo* (1939), he also endowed the character of 'the thinking men who find a cause' with a combination of self-effacing irony, political passion and otherworldliness.[1] The range of his Hollywood roles included the dashing double-faced *Scarlet Pimpernel* (1935), the brilliant and quirky Henry Higgins in *Pygmalion* (1938) and the erotically challenged Ashley Wilkes in *Gone with the Wind* (1939) (a role he hated). Howard's screen persona as witty, elegant if absent-minded intellectual won him critical and popular acclaim on both sides of the Atlantic.[2] His success afforded him a glamorous and comfortable life in both Los Angeles and New York, but in 1938, after the Munich debacle, he made the crucial decision to return to Britain and did so a week before war was declared. His artistry was thereafter shaped and defined by his political activism.

Howard's career as propaganda artist came to a tragic end when his civilian aeroplane was shot down over the Bay of Biscay by the Luftwaffe on 1 June 1943.[3] As Estel Eforgan reports, Howard's son Ronald felt that by 1940, his father had 'become a "V-Personen"', the Germans' term for unofficial spy (*In Search*, 127). Gossip intensified this rumour, especially as lurid accounts about Howard's affair with a 'mysterious female spy' were circulating (127). Eforgan's rigorous research and analysis dispel these stories, leading her to conclude that 'No evidence has ever connected Leslie Howard to any intelligence agency' (127). Nonetheless, even without such connections, Howard had supporters in the British government who substantiated his film treatments of Nazi Germany's plans for world conquest.

With fervent belief in the propaganda power of film and radio, Howard offered his services to the war effort. He worked with the Ministry of

Information, the government agency 'whose prime duty on the home front was to sustain civilian morale' through 'the release of official news; security censorship of the press, films and the BBC [...] the conduct of publicity campaigns for other departments; and the dissemination of propaganda to enemy, neutral, allied and empire countries' (McLaine 1, 3).[4] By arrangement with the MOI, which chose speakers for the BBC, Howard joined J. B. Priestley's BBC radio programme, 'Britain Speaks', to transmit twenty-seven broadcasts to the United States and Canada between 16 July 1940 and January 1941. Priestley's programmes were extremely popular both at home and abroad because, unlike those radio voices that were 'too impersonal' and 'academic' to be personally appealing, Priestley's speakers were 'unpatronising' and expressed their ideas clearly and unpretentiously (McLaine, 99). In addition to his broadcasts, Howard also worked with British filmmakers to design, produce and star in a series of films to be distributed in the United States and Canada.

Working with a complex weave of official government ministries and divisions, the Foreign Office and the co-operation of American journalists stationed in London, Howard's combined efforts would convey the necessity for North Americans to support Britain in its efforts to defend itself and defeat Hitler.[5] He would have agreed with Jacques Ellul, who asserted that to be a propagandist for morale was not 'to modify ideas, but to provoke action' (qtd in McLaine, 9). Howard's individual contribution would be to embody 'the visionary aspect of Englishness [...] a quiet, thoughtful spirit roused to action by an evil more monstrous than the world had ever known' (Richards, xiv). Although he agreed with some of the government's official war aims, his wartime work performed a personal call to preserve individual and collective freedom and thus activate democratic ideals and practices. The result counters the government's assumption that ordinary Britons were 'unlikely to respond "to such abstract concepts as Freedom" but were "at least averagely susceptible to propaganda" [...] as long as it didn't provoke their sense of the ridiculous' (McLaine, 22).

According to his son Ronald, the outbreak of war signalled a 'revolutionary' departure from Howard's earlier career of romantic and light roles (*Trivial Fond Records*, 151). Unlike others in the film industry for whom the war was very unsettling and who reacted with an 'inertia, which strikes artists of all kinds in times of violence and destruction', Howard developed a new creative outlet, becoming a political artist, as he said in his recording 'English Films and the War', for the BBC *Radio Newsreel*.[6] In April 1940, despite 'fragile' relations with France, the Anglo-French Propaganda Council sent Howard to meet with writers and the French Minister of Information to discuss collaboration on propaganda films and also to meet with filmmakers in neutral Spain, Portugal and Ireland (Eforgan, 135–6). Not that this commitment easily translated into action, for few with power either in the film industry or government shared 'the agitations of a film star, however important, recently landed from Hollywood' (Howard, *TFR*, 151).

With very scarce material and human resources, including film stock and technicians in military service, and because each turn of the war changed the attitudes of both the government and public opinion, the British film industry constantly had to plead for support. Both the government and the BBC responded according to their 'calculation of the audience's wartime needs and by reference to the extraordinary conditions being endured' (Gledhill and Swanson, 2). Among the factors to assess the appropriateness of a film were styles, subjects and genres and whether they would appeal to audiences across the national spectrum: 'class, gender, age, region and ethnicity'; it would be more persuasive 'to tap into historically specific circumstances and dilemmas – whether through realism *or* fantasy' (Gledhill and Swanson 2). As Howard expressed this dilemma, one of the

> profound psychological deterrents [. . .] is the conviction that film entertainment is a trivial occupation in times when there remain such tremendous and historic tasks to be done. It is doubtless for this latter reason that practically every film made in England during the war has had a war-time or propaganda theme. But it is beginning to become evident that the public has had enough of these. As usual, the public's principal demand from the cinema is entertainment. ('English Films', *TFR*, 156)

Following his own advice, Howard's anti-Nazi propaganda films were designed to be entertainments, combining comedy with politically inflected suspense. With a canny talent for persuasion, his films also integrated narrative and cinematic experiments that expressed the historical urgency of his propaganda cause.[7] His production of *Pimpernel Smith* (1941) and his performance in *49th Parallel* (1941) would deliver crowd-pleasing, plot-twisting surprises, but before North American audiences could settle into the comfort of the expected, they would feel the ominous jolt of a Nazi rhetorical threat. British audiences would have reacted differently, seeking escapism from bombing, retreat and uncertainty about the future. By contrast, it was hoped that American audiences would be shocked into becoming what Ina Rae Hark has termed 'active spectators', taking their fates into their own hands by supporting anti-Nazi intervention rather than being 'content to sit quietly in the audience while the spectacle of world affairs unfolds before them' (12–13). In their appeal to North America, like the fiction of Eric Ambler and Helen MacInnes, these films attempted to build a transatlantic community that would defend and preserve their shared democratic values as they were being overwhelmed by the Nazi occupation of Europe. The challenge lay in the assumption of shared values based on a romantic political sense of conjoined destiny. The vision remained to be tested.

From 1940 through to his last film, made in early 1943, Howard became both a critical and popular voice advocating for Britain, its people and Hitler's targeted victims. Implied in this mixed media political career was a rebuttal to the negative connotations of propaganda that remained in the nation's consciousness since the misguided campaigns of the First World War that emphasised atrocities. His broadcasts can also be viewed as countering those of Lord Haw Haw (William Joyce), whose pro-Nazi radio programme, 'Germany Calling', reached Britain from 18 September 1939 until 30 April 1945. Howard's broadcasts to the US and Canada on 16 and 17 December 1940, 'That Unspeakable Word', begin with a self-ironising acknowledgment that 'by nature', the British 'take the view that a thing that is good speaks for itself and that the constant proclamation of the virtues of any article or idea is tiresome and defeats its own object' (1). His own rhetorical strategy was to identify with his British listeners and mock the Nazis' mind-numbing proclivity for repeating lies so often that they acquired the sheen of unassailable truths. Such mockery becomes withering disdain in his response to the hammering voice of Nazism in *49th Parallel*.[8] His radio broadcast was more direct. To drive home his distinction between the content, rhetoric and goals of British propaganda and that of the Germans, he indicts the Nazis' supremacist and expansionist declarations: 'It was, indeed, German propaganda that largely brought this about [...]' ('Unspeakable Word', 2).

Howard's efforts to forge a mutually sympathetic transatlantic community would be based on nostalgic memories of his years in the United States. Although his American films never lost an opportunity to highlight his Englishness, one of his broadcasting goals was to topple the image of a 'mythical ideal' Englishman (Rattigan, 24). Instead he would capitalise on the sense he developed from his American years that he had created a hybrid identity. He had melded his sense of England as his home and of the United States as his adopted culture. This dual cultural identity inspired him to feel an easy rapport on which he could depend when he volunteered to send his voice across the Atlantic on Britain's behalf. As Neil Rattigan observes, Howard's presence as a film actor and 'as a "real" person [...] suggests this image merged the boundaries of cinematic fiction and real life' (24). Howard told his American listeners in his broadcast titled 'Shopkeepers and Poets' (14–15 October 1940), he forgot he 'was an alien' and had made 'the American way of life and attitude of mind' his own (1). This cultural and social familiarity would supersede the MOI's advice to the BBC to replace 'the Oxford Accent disliked by Americans with a Canadian or Scottish accent' or the voices of such 'ordinary people' as 'cab drivers, dockers, and housewives' (Brewer, 49). Although it is difficult to estimate the size or precise responses of his shortwave radio audiences, his intention was to be 'the persuader [who] is a voice from without speaking the language of the audience's voices within' (Jowett and O'Donnell, 28).

One of Howard's primary broadcasting goals was to show his respect for Americans, and so he appeals to their 'deep and instinctive understanding of the state of the world, and of the supreme danger in which human freedom stands' ('Unspeakable Word', 2). His appeal would also assume a sympathetic union between Americans and Britons as non-ideological, ordinary people of good will, debunking the criticism of propagandist manipulation as pretentious and digressive: '"I say to hell with whether what I say sounds like propaganda or not. I've never stopped to figure it out, and I don't think it matters any more. The British Commonwealths and the United States have surely got beyond the point of those niceties. We've arrived at the stage at which we must tell each openly what is in our hearts and in our minds"' ('UnspeakableWord', 2). That he made his broadcasts from the site of the Blitz validated his assumption that open and honest propaganda would also appeal to his fellow Britons. One observer, Guy Morgan, remembered Howard as '"something of a symbol to the British people" because "he came home from America to help us when times were bad [. . .] The public liked and trusted his quiet voice and whimsical judgement; he had, and always will have, a very special place in his country's affections"' (qtd in Lant, 111). Howard's radio broadcasts and films can be read as intertexts, composed of mutually reinforcing messages that experiment with the narrative properties of each medium and the roles he would play as both actor and director. For example, he combined satire, suspense and peroration as actor and director of the rescue spy thriller *Pimpernel Smith* (1941) and applied his knowledge of producing dramatic suspense in his acting and direction of the story of R. J. Mitchell, designer of the Spitfire, *The First of the Few* (1942). He combined documentary and Expressionist camera styles with his voiceover in directing *The Gentle Sex* (1943), a celebration of women's war work.[9] His voiceover narration of other documentary films enhanced their intentions with his familiar wry, sonorous tones.

Radio's Personal Propagandist

Howard would concur with Priestley's distinction between his broadcasts and government propaganda in describing himself as 'simply a private person giving his impression of what is happening. I have no official standing [...] No official tells me what to say. There are no strategy and tactics in the background [...]' (Priestley, 232).[10] Although he differed from Priestley in 'being basically apolitical' and as his son reports, 'liberal and laissez-faire', his mission and strategy accorded with the government's campaign to encourage American support for the war effort (*In Search*, 77). Susan Brewer explains the need to overcome American ambivalence: by summer 1940, 'a majority of Americans supported the Allies against Hitler and approved of aid, but they did not want to go to war' (38).[11] To appeal to United States officials and the public, an American advertising executive urged the British Foreign Office to 'consider American attitudes, such as loathing of Nazism and distrust of Britain, [to] recognize the importance of appealing to people's fears, and use [...] the new media, especially radio' (Brewer, 48).[12]

During the summer of 1940, following the fall of France, Howard broadcast an appeal on 'Britain Speaks' to his British and American audiences to share his '"curious elation"' at Britain being '"singled out of all the nations of the world for the rare honour of fighting alone against the huge and ruthless forces of tyranny"' (qtd in L. Ruth Howard, 271). As the Blitz began in earnest, on 30 September 1940, this 'curious elation' is clarified by his pride in Britain's progressive record, when he invokes the nation's historical struggle for democratic 'authority' as 'slowly wrested from feudalism and autocracy through many centuries of blood and toil' ('The Tree of Liberty', 1). Throughout his broadcasts Howard combined a Churchillian register with a more personal voice to honour the nation's collective and individual courage.[13] Shifting between 'I' and 'we', he appealed to a shared epic history. This approach, he hoped, would provide a broad context through which to illustrate Britain's aims and role in the war. Nonetheless, he knew he needed to craft his radio talks with awareness of the deep division between Americans' sense of their ideological, political and popular commitment to capitalist democracy and Britain's desire to preserve the Empire even as its post-war future might lean towards national welfare. The connection he chose was the fight for survival (*In Search*, 58). Regardless of the political and social disjunctions emanating from America's Revolutionary War, Howard deployed quotes from the Declaration of Independence and his knowledge of American political history to appeal to the two nations' shared democratic values and the need to preserve them by defeating Fascism.

In his broadcast titled 'The Fighting Democrat', Howard intervenes in America's debates about supporting Britain's war effort. Just as he invoked British history to rouse awareness, sympathy and pride for its current forbearance, so he enrolls the founding fathers in his story of America's conflicted attitudes towards defence. The dangers of 'diplomatic isolation' originate with the nation's 'father of American Democracy', Thomas Jefferson, while a more vigorous protector of American democracy is the present Franklin Delano Roosevelt (*Trivial Fond Records*, 175, 174). For Howard, integral to Jeffersonian individualism and republicanism was a 'parochial' vision that profoundly opposed 'armament of any kind' (*TFR*, 175). Although Howard concedes that Jefferson 'might have been forced to a policy of rearmament' had he lived in 1940, 'what the world is desperately in need of now is not the gentle, philosophic democracy of Jefferson, but the outspoken, militant and ringing democracy of Roosevelt, representing the righteous anger of the free people of the world aroused against the cynical arrogance of the totalitarian feudalists' (*TFR*, 175). This broadcast abandons the gentle, understated voice that had produced Howard's popularity and persuasive powers. Although the historicity of Howard's political contrast might be challenged, his Churchillian endorsement of Roosevelt argued on behalf of a bond not only between the two nations, but also between the American President and people. Forging the identity and character of the United States as a freedom fighter, Howard abandoned his self-identified private status to enter a contentious public sphere.

Howard's continued broadcasts and films would construct democracy as a middlebrow narrative. His interpretation would engage human interest stories that would garner sympathy for their recognisable concerns with home and family. In turn, these homespun tales would humanise more abstract ideas about freedom and self-determination and less familiar historical allusions. Such stories are easily assessed as conservative, 'lacking aesthetic and ideological self-consciousness, counter-culture intellectual voices, and remaining averse to narrative experiment that might risk challenging or even alienating its audiences' (Lassner, Rea and Brassard, 7). Howard's work challenges this assessment by combining such elements of popular culture as comic and irreverent jokes, melodrama and romance with testimonies and depictions of exile, loss, and irreversible discontinuity and disorientation. The interweave of these narrative traditions creates a political and cultural discourse that asks more of its audience than ideological allegiance or agreement, intellectual or aesthetic satisfaction or pleasure in the moment.

One of the most challenging and yet humane of Howard's political and aesthetic innovations is his insistence on the presence and voice of the persecuted other, a subject that was ignored or marginalised in other propaganda campaigns. Unlike British propaganda campaigns of World War I and the beginning of World War II, which featured warnings about citizens' risky behaviour or the barbarism of the enemy, Howard pleaded for the creation of empathy for Hitler's targeted victims.[14] The inspiration for this empathy may have derived from his family's move to Vienna for five years when he was five years old. Although his parents lived in a community of secular Jews and 'assimilated Jews were making their mark in Vienna', the pronounced antisemitism of the city created 'suffocating restrictions' that motivated a return to London (Eforgan, 8).[15] Howard's propaganda campaign worked against the persuasive power of xenophobia, forging likenesses amongst Britons, North Americans and Europe's deracinated others. Like the other writers studied in this book, he inserted the unprecedented, unimaginable stories of those who were strangers to both high and middlebrow cultural production and made them matter to all his audiences. The form he developed to express this agenda coalesces as pleasurable propaganda.

In his 20 July 1940 broadcast titled 'London Today', Howard submerges his personal vision into that of a legendary city which personifies independence and freedom for all. Upheld by 'the rugged unity of its corporate structure combined with the toughness of its inhabitants', the city represents a historical saga of overcoming conquest, from the Romans to the Normans and Danes, and threats by the Spanish, Dutch and French, with the indomitable 'fibre of her citizens' (*TFR*, 153, 154). With metanarrative flourish, he combines myth, historical 'fact', and dystopian speculation to warn of the 'Nazi enslavement' of Europe if London, 'the capital of European civilisation' were to be destroyed and if invasion were to succeed (*TFR*, 154). A crucial implication of this rhetorical strategy is its contrast with previous invasions. In the past, invaders of Britain became domesticated, insinuating themselves into the nation's culturally and politically complex character. In contrast, a Nazi invasion would produce a brutalising occupation, maintaining a hierarchical distinction between the Aryan nation and its subjugated Britons. Such a scenario is imagined in Katherine Burdekin's 1937 dystopia, *Swastika Night*. All the world's Jews have been exterminated, Africa is a crater and Britons have devolved into feudal servitude. Uprooted in their own nation, Britons are deprived of historical memory and consciousness and therefore have no basis for re-forming a collective identity and sense of purpose. The sovereign state has been devoured by Nazi domination, producing a world of stateless populations; the claims of citizenship and human rights have been obliterated.[16] While focused on Britain, particularly 'Londoners', the dystopian implications of the broadcast coincide with the film *49th Parallel,* which imagines the consequence of a Nazi invasion of Canada to be the decimation of its culturally and politically heterogeneous population.[17]

Howard's narrative method resounds with 'the propaganda imperative' that would later solidify as 'the people's war', heralding a unified and intrepid Britain standing alone, beating back the evil empire (Rattigan, 15).[18] As James Chapman explains, this 'myth' is largely indebted to the wartime film images of the British at war that featured 'the part played by ordinary men and women' and which the government encouraged 'to mobilise popular support for and participation in the war effort (*British at War,* 161). At the moment of Howard's broadcast, however, this is more of a hope than a perception or construction of the more complex experiential realities of the ensuing Battle of Britain and the Blitz. In response to the 'dismal record of failure' of the government's propaganda early in the war, Howard fully understood the primary need to combat 'declining morale and enemy propaganda' (Fox, 23, 24). As Jo Fox explains, a primary task for the British Ministry of Information was 'to present the British and Allied case as widely and fully as possible to the world in all its aspects' and 'to watch and check enemy news and propaganda in all countries and to undertake counter-prop and [a] counter news service to ensure that the British position [is] fully understood' (24).[19] Howard's response to this imperative was to represent those 'aspects' of the British cause by familiarising his audiences with the forbearance of ordinary Britons and the suffering of embattled Central Europeans. Howard here is forging a wider unity under fire, stretching from Nazi-occupied Europe to the British Isles and across the Atlantic. Lurking between the lines that celebrate Britain's inherent heroism is an anxiety that accompanies fears of defeat and desolation. As Neil Rattigan notes, 'one of the astonishing aspects of British film during this time was their virtual silence about any postulated certainty of British victory' (17).[20]

As demonstrated in his content and discursive shifts over the course of his broadcasts, Howard implicitly agreed with changes in the MOI's propaganda policy. Like the Ministry and liberal academics who studied propaganda, once the Battle of Britain and the Blitz began, he understood that the 'exhortational emotion' required to argue for 'the righteousness of our cause' needed to be balanced or even replaced by 'reasoned argument and factual information' (Chapman, *British at War,* 45). Howard complies with this shift by creating a rhetorical boundary between his previous heroic register and objectifying the war's contingencies. His test case is the Battle of Britain and the Blitz. Debunking the mythic idyll of England as a green and pleasant land, he replaces its lyrical celebration of an organically conceived nation with the denaturalising objects of defence: 'trenches, machine gun emplacements, block houses, pill boxes, concrete shelters, tank traps and land mines' (qtd in R. L. Howard, 272). Devoid of humanity, eschewing irony of any sort, the image constructs its warning by populating it with the war's detritus.

Howard mediates between objectifying and personalising the home front experience by positioning himself as witness and survivor in his broadcast of 23 September 1940, 'First Fortnight of the Battle of London'. Recounting a direct hit to his own home in serene Surrey while relaxing with his son on leave from the Navy, Howard conveys the melodramatic shock of 'a sound which is like no other [. . .] rather like a streamline train rushing towards you' or 'a sheet of tin being shaken as they do it to represent thunder in amateur theatricals' ('First Fortnight', 2). The propaganda artist has created a performative bridge between radio, theatre and film through the evocation of sensory experience: audio and visual expression. In his roles as film director, he would translate this visceral sense of being bombarded into his characters' reaction shots. Both inside this scenario and outside, his reportage attains authenticity by dint of his experiential presence. Howard's report then projects his individual response into the audience which is being asked to form a community through empathy with the broadcaster. If it works, according to Miriam Hansen, this experiment will create a shared experience of sensory responses that inspires the mass audience's 'liberatory impulses' (341). Because Hansen is referring to classical Hollywood film, it calls attention to Howard's intermedia propaganda as a narrative experiment.

Howard's broadcasts during the Blitz emphasise his experience as collective in order to demonstrate that the will to freedom would remain inviolable only with shared activism: 'To have lived in and around London during the two weeks ending September 21st, 1940', Howard told America, 'is to have lived through the most menacing, dangerous grueling fortnight in the long, valiant history of this metropolis' (qtd in R. L. Howard, 273). The city and its people are unified in an image of indomitability. Londoners' valour is accessible through graphic details of nightly bombings that would, he hoped, produce Americans' empathy and support. Because, however, he remained aware that the failed propaganda campaigns for World War I contributed to American isolationism, his radio scripts eschew any sense of Londoners as victims or Germans as brutal warriors. For Howard, there is no continuity between the bombastic, inflated propaganda of World War I and the language and forms that will be needed to face a unique global menace.

He also avoids the propaganda pitfall of inciting bathetic or bitter memories by acknowledging the problems with glamorising this war: Now 'there are none of the crowds, none of the light-hearted gaiety [. . .] no music halls, no opera, no "Tipperary"' (qtd in R. L. Howard, 273). Instead, he presents Londoners as

> a people facing the worst menace in their history, committed to a life or death proposition and knowing full well all the implications. A people without illusions, but with a stronger, I swear it, more profound conviction that no matter what the cost or how long the time, once again they will triumph. (qtd in R. L. Howard, 273)

These Londoners occupy a narrative space in which mythic heroism and the historical moment are synthesised in creative tension. Intrepid but knowing the score, Londoners are the fount of pragmatism and hold no truck with sloganeering propaganda. They will win the support of Americans because like them, they will not be fooled by promises of glory, only the 'triumph' of survival and self-determination. Reporting from a Hurricane Squadron base reinforces Howard's aim to create empathy from a distanced perspective. He presents his impressions in the first person to announce his own position as outsider-observer, an onlooker to heroism that will hopefully inspire his listeners to support 'these smiling men in blue' who model the forbearance necessary to defeat 'Hitler's war of total annihilation' (qtd in R. L. Howard, 272–3).

Despite official doubts about the presence of a movie star and filmmaker, Howard also volunteered his service to the Ministry of Information's Ideas Committee.[21] Jo Fox attests that 'in the early years of the war, MOI expressed little confidence in the British film industry's ability to produce entertainment features with propaganda value. Escapist entertainment was to be left to the Hollywood dream factory. This, in part, also reflected the government's concerns over investing in such an unpredictable medium as the entertainment feature film for propagandistic purposes' (33). In co-operation with the Ministry and on his own, Howard exploited this unpredictability by combining different cinematic styles to make feature films and documentaries that linked Britain's war aims to the integrity of different European cultures. For example, his voiceover plea in the film *The White Eagle* (1941) supported the efforts of Poles who had joined the Allied forces in Britain to maintain their culture.[22]

With their transatlantic reach and audience approval, his broadcasts and films also countered the pejorative connotations of propaganda.[23]

Rather than intone nostalgia for a glorious English past and a salute to Britain's wartime progress, Howard's scripts created a British war that focused on creating sympathy for others. He became aware of Nazi Germany's assault on its neighbouring nations by listening to broadcasts from Poland and the Balkans. In turn, he created sympathy for the besieged by translating Germany's conquest of nations into the personal experiences of those who were exiled from their homes and homelands as a result. Relating the destruction of British homes in the Blitz to the losses suffered by those on the Continent, he declared in his broadcast 'About Home': 'The real effect of war, its standard measurement in terms of ordinary, everyday lives, is its impact on people's homes [...] the disruption that *counts* to people like you and me – is the breaking up of families and the homes they live in' (*TFR*, 171). Giving full recognition to differences between the British and European experiences, he also created an equivalency among them. Traumatic loss was becoming a universal, unifying response to the Nazis' brutal conquest: 'In Poland people like you have been turned out of their houses at half-an-hour's notice, without food, money or warm clothing, in the depth of the bitterest winter Europe has known for years, and told that they must walk to a town twenty, fifty, a hundred miles away if they want work, food or shelter' (*TFR*, 172).[24]

With graphic detail as evidence, this depiction conveyed the reality of a human tragedy that was 'denounced [...] as atrocity propaganda' by American isolationists when the British government issued a 'White Paper on Nazi Persecution of the Jews' in the autumn of 1939 (Cull, 55). Despite the great immigrations to North America and Britain in the earlier part of the century, like the Jews, Poles and other Central and East Europeans remained too alien to be considered integral to their adopted countries. The persuasive power of racialised and antisemitic stereotypes contributed to misreading the refugees' customs and characters as unassimilable to official and popular imaginations. Although official Allied war aims to defeat Nazism did not include efforts to rescue Hitler's victims, Leslie Howard extended his anti-Nazi activism to stake his career and then his life in garnering concern for imperilled Europeans. Like Storm Jameson, Rebecca West and Phyllis Bottome, Howard's wartime career defied wilful ignorance and indifference to argue that Britain's future as a democratic nation depended on activating empathy for those who had become stateless exiles within and beyond their homelands. By 1 June 1943, when Howard's plane was shot down, Howard had won two victories: in 'a battle against apathy', he showed that 'artistry could survive – jolted by new dangers and adversities to unexpected fruition' (*In Search*, 14).

Filming Nazi and Anti-Nazi Intrigue

If the warnings and prohibitions that characterised British propaganda posters failed to win enthusiastic support for the war effort, various forms of popular culture, such as pulp magazines and films like Howard's attracted large audiences. In 1940, an editor invited submissions as follows: 'We are accepting pulp fiction dealing with the present European War. The former ban on anti-German stories has been lifted. For *Air Adventures* we would like [. . .] writers to make their heroes English, French or American adventurers. For *Fantastic Adventures* and *Amazing Stories* we will welcome stories dealing with Nazi intrigue in the United States' (qtd in Cull, 63). Concurrent with the propaganda value of popular fiction, filmmaker John Grierson explains the mass appeal of film:

> The film appeals to all classes and speaks in a universal language. It is brief, vivid and simple in getting across its message [. . .] As a means of disseminating public information and propaganda it is often more striking and thus more effective than the written or spoken word [. . .] Under present circumstances no considered public service of information can disregard the tremendous value of films. (qtd in Fox, 1)

Robert Murphy underscores the significance of popular film for the war effort: 'Film, whether fiction, newsreel or documentary, became such an essential part of wartime culture because of the way in which it reflected and shared commonly held hopes, beliefs and fears' and appealed to audiences of wide ranging class and regional affiliations' (4).[25]

In 1941 this effort to build a community of shared sympathies resulted in a short official film, *From the Four Corners*, in which Howard shared the platform with a Canadian, an Australian and a New Zealander to portray the nations of the British Commonwealth as unified in being 'a democratic alternative to Hitler's "New World Order"' (Chapman, *British*, 56, 57). In his feature film made later that year, *49th Parallel*, Howard also performed an ensemble role that would complement Commonwealth unity with the collective portrait of Canada as a multicultural nation. Both films would use the technique 'of suture' where as Wollaeger explains, 'spectators are encouraged to align their vision with the characters on the screen, who function as their mirrors or representatives' (235).

In popular fiction and film, private and public stories merged to synthesise anxiety and resolve into fictions depicting the imminent threat to dissolve distinct European nations into a unified Axis empire. This threat would rely on a homogenising and universalising myth of racial supremacism, and from 1933 to World War II, would inspire the building of ghettos, slave labour, concentration camps and killing centres designed for both slow and instant extermination of Nazism's *untermenschen*. By the late 1930s, the threat of Fascist power had inspired many British writers and filmmakers such as Alfred Hitchcock and Michael Powell and Emeric Pressburger to envision legions of trains leaving Waterloo station for the Continent and to reach out to North America through radio broadcasts. Their brief was to create an inclusionary propaganda mission that countered stalemated official debates. A key feature of these films was their representation of a cohesive British voice arguing that to combat 'a very great evil for everyone concerned' would involve an outward-looking, desperately sincere effort to engage Britain and its Allies in the world through writing and other media.

Howard's Hollywood career developed his knowledge of film's persuasive power that he would apply to his wartime work. He would deploy suspense, romance and comedy as well as the atmospherics of Expressionist film to prod audiences away from the comfort of conventional film values, such as the homogeneous, Anglo-centred face of heroism. His audience included the British government from which he solicited support for documentary films and speakers to make the case for Britain's war aims as he shaped them to fit his own transnational political vision. At the end of the 1930s, when the remains of any hope for peace had been dashed, when Hitler's agreement with Chamberlain proved to be fraudulent, Howard's *Notes on American Propaganda* conveyed the desire to produce '"an exciting and dramatic documentary"' to let the American public know '"why we declared war and clear the air of misapprehensions"' (*TFR*, 57). Denoting the empathy he wished to create, he argued for the declaration of war over Germany's invasion of Poland: 'With nothing to gain we have voluntarily undertaken the obligation of fighting for a remote state for no other reason than that we cannot stand by and see an ever increasing area of the civilised world dominated by a bully and subjected to gangster force' (*TFR*, 57). Howard was very specific that in a series of documentaries,

> The first of these films should concern itself with placing the war-guilt irrefutably upon the Nazis [...] the second [...] could deal with the outbreak of war, its effect on the ordinary citizen, the evacuation of children, the tremendous and immediate change in every day life, the rush to join the colours, the A.R.P. arrangements, the blackouts, the whole changing face of a great city within twenty-four hours. (qtd in L. R. Howard, 269)

Howard's daughter Ruth reports that a lack of government interest in his propaganda films led him to focus on 'one feature film in which the cause of freedom and Britain's part in it would be clearly defined' (269). This change coincided with the government's recognition that 'commercial feature films' represented 'excellent opportunities for disseminating, if not direct propaganda, an impression of the British attitude both to the issues of war and to war-time conditions' (*Thirteenth Report from the Select Committee on National Expenditure* [1940], qtd in Chapman, *British*, 58).

Howard's first propaganda feature film was *Pimpernel Smith*, which was also the first of Britain's war films. It is an entertainment that experiments with narrative and cinematic forms to politicise the language of popular film, especially spy thrillers. Rather than establishing escalating tension from the start, his direction and performance would set the film's pace with his familiar ironic understatement that would remain the signature of his wartime activism. The film, which he produced and directed, capitalised on his celebrity persona as a self-effacing, idealistic, adventurous man of few but persuasive words.[26] His image was not that of a matinée idol, but instead, as Rattigan argues, the actor's wartime roles naturalised upper middle class leadership 'as mythical ideal' (24). Aldgate and Richards describe Howard's appeal as projecting the humanisation of the intellectual, 'brought down from the heights of academe to discover personal commitment and the real world' while maintaining a 'dreamy, other-worldly air' (53).[27] Howard's interpretation of the iconic Englishman, the absent-minded apolitical amateur who with little visible effort morphs into heroic rescuer, also represents what Neil Rattigan describes as

> a certain image of what an English, and the regional specificity is significant, hero might be. The class structure of British society makes a notion of a universal, cross-cultural 'every man' unthinkable [...] It is difficult to discuss these characters as distinct from Leslie Howard, the actor playing them. The use the Ministry of Information made of Howard as both an actor in films and as a 'real' person able to speak on behalf of Britain, suggests this image merged the boundaries of cinematic fiction and real life. (24)

The fusion of Howard's off and onscreen persona is also identifiable in the self-conscious reflexivity of his iconic voice. Self-questioning, self-mocking and modestly authoritative, his voice and screen presence embody the learned traditions of Oxbridge while issuing a clarion call to abandon its ivory towers and activate its time-honoured humanist curriculum.

Howard was inspired to make the film in 1938, just before the *Anschluss*, when he met the artist Alfons Walde while on a ski trip to Austria. Walde's stories of the Nazi persecution of artists and intellectuals crystallised as the idea for a plot shortly after Howard heard the story of the writer Wolfgang Wilhelm's escape (*In Search*, 64). Howard's film accorded with British propaganda policy to adopt the 'strategy of truth', but with one exception (Brewer, 31). He remedied the policy's exclusion of any available facts about Hitler's victims. The catalyst for his resistance was *Kristallnacht*, the Nazis' pogrom on 9 November 1938 that decimated Jewish homes, businesses and synagogues throughout Germany and Austria, and that began the systematic round-up of Jewish men. Leonard Woolf reported the British reaction with biting sarcasm:

> It has never been the custom of civilised and Christian men to take any notice when a sparrow falls; to-day we take as little notice when a thousand innocent human beings are beaten, tortured, and killed by a government round the corner. 600,000 seems, however, to have been a bit too much. Even so, all that can be said is that 'public opinion has been shocked'. (26)

From that moment on, Howard followed the news of intensifying Jewish persecution as closely as possible. But it was only after the hard won Battle of Britain and during the Blitz, when the war had come home, that Howard consolidated his activism into a film about rescuing Hitler's victims. Once the film was approved by MOI, he took 'unchallenged control' over its design and execution (Eforgan, 152). The film, which 'declares itself a fantasy', is dedicated to the actual 'exploits of a number of courageous men who were and still are risking their lives daily to help those unfortunate people of many nationalities who are being persecuted and exterminated by the Nazis' (qtd in Aldgate and Richards, 58).[28] Testimony about persecution and expertise in film design were consolidated in the contributions of German refugee filmmakers who had found shelter in Britain. Among them was Wolfgang Wilhelm, who would guide the construction of sets employing visual metaphors to suggest the strangling atmosphere of Nazi Germany. Help with the storyline was provided by five writers, including the novelist A. G. Macdonell and the Russian refugee filmmaker Anatole de Grunwald, while the cinematographer was a German Jewish refugee, Max Greenbaum, whose experience with German Expressionist film shaped the film's unsettling atmospherics of satire and terror.

While the government made use of Howard's popular image, the posters advertising *Pimpernel Smith* are integral to the propaganda campaign he had suggested in his 1939 *Notes on American Propaganda* and in the report he wrote with filmmaker Anthony Asquith, *The Film Industry in Time of War* (Eforgan, 140). Close reading of the film reveals a narrative progression that calls upon the audience to share its process of discovering and resisting the reality of Fascist ethical, material, and experiential devastation. Although the film was a box office success,

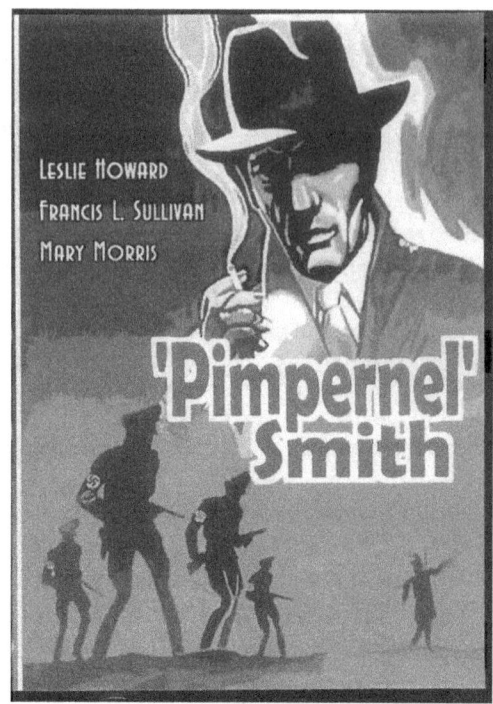

Figure 3.1 Leslie Howard's 1941 film *'Pimpernel' Smith* (British National/Anglo-Amalgamated)

the influence of its propaganda messages cannot be known. Raoul Wallenberg, the Swedish diplomat who rescued thousands of Hungarian Jews while he was stationed in Budapest, told his sister that he was inspired by the film.[29]

Exile as Rescue

Pimpernel Smith was a contemporary adaptation of Howard's 1934 film *The Scarlet Pimpernel*, based on the novel by Baroness Orczy, in which he played Sir Percy Blakeney, an effete English aristocrat who also rescues victims of Robespierre's reign of terror. In *Pimpernel Smith*, Howard plays Horatio Smith, a misogynist, ivory-tower Cambridge professor who rescues victims of Nazism. Estel Eforgan explains the pitfalls of the adaptation: 'The film equated the Terror in revolutionary France with that of modern Germany, but it was not a message anyone wanted to hear' (103). Although Howard disdained the comparison between a story of oppressed aristocrats and Hitler's victims, the Scarlet

Pimpernel's quotation from Shakespeare's *Richard II* retained its rhetorical power as a patriotic mantra that resonated throughout World War II: 'This blessed plot, this earth, this realm, this England!' Punctuated throughout *Pimpernel Smith*, victims of Nazism equate the hope for freedom with the wish to be rescued to England, the remaining site of active resistance against German conquest of Europe. To ensure the audience's identification with England as Europe's last standing sanctuary of democratic values, the film elides domestic complications. For example, neither the film nor any of Howard's statements alludes to the British internment of refugees from German controlled lands who were suspected of being fifth columnists because they would have needed Nazi permission to leave (Kushner, *HLI*, 151).[30] While one of the film's rescued victims is a scientist who disproves Nazi racial ideology,[31] the official British rescue effort included the internment of refugee Jewish scientists offering their talents to the war effort (Murphy, 43). As Tony Kushner reports, 'The exclusive framework of Englishness was such that all "aliens" could be seen as essentially other"' (*HLI*, 151). That Howard's father, Ferdinand Raphael Steiner, had been a Hungarian Jewish refugee decades earlier may very well have forged Howard's commitment to Britain as a refuge and repository of the democratic values on which he would stake his wartime career.

While *Pimpernel Smith* was as popular and patriotic as its antecedent and resonated even more obviously with the current threat, it also generated some complaint. The translation of a historical fantasy of *noblesse oblige* into urgent propaganda did not please some critics. Objections to *Pimpernel Smith* included

> little to portray the war effort of ordinary people, that fighting the war was an adventure which was best left to the gentlemen of Cambridge University, who could be trusted to stand up for democracy [. . .] and run rings around the Nazis [. . .] Films of this kind are bad propaganda because they present the war in absurdly romantic terms and their entertainment value is impaired by the conflict in the mind of the audience between the hard facts of real war and its glamorous embellishments in the film. (Chapman, *British*, 170–1)

Although Horatio Smith, the film's spy, is no ordinary person, one side of his duality captures the urgency to attempt the documented risks of rescue, of poaching on Hitler's domain. His cover is complicated in another way. Cohering seamlessly with his familiar Hollywood persona, Howard's role as intellectual aristocrat is self-mocking, mimicking its Oxbridge accent and confidence as integral to his privileged status.[32] Cross-cutting between Cambridge and Germany, Howard's black and white film shows how nostalgia for 'Deep England [. . .] a way of life encapsulated in images of rural village Britain' has been superseded by visual metaphors confronting the interdependent fates of Britain and Europe (Rattigan, 22).[33] Once the sunlit, softly-focused cloisters of Cambridge University are left behind, the film's lighting style shifts dramatically to underscore the terror of Gestapo headquarters, arrests and imprisonment with piercing light and darkness. The shift can also be read to signify the film's commitment to extending Britain's war aims to include the fate of Europe's 'others' and to move away from the home front films that characterised British wartime production (Lant, 44).

As in *The Scarlet Pimpernel*, in *Pimpernel Smith* Howard plays a man of split personalities, but now the risks of political passion replace the security of aristocratic privilege. Played for both comic and ideological purposes, Horatio Smith appears to be both absent-minded and a committed misogynist as well as a rescuer of endangered anti-Nazi intellectuals and artists. Aldgate and Richards note that the film's focus on rescuing artists and intellectuals 'is elitist', but accords with Howard's interpretation of the war that 'progress and civilization depend in every age upon the hands and brains of a few exceptional spirits' (61). This interpretation is evident in an incident on the train to Berlin. Maxwell, a stereotypical American rich kid, played by Hugh McDermott, confesses that he converted to Smith's cause only when he realised the danger to democracy in the Nazis' extermination of artists and intellectuals: 'It's hard to stand by while the most gifted are endangered.' Howard found support for his view in the fact that those intellectuals and artists who had not already fled Germany and Nazi-occupied Europe were being hunted and killed. Among those who found shelter and work in England were Alexander Korda and Emeric Pressburger.[34] Although he would be joined by Pressburger in his next anti-Nazi film, *49th Parallel*, at this moment, Howard is the lone voice in the British film industry making the plea for rescue. In fact, although there were many already in the industry of Jewish identity or background, and more among the refugees, they preferred to resist quietly, responding to the prevailing anxiety about an antisemitic backlash. As Eforgan reports, although Korda aided many Jews in their escape efforts, he neither wrote his memoirs nor admitted his Jewish heritage, while Michael Balcon, head of Ealing Studios, had presented a positive image of the Jew in his film *Jew Süss*, but made no public statement about Jewish persecution (165).

Amidst fears of resurging antisemitism and of a Nazi invasion of Britain, the British Fascist newspaper *The Blackshirt* fed on pre-existing myths about Jewish venality and clandestine plans for a global economic takeover. Eforgan notes, 'Those who dared to mention the subject were at deadly risk, as Britain stood alone against the terrifying power of the German army as it cut through Europe' (167). Between this context and the content of Nazi persecution, the refugee as imperilled other creates an identity category that challenges the British obsession with class and Howard's goal of creating audience empathy. Stateless and therefore classless, an outsider to all European and British social cultures, the overdetermined figure of the refugee is alienated from familiar identity categories. The goal of Howard's radio and film work was to overcome this alienation by representing a common experience forged by the threat of racialist supremacism. The danger to his targeted victims lies in the Nazis' racialisation of their characters, communities, talents and allegiance to democratic principles, qualities with which Howard hoped his audiences would identify.

Comedy as a Double Agent

The project that serves as Horatio Smith's cover and grants him a travel permit to Nazi Germany is to unearth an ancient Aryan civilisation on German soil and therefore validate Nazi claims for racial supremacy. The plot is both deadly serious and a hoot, with Smith's character iterating 'Britain's war culture' as 'a mixture of idealism and stoical humour rather than patriotic chauvinism' (Murphy, 4). As Robert Murphy explains, the anxieties produced by setbacks in the war's first years inspired 'spy thrillers or stories of resistance to the Nazis' (34). Set in 1939 Cambridge and Berlin, the film opens by announcing its intermodern mix of popular culture and political seriousness in its depiction of Smith's dual persona. As the credits roll, a shadowy, silhouetted image of Pimpernel Smith appears behind them, adorned with hunting cap and pipe, an image that aligns him with the iconic and peculiar master of detection, Sherlock Holmes, so very British and yet like Horatio Smith, easily performed as self-parody. Smith's rescue machinations are equally camp; his mysterious image as 'The Shadow' is accompanied by whistling the ditty 'There is a Tavern in the Town'. As the film's drama begins, however, a darker Expressionist palate conveys the tragedy taking place in Berlin where the Gestapo are about to arrest a scientist for his humanitarian research.[35] The film responds with a sign of resistance, combining, in Jennifer Barker's formulation, 'both content and form, and by different means – satire and sincerity' (109). Smith's calling card to the scientist and film audience aphoristically proclaims that 'The mind of man is bounded only by the universe.' Contrasting the depredations of physical imprisonment and anxieties of escape attempts, the film also depicts men and the woman protagonist with minds that express political freedom. To complete his masquerade, Smith presents his own mind as bounded by a sexist rejection of women's presence in the university and a celebration of the gendered separateness of ancient Greek culture.

The film calls attention to its propaganda goal of distinguishing political ideologies by counterpoising mythic icons of democracy and Nazism. Instead, however, of representing a modernist 'mystic epiphany', these icons demystify and mock both their pretentious, tendentious mythic allusions and British political idealism.[36] For example, when the opening scene switches from the portentous fog of Berlin to sunlit Cambridge, Smith is exposed, not as a fount of ancient Greek philosophical learning or of political critique, but as zealously smitten with a Greek statue of Aphrodite, a visual comment on his frozen attitude towards living women.

While the scene is clearly played for laughs, and Smith is unabashedly performing his cover, the location of the statue in a Cambridge museum and Smith's position as a British archaeologist suggest a cultural critique in the guise of farce. Aphrodite's physical beauty can only achieve perfection when Smith dusts her off with his handkerchief. As silly as it is, the gesture suggests important questions about his interpretation of Aphrodite representing the 'blindness and ignorance of the world'. To be sure, his target is the wilful avoidance of integrating the rescue of Hitler's victims into the war's aims. At the same time, his analysis allows Smith to revel in his own superior mind and penetrating foresight.

The instrument of critical inquiry turns out to be the statue's modern historical and aesthetic contexts, questioning not only the cultural prestige and otherworldliness of Cambridge University but also Nazi Germany's claims for cultural supremacy. For a start, Britain's possession of the statue has nothing to do with British cultural production. Aphrodite's representation of ideal beauty, love and harmony originates in classical Greek culture. That the statue is lodged in a British museum assumes it belongs there, but at the time the film was made, its actual provenance would not have been questioned as such antiquities are today. Nonetheless, combined with Smith's dotty devotion, the scene embeds a challenge to the ideological and cultural superiority of Britain as sanctuary for the aesthetic harmony of ancient democratic ideals. In its monumentality, the Aphrodite also alludes to Nazi Germany's appropriation of classical aesthetics that materialised in Berlin and Rome as colossal statues, arches and buildings. In the film, sculpted images of mythical muscle power adorn the Gestapo's office, reminding audiences of the Reich's propaganda claim to be a Master Race of supermen.

Among these images is a travel poster advertising 'Come to Romantic Germany', depicting the ideal woman of the Third Reich as domestically all powerful, overwhelming the poster's text in a *volkish* dirndl. Appearing both at the beginning and end of the film, and suggesting a riposte to Josef Goebbels, Hitler's propaganda minister, the poster signifies Howard's propaganda message, that the invitation to leave home for Fascist enlightenment is tantamount to entrapment in Nazism's mythic romanticism, a one-way ticket to elimination. The poster's pastoral background, complete with mountains reaching to infinite open space, is undercut by the sound track – Hitler's ravings, pounding goose steps and gunshots. The insertion of a poster within the film also highlights the representational import of propaganda. Antonia Lant's comment that 'The poster as a representational form has no original' is applicable to Howard's film which, in its opposition to British wartime posters, provided 'a responsible, moral reading of the scene consonant with national concern' (*Blackout*, 37). The German travel poster is also 'a peculiarly wartime document', carrying 'the power to address the viewer', but the 'fantasy state [it] cuts into' is the Nazi idyllic perspective on its fatherland (*Blackout*, 37). Unlike the critical reflexivity of the Aphrodite scene, the German travel poster suggests a solipsistic, male-empowered self-congratulation.

If Smith's donnish eccentricities mock an inward turning Anglo-satisfaction, isolated from ordinary people or even Cambridge colleagues, his formation of a multi-cultural community of student activists signifies an outward-bound concern for others. At the beginning, the professor is certainly portrayed as a static, self-centred introvert. But when the film's fulcrum of attention leaves the hallowed halls of Cambridge behind and boards the train to Germany, Smith and the film reveal their protean characters, resisting Fascism's simplified, static aesthetic with 'the multiplicity and nuance implicit in [cinematic] collage and montage' (Barker, 6). We learn that this is only one of Smith's many trips that will revise the meaning of alienation from the Nazis' unassailable category of subhuman to the indeterminacy of rescue, exile and the possibility of self-determination. The group's travels to Germany will produce an ethnography that confirms 'the anxieties and perplexities of the period' and confronts 'the fogs of political confusion' that mark Nazi rhetoric and ideology. *Pimpernel Smith* presents the British case and responds to Nazi propaganda by encoding one within the other. Triumphalist Nazism is represented as an expanding danger with the arrests of a dissident scientist and journalist, but also threatened with defeat by British daring and humour. A 1940 Mass Observation report stated that the public had become critical of film representations of the enemy, that 'horror scenes cause disgust among the audience and the usual scenes of marching Germans [. . .] only boredom' (Fox, 141). As a

Figure 3.2   Leslie Howard and Francis X. Sullivan in *'Pimpernel' Smith*

result of this response, the MOI wanted films that portrayed the Gestapo 'as more easily credible, the sinister rather than the sadistic aspect' (Fox, 141). As McLaine reports, 'the language of hate was too exhausted to describe the enormity of what had been done in occupied Europe when it became known' (166).

Menace and mockery combine in Francis X. Sullivan's performance as Gestapo General Von Graum, a big-bellied stand-in for Hermann Goering, Hitler's Reichsmarschall. The send-up is complete with Von Graum's imposing book-lined desk, containing objects of scorn for the General's self-serving misreadings, which include his insistence that Shakespeare was German and conclusion that *Punch*, Wodehouse and Lewis Carroll contain neither humour nor meaning. That the irony of British humour is a form of deception, another espionage tool, lampoons von Graum's cultural and espionage illiteracy; even as he performs Smith's signature ditty on the piano with symphonic bombast, he cannot decipher it. Likewise, a blanket of red pins marking Smith's border crossings only obliterates the map of Europe, covering the tracks of the British spy. The useless map can now be read metonymically, suggesting Hitler's self-annihilating plans for conquest, especially as 'Rule Britannia' resounds in the background. Blending satire and seriousness, Sullivan's performance of Goering is constructed as both caricature and critique. Although the portrait could easily be discounted for relying on the stereotype of the humourless Hun, the mirroring effect of satirising Smith's self-righteous chauvinism invites a view of the film as self-consciously examining its propagandist intent and structure. The Reichmarschall's dour celebration of German cultural superiority is inseparable from his fervid allegiance to the Reich's millennial designs.

With parallel import and his characteristic irony, Howard offered a critique of Fascist modernity in his radio broadcast of 9 September 1940:

> All Nazis and Fascists still remain enthralled and amazed at the newness and originality of a form of government which puts every citizen under the [...] domination of one man and which forbids those citizens any deviation, in thought, from [his] principles [...] and which imposes penalties of violence and death for any such deviation. The dictators assure us that these great and new political conceptions will build a new and better world for mankind, and they are trying to implant in our minds the suggestion that our famous Democracies are tattered, shabby and old-fashioned ideologies, that the world needs something new, and that they have got it. Their patience is exhausted with people who are so hopelessly out-of-date. ('The Tree of Liberty', 2)

The broadcast echoes Frances Myles' anti-Nazi critiques in *Above Suspicion*, arguing that the inflexibility of Nazi ideology and politics, akin to a lack of self-irony, would lead to the Reich's defeat against its 'agile and imaginative opponent' (Ronald Howard, *In Search*, 99). The reference to Lewis Carroll, including 'The Jabberwocky' recited by both Smith and von Graum, establishes a central trope of the film as the decoding of nonsense. For Germany is indeed, as von Graum insists, 'a wonderland'. Resting on a fantasy that myth can produce reality, Nazi Germany's self-image highlights a world in which illogical but perdurable moral and rationalised principles reverse the critical values embedded in the humanist heritage of both Shakespeare and Germany. Extending the structural trope of Alice's looking-glass, the film shifts back and forth from Nazi threats to Smith's mission, and from the sense of urgency to self-reflexive humour. For example, Smith conjures a scheme in which, with a self-mocking nod to British and North American filmgoers, he satirises imperious Germany by impersonating a German official dressed as a British parliamentarian. Decked out with moustache, striped trousers, bowler hat and umbrella, the multi-faceted caricature also invites his 1941 audience to share his pleasure in performing a dual homage to the two great film satirists of the period: Groucho Marx and Charlie Chaplin – what would amount to a transatlantic riposte to 'The Great Dictator's unassailable stature.[37] The goal of the fake official is equally deceptive and self-ironising: he demands travel permits for six American journalists who will pretend to serve the Reich by broadcasting reports of how 'everybody's happy' in Nazi concentration camps. Of course the journalists are Smith's masquerading students and their real mission is to free the imprisoned dissidents by disguising them in the uniforms of the Nazi officers now lying unconscious and trussed in propagandist poetic justice.

The film's propaganda campaign embeds messages Howard delivered in radio broadcasts about preventing 'the horror of war' and the urgency of fighting 'the cynical arrogance of the totalitarian feudalists' for freedom and democracy (qtd in Aldgate and Richards, 60). Alternating with satire, the mode of transporting this message consists of images of trains racing between England and Germany and that enable Smith to pursue his mission – trains that carry imperilled human cargos, trains that cross endangered borders, trains that defy the stasis and rigid identity categories to which the Nazis have subjected their victims. As in Ambler's *Background to Danger*, Hitchcock's 1938, *The Lady Vanishes* and Carol Reed's 1940 *Night Train to Munich*, trains representing attempts to escape the Fascist threat are ubiquitous, intensifying the risky necessity of becoming unstuck from apathy.

In a telling sequence in Germany, just as Smith's students are preparing to escape with their human treasures, the film burlesques the pseudo-scientific rigidity of Nazi racial ideology through the trope of archaeology. When von Graum and his men visit Smith's dig, ostensibly to celebrate evidence of an ancient Aryan civilisation, Smith picks up a human skull and riffing on the General's muddle over Shakespeare, intones, 'Alas poor Yorick [. . .].' Like a wink, the camera's close-up of a skull invites the audience to share Smith's joke, that this human shard is material evidence of nothing, an absence of Aryan civilisation on German soil and the empty-headedness of Nazi racial ideology.[38] The real target of the Nazis' search, the hidden non-Aryan dissidents, represents the urgency of the film's role as witness; otherwise, the story of Nazism's victims remains a shard of history. The film responds to this dual threat by authenticating the treasure the Nazis would prefer to bury – the fluidity of self-determination and open inquiry.

A Woman's Critical Voice

The film dramatises this fluidity as the transformation of Horatio Smith's character and the intrepid double agency of its sole female protagonist, Ludmilla Koslowska, the daughter of a Polish dissident journalist. Ludmilla embarks on her own espionage adventure when she agrees to work for von Graum to save her father from imprisonment. Her share of the bargain is to identify the British rescuer while her own mission subverts the effort. At a British embassy reception, the triangular duel between Smith, von Graum and Ludmilla becomes the main event, filmed from the perspective of a grand staircase, where the camera's panoramic high angle sweep joins the sharply defined black and white colouration to showcase the suspense. Although subject to von Graum's threats, Ludmilla becomes her own agent, recognising Horatio Smith as the British spy. Instead of denouncing him to von Graum, she chooses her own cause and goes to Smith's room to seek his help. It is here that the film's overall comic tone and its particular incarnation as bedroom farce are radicalised by political intrigue. Propped up in bed reading, resembling a skittish ingénue more than a daring rescuer, Smith insists that Ludmilla leave him alone. Smith's misogynist dottiness is finally overwhelmed when political urgency becomes the catalyst for sexual frisson. Ludmilla's beauty and sexuality are defined as political courage and Smith's consent to help transforms his sexist asexuality into respect and love for a woman's audacious intelligence. More than a makeover, however, the cinematography signals a move towards a reflexively critical heterosexual romance. Each time that Smith and Ludmilla are physically close, the lighting casts their silhouetted shadows across each other's faces. Nowhere is this metamorphosis more apparent than when after Ludmilla has been saved from arrest. On the train to Britain, Smith tears up his photo of Aphrodite. Unlike the Nazi poster of the ideal German woman which inscribes male domination, the image of Aphrodite is replaced by a woman who is Smith's equal.

Although Ludmilla does not appear after this scene, the film leaves its audiences with the assumption that she will join her father in Britain and together they will bear witness on behalf of Hitler's victims. Smith, however, does return, to confront von Graum. With quiet bravura, enveloped by the shadowy atmospherics of Expressionist ambiguity and disorientation, he appears and disappears in a smoky haze to outwit the General who articulates his universal threat. The train station setting reinforces Smith's announcement that he will return again and again, that rescue efforts will continue and that Nazism will self-destruct. With the syntax of proclamation, Smith orchestrates his final confrontation with von Graum so that no audience will fail to understand the sinister but self-destructive itinerary disguised by the General's bumbling intellect:

> 'Tonight you will take the first step along a dark road from which there is no turning back. You will have to go on, from one madness to another, leaving behind you a wilderness of misery and hatred, and still you will have to go

Figure 3.3 Leslie Howard in *'Pimpernel' Smith*

on because you will find no horizon, you will see no dawn until at last you are lost and destroyed. You are doomed, captain of murderers, and one day sooner or later, you will remember my words.'

The war had been raging in Europe for twenty months when the film was released on 26 July 1941 in Britain, and Americans did not see it until March 1942, three months after the United States entered the war. Despite the Allies' efforts, Germany showed every sign of going forward with its conquests far beyond the European horizon. There was no evidence that the Reich's goals for global conquest would be self-destructive. On the contrary, as Nazi Germany continued to gain ground, the destruction of Central and Eastern European communities and people was escalating to the point of no return. Although Howard could not have known the extent of this tragedy, as Estel Eforgan observes, 'What emerges most strongly from the film is Leslie's anger' (152). As the film's dedication declares and Howard's radio broadcasts confirm, his propaganda art expresses his personal conviction that the war must be fought to try to save 'those unfortunate people of many nationalities who are being persecuted and exterminated by the Nazis'.

Enemy Agents in Exile

At the same time that Leslie Howard was filming *Pimpernel Smith*, he was approached by Michael Powell and Emeric Pressburger to act in another anti-Nazi spy thriller, *49th Parallel*. Howard's part in this film extends his wartime propaganda career to an ever-greater collaborative effort. Neither the star nor a lone voice, his role harmonises with the film's other anti-Nazi voices, contributing to an ensemble of perspectives on the meanings of invasion and defence, both of which corroborate the propaganda messages that shaped his radio broadcasts and *Pimpernel Smith*.[39] In fact Howard's role as ethnographer and cultural critic Philip Armstrong Scott augments the intellectual activist character of Horatio Smith by eliminating his sexist send-up, while his speech to the German invaders is performed in his iconic style and tonal register. Although Pressburger was annoyed that Howard inserted his own lines into the prepared script, he endorsed the actor's politics and performance (Eforgan, 179).

49th Parallel, released in the United States as *The Invaders*, was the first commercial full-length film financed by the MOI. As James Chapman reports, it dramatises principles outlined in Kenneth Clark's Programme for Film Propaganda: 'it vocalises the ideological differences between democracy and Nazism; it addresses the theme of why the British Commonwealth was fighting the war; and it provides the good entertainment value which was considered desirable for film propaganda' (*British*, 70). The film was produced and directed by Powell and Pressburger who hoped it would convince North Americans that Nazi Germany's plans for conquest extended across the Atlantic and was therefore a boundless threat. Pressburger claimed that it was 'one of the very first important films about the ideology of the Nazis and our own' (qtd in Williams, 42). Pressburger had a personal commitment to the film. At the time of its production, he was confronting his own precarious fate, caught between Nazi persecution and British rescue politics. A Hungarian Jew, he had immigrated to Britain in 1935 to escape Nazi imprisonment. Because his passport declared him stateless, however, he was designated an enemy alien by British authorities. When he returned to Britain after filming in Canada, he was imprisoned and threatened with deportation until Powell and the Ministry of Information intervened. His contributions to wartime British cinema expressed only gratitude and allegiance to the nation that ultimately offered him safe haven.[40]

49th Parallel won transatlantic audiences and critical acclaim for its affirmation of Canadian and American democracy and multi-vocal opposition to Nazi Germany's lethal supremacism. The film's unrelenting dramatic tension gave its propaganda message an entertaining edginess. James Chapman notes, '*The Times* lauded the film for offering the same kind of pleasure that we get from a John Buchan novel. The incidents are sufficiently exciting to carry the patriotic theme' (*British*, 74). It was the most profitable British film in 1941 and Pressburger's screenplay won an Academy Award in 1942 (Aldgate and Richards, 40). Inspired by reports of German U-boats operating off the Canadian coast, Pressburger devised the story line: 'I think we wreck a German submarine somewhere in Canada and then follow the survivors all across Canada and that way [...] we've got a good suspense story' (Aldgate and Richards, 29). According to Robert Murphy, Powell researched details to ensure the film's 'authenticity' which, 'combined with extensive location shooting gives *49th Parallel* a different aesthetic to ideologically very similar films such as *Pimpernel Smith*, but this realism is not like documentarists' (135). A major attraction of the film was its star-studded multi-cultural cast: Leslie Howard, Laurence Olivier, Eric Portman, Anton Walbrook – a Hungarian Jewish emigré – and Canadian Raymond Massey. The film also introduced Glynis Johns as a young Hutterite woman representing the yearning for peace and an accepting homeland.

The producers investigated the Canadian landscape to find locations symbolically resonant with the film's propaganda purpose. Using naturalistic settings and aerial cinematography, the film exploits Canadian vistas to convey the nation's epic vastness as representing the Germans' expansive plans for invasion and Canada's resistance. The associations of this naturalism with the openness of democracy recalls the linkage between the Nazis' contrived monumentalism and its despotism in *Pimpernel Smith*. In *49th Parallel*, from the Gulf of St Lawrence and the Labrador coast up to Hudson Bay, across the provinces of the great plains and on to the Rockies, with a rousing musical score by Ralph Vaughan Williams, Canada is represented as a boundless repository of democratic principles and practices, fully capable of opposing Nazi plans for conquest. The title refers to the unguarded boundary between Canada and the United States as a testament to the two nations' shared humanistic values and trust. The opening voiceover proclaims:

> I see a long straight line athwart a continent. No chain of forts, or deep flowing river, or mountain range, but a line drawn by men upon a map nearly a century ago, accepted with a handshake and kept ever since. A boundary which divides two nations yet marks their friendly meeting ground, the 49th Parallel, the only undefended frontier in the world.

The threat to North America's shared democracy is filmed as a German submarine cruises the Gulf of St Lawrence, destroys a merchant ship and ruthlessly throws its civilian crew into the freezing water. With cinematic justice, the submarine is destroyed by Canadian fighter planes. The surviving crew of six, including the leader, Lieutenant Ernst Hirth, sets out on a double mission: to avoid detection and plant the flag of the Third Reich on Canadian soil as the sign of conquest.

As the crew makes its way across Canada, the Nazi plan for domination of the continent, to be constituted as a despotic diaspora, establishes the framework for propaganda as a spy thriller. Each encounter with different communities devolves with greater intensity from rhetorical persuasion to brutality. The cumulative effect anatomises both the Germans' escalating alienation and resistance by those who would be marked as undesirable and victimised by German occupation. But as one would expect in a thriller, resistance only exacerbates the antagonists' resolve. Instead, the film defeats the invasion, not by featuring Canadian armed resistance, but by creating its own ideological weapon: passive resistance. The plot constructs the Nazis' purpose as increasingly self-destructive. Isolated from German military, administrative and cultural support, dislodged from Nazism's ideological context and victories and rejected ideologically and experientially by Canada's multi-cultural societies, the crew no longer has a place to belong. Unlike Odysseus, who returns home and re-establishes his power after a ten-year return from the Trojan War, the itinerary of the German agents traps them in their celebration of 'wars that go on forever'. As though reversing the trope of the Trojan Horse, the Germans deceive themselves and are attacked from within by their beliefs. The battlefield is reimagined in this film as Nazism's never-ending state of temporal and ideological disorder. The result is constituted as an all-encompassing exile.

With a sense of immediacy, as though a clandestine Nazi invasion is imminent, the film follows the German crew episodically across Canada as it seeks provisions and shelter and encounters distinct ethnic communities representing the nation's multi-cultural democratic union. And yet despite this unified multiplicity, as with *Pimpernel Smith*, the film is primarily a man's story. With only one exception, the Hutterite woman Anna, protagonists and antagonists are men who serve as spokesmen and fighters for the opposing ideologies of democracy and Nazism. In scenes featuring violent attack and self-defence, Canadians exhibit their ethical dissociation from the enemy and indebtedness to Britain's 'special contribution' to warfare – the lesson of 'fair play', derived from the playing fields of boys' public schools (Harper, 195). As Harper argues, in 'official film policy in the Second World War [. . .] there was no consistent address to female audiences' (197). Despite official remits that gendered wartime films, the actual productions offered characterisations and scenarios that question stereotypical assumptions about the responses of women audiences, including a nexus of relations between representing violence and reconstituting the genre's conventional enactment of masculinity.

A case in point is the film's depiction of the unbridgeable ethical distance between the Nazi invaders and Canadians.[41] Only when confronted with Nazi violence do any of the Canadian characters or groups respond in kind. Instead, a male spokesman for each of the featured communities rebuts with philosophical arguments for freedom as the most potent form of opposition to the Nazi rhetoric and takeover. The cinematography, however, represents a different narrative of Canadian shared values. Although they are intended as integral to the nation's multi-culturalism, the Inuit never speak, the camera hardly shows their faces and they therefore lack individuality. As a group, however, they are represented as a vulnerable minority, included in Canadian national identity. In the first confrontation between the Germans and Canadians, at the Hudson's Bay trading post of Wolstenholme, the camera expresses sympathy for the Inuit as it pans them scurrying for safety when the Nazi crew fires on them. Although this signals the Germans' inclination towards mass murder of *untermenschen*, unlike a 'staple of propaganda' in the campaigns of World War I, the film refrains from depicting German atrocities as it would if it intended to appeal to audience's expectations of 'uncomplicated savagery' (Wollaeger, 27). Instead, using rapid intercuts, the scene dramatises the conflict between the Nazi crew and its French Canadian victims with individualised, face-to-face confrontations, shifting the points of view with close-ups and reaction shots. Among the different responses to the attack, the episode features Johnnie Barras, a French Canadian fur trapper, played with boisterous élan by Laurence Olivier. His over-the-top performance is also a function of satire, the target of which is the rugged masculinity associated with toiling in the wild, with animals his only companions. His return to civilisation, portrayed as a mutually caring commune of trappers, domesticates the militaristic overtones of masculinity. Sharing the bounty of the Canadian tundra with the Inuit contrasts sharply with the Germans, all of whose relationships express the escalation of Nazi supremacist ideology into violent aggression against others.

The film romanticises Canadian ethnic harmony to valorise shared democratic ideals. Ignoring the nation's fraught political and territorial relations with its indigenous peoples and French Canada, the script and cinematography represent them as an internal dominion, distinct yet interdependent. A sense of mutuality within the national collective is apparent in Johnnie Barras' rebuttal of Hirth's declaration that German occupation will liberate French Canadians from their status as an 'oppressed minority': 'I am free. We French Canadians have always had our own schools, our own church, and the right to speak as we want.' Asserting a distinct French Canadian cultural character and autonomy signifies a self-determining political and cultural choice. The threat of oppression materialises not from within the nation, but only with German violence, implying that Canadian multi-cultural ideology and practice are integral to its democratic identity and endangered by Nazi Germany's exclusionary ideology and war. And yet, even as the film features disparate ethnic communities, it never depicts any interaction among them, implying that its propaganda mission needs to include the construction of a culturally heterogeneous nation in order to form a unified fighting force.

The domestic self-enclosure of the trappers' scenario provides a stable base of interdependent relations that aligns Canada's endangered ethnic communities with Europe's. A Scottish workmate informs the others about the Nazis' atrocities in Europe, including the destruction of Warsaw where they 'machine gunned down the refugees, poor women and children', the same targeted victims for whom Leslie Howard asked compassion from his radio audience, and Helen MacInnes, Ann Bridge and Eric Ambler from their readers. Similar to the response Howard anticipated and addressed, the trappers register indifference and self-interest: 'What does it mean to us?' they ask, extending the script's political and ethical implications. Echoing concerns that compelled other anti-Nazi British fiction, the question is addressed to multiple audiences. For Emeric Pressburger, this would include its immediate British audience, especially the officials whose policies expressed deep ambivalence about European others. For Canadians as well as Americans, who left European oppression and warfare an ocean away, it asks whether the fate of conquered others should be their concern. Compounding this question is the trappers' protective illusion that 'The Germans are ordinary men, same as you and me [. . .] I wouldn't do a thing like that.' The universalising construction of a shared humanity embeds the failure to recognise Nazism's exclusionary doctrine. Fused by Nazi racialist ideology into one subhuman mass, North Americans would all be subject to the Reich's vilification and violence, as voiced by Hirth, the German crew leader: 'Eskimos are racially as low as Negroes [. . .] Negroes are semi-apes, only one degree above the Jews.' Legitimising his diatribe, he announces that these words originate in the Führer's portentous tome, *Mein Kampf*. With an anxious flourish, the segment ends by dramatising the dire consequences of isolationism and non-intervention, which Pressburger scripted as the Nazi crew's slaughter of Johnnie and the Inuit.

The film's depiction of native, settled and immigrant Canadians represents an attempt to unify its transatlantic audiences by constructing a shared multi-cultural character and a cause of mutual interest. The idea that a 'unified subject' is an 'illusion' constructed to 'manage' audience 'reception' is part of a larger discussion engaged by Mark Wollaeger to show stylistic commonalities between modernist and propaganda films in the 1930s and 1940s (220–1). While it has been claimed that such audience management can only be attained 'by suppressing difference, discontinuity, and the process of production', Wollaeger argues that experimental film both exploits and undermines the audience manipulations of propaganda (220–1). Whereas Wollaeger situates the wartime propaganda films of Hitchcock and Welles within cinematic aesthetic and production history, the propaganda films of Leslie Howard and Powell and Pressburger represent the history of the war's targeted victims as ideological perspectives. This intervention would emphasise Nazi ideology as the agent of 'suppressing difference' and inciting a threatening discontinuity from the liberal democracy on which North America based its identity. *Pimpernel Smith* and *49th Parallel* were motivated by an ideal of creating propaganda art that would activate the mutual empathy of a united community.

The cohesion of different ethnic and cultural identities into a Canadian national identity underscores its contrast with the German goal of creating a master race by eliminating its undesirable others and their cultures. With cinematic irony, this oppressive supremacism becomes a potent form of critique. For example, later in the film, one of the Germans tries to melt into a crowd of Indian Day revellers, but is exposed by the keen eye of a Canadian Indian for cultural difference. Even if this exposure is read as a reflection of the First Nation's tense political position, there is no doubt that the ideology of an inimitable, indomitable Master Race has backfired. Both indigenous and other, in all his native regalia, head above the crowd, the Canadian Indian reinforces the Allies' collective opposition to Nazism and signals his nation's equal status with the United States and Britain. Overall, in this scene and in all the encounters of the Nazi crew with Canadian communities, the film represents Canada as an independent, sovereign nation, identifying its political position as a Dominion, loosely but definitively confederated with the British Empire.[42] This confederation alludes obliquely to the British Commonwealth nations as a model of shared Allied power – Australia, New Zealand, South Africa, Northern

Ireland and Newfoundland – all of whose military contributions to the war effort would prove crucial.[43]

As the film charts the Germans' trek across Canada, the divide between their ideological commitment to conquest and an escalating Canadian resistance sculpts a Canadian national character. As Christine Geraghty maintains, 'British war films' create a cohesive 'national identity' by having 'different groups – men, young and old, aristocrats and "ordinary people"' cohere around the cause for which they fight (232). Jo Fox argues that a critical problem with this homogenising representation was registered in a complaint 'that the Germans look, and were, the same as Englishmen. This tended to prompt a strong feeling of "sympathy" in the audience, where the Nazis are "only misguided" and "disappointed heroes"' (144).

In contrast to *Pimpernel Smith*'s broad satire, *49th Parallel* maintains a serious if occasionally melodramatic register to debunk the rhetoric of German triumphalism. Instead of building suspense by orchestrating a climactic scene that denounced the Nazi presence, the overt didacticism of *49th Parallel* builds its suspense through a series of emblematically contrasting encounters, each one exposing the Nazis as increasingly trapped within their own dogma. Illustrating the MOI remit that Germans 'be shown as making absurd errors of judgement', the film avoids cartoon-like stereotypes and mockery (Aldgate and Richards, 34). Instead, close-ups of the German crew members expose a spectrum of responses to the resistant continent they encounter. Rage, fear, shame and even compassion humanise and individualise each team member, in suggestive opposition to the essentialist practice of Nazi ideology. With rapid-fire transitions, the camera also creates a critical exegesis. As it cuts from one sharply etched emotional expression to another, the recursive style of its juxtapositions suggests a collage of individual responses to the Nazi mandate. The political effect of this aesthetic is to remove any doubt that both individually and collectively, the Germans are responsible for their own fate. Without provocation, their own irrational will to conquer produces a series of disastrous effects, including misreading the fuel gauge of an escape plane, just as they will misread Canada, and crashing literally and figuratively as a result. Despite these mis-steps, however, the film's suspense builds as the Germans rebound each time, performing a phalanx of indomitability. Even the resistance of Vogel, a team member characterised as a religious humanist, resisting the brutal fiat of their zealous leader, is overpowered and he is rendered an ineffectual actor and voice. Metonymically representing the ordinary German populace sympathetically, as objects of coercive policies and practices, Vogel appears to have no recourse but to follow his leader. When he protests, he is accused of treason and shot.

Contesting religious ideologies shape the locus of meaning in the team's encounter with a Hutterite community in Manitoba. Identified as Germans who immigrated to Canada to escape religious persecution, the Hutterites seek only peace and acceptance. From their Austrian origins in the sixteenth century, they base their faith on absolute pacifism, a belief and practice that the film honours but also deploys to highlight Nazi Germany's rabid militarism. Eric Portman's celebrated performance as Hirth in this segment is calibrated to expose the zealous religiosity underpinning and activating Nazi ideology. As Gordon Williams observes, Hirth's character provides structural and critical coherence to a film that could be viewed as loosely episodic: 'In moral terms, there is a strong feeling of wasted potential, of nobility perverted by a false doctrine' (42). Hirth's declaration of German supremacism echoes that of the Führer in decibels and slogans. In a slowly escalating bombardment of racialist vitriol, he mythicises and celebrates 'blood' as determining 'the supremacy of the Nordic race, of the German people' and in a gesture of magnanimity, invites the Hutterites to embrace their Germanness and join the 'brotherhood'. The shift from his commanding presence and certainty to frenzied bombast registers impending defeat as the steady state of the camera contrasts with Hirth's twitching face. The final blow to Nazi command, wielded by the Hutterites, is a subdued but passionate testament. With quiet resolve, as performed by Anton Walbrook, their leader Peter responds by declaring Germany 'dead', an 'evil' force whose national identity rests on the 'persecution' of others. The Hutterites by contrast, reject all military activity, including its symbolic uniforms, salutes or an anthem that celebrates a nation's power as its core identity.[44] Instead, 'We sing because we like to [. . .] We are not Europe. Our children are free, not forced into uniforms.' The only hatred affirmed by the Hutterites is 'the power of evil'.

Vigorously self-sufficient, the Hutterites contribute to Canada's ethnic multiplicity while countering stereotypical claims that immigrants espousing alien beliefs are unassimilable and cannot fulfil the responsibilities of citizenship. With an implied response, the film depicts the Hutterite community as creating a diasporic place of belonging in Canada where, as Peter declares, they 'have found security, peace, tolerance and understanding'. Rather than clinging to an outsider identity as displaced exiles, they find fertile ground on which to sustain their traditional beliefs and practices. Panoramic shots of wheat fields, reflecting both their self-sufficiency and a harvest far too vast for internal consumption, show the Hutterites to be essential to the nation's basic needs.

As this segment of the film proceeds, its narrative message is that such productivity would be disdained and rejected by Nazism because the religious belief system that generates peaceful collaboration would be racialised as undesirable. Completing the opposition between the Nazi crew and the Hutterites, the Hutterite community enacts the rejection of a Nazi German diaspora in Canada.

In spirit with the Hutterites' self-confidence, the film shows that their lack of animus towards the invading German party includes offers of shelter, food and even work. This respect for the intruders reflects the Hutterite communal structure, where social and political hierarchies have no place and where the physical act of work is a creative process of community building. Nonetheless, as Sue Harper argues, like the other communities invaded by the German team, the Hutterite community has 'rigidly stereotyped' gender roles whose 'permanently headscarved women' are 'asexual and malleable', and 'generally content in traditional tasks' (199).[45] While this critique describes the Hutterite women accurately, it omits the community's faith tradition and division of labour as an important context and intervention. In Hutterite tradition, women cook, provide fabric for clothing, manage medical care and participate in communal decisions at the level of social discourse and interaction. But the film also shows men performing domestic roles, baking and serving food. Following Hutterite religious principles, sixteen-year-old Anna, orphaned by German submarine attacks, is nurtured and fully integrated into the community's social structures, including tending to the Germans' lodgings. Yet she emerges as a confident voice of protest to the Nazis. When Hirth is startled by the Hutterites' lack of a dominant leader, Anna retorts that the role consists of following people's needs. Recounting how her parents were killed by the Germans, her voice intensifies until she screams, 'I hate you!' Her refusal to make up the crew's beds may seem trivial, but in light of her assigned role, this is a proclamation of independence that reverberates in Peter's response to Hirth and therefore assumes an active role in sustaining the integrity of the community and affirming the cinematic complexity of her character. Anna's role contrasts with the Nazi poster of idealised German womanhood and recalls that of Ludmilla in *Pimpernel Smith*. Anna and Ludmilla are both motivated to resist by the loss or threatened loss of parents perpetrated by Nazi ruthlessness. While their roles are subordinate to male authority, and in Ludmilla's case, to romance, their voices powerfully enunciate the war effort on behalf of family and community, thereby humanising the abstractions of the men's ideological and political speeches.

While the harmonised work of the Hutterite men and women is

choreographed in reverent silence, graphically representing the abstract meanings of freedom and self-determination, intellectual work is shown to be a form of political activism in the Germans' encounter with Philip Armstrong Scott. Living contentedly in a teepee lined with books and paintings, Scott studies Indian life and culture. As Aldgate and Richards observe, he is also 'self-critical, self-aware, acutely conscious of the quaint image he must present to an outsider' (36). Performed by Leslie Howard, Scott resembles Horatio Smith in combining his passions for art and political and cultural freedom. Unlike Smith, however, Scott's life, surroundings and art work remain devoid of women, highlighting the film's construction of Canadian cultural expression, integration and political protest as male defined. As though forming a chorus or canon of anti-Fascist art, the works of Hemingway, Thomas Mann, Picasso and Matisse are deployed to support Scott's polemics. Modernists all, but resisting an apolitical aesthetic, these artists remind the audience of the consequences of Fascist conquest. When Scott shows Hirth and Lohrmann Picasso's painting of a mother and child, its humane tranquillity is disturbed by the absent presence of the artist's anti-Fascist 1937 painting *Guernica*, with its silent screams. That the crew will burn a still life by Matisse suggests that at this moment, as the war rages in Europe, the painting's open window can remind its viewers of destroyed freedom of expression. With similar import, Hemingway's 1940 novel *For Whom the Bell Tolls* narrates the Republicans' doomed anti-Fascist resistance. The support needed by the novel's lone American partisan never arrives.

The script's reference to Thomas Mann's 1924 dialogical novel of ideas, *The Magic Mountain*, condenses a multi-faceted narration. It resonates with the novel's response to World War I's devastations and with Mann's escape from Hitler's oppression, first to Switzerland in 1933 and then to the United States in 1939. In relation to the film, Mann's title serves as a metaphorical subtitle, offering a reflexive critical gloss on both Mann's and Scott's iconography. Both texts are set atop isolated mountains, redolent of fairy-tale wonder worlds from which a deadly *Walpurgisnacht* explodes. In 1924 and 1940, the Swiss Alps may represent a safely neutral space in which to engage in political and philosophical debate, but the isolation of the Canadian Rockies in 1940 troubles that narrative. The Nazis' invasion of Scott's secluded campsite and destruction of modernist art accentuate the urgency to replace dialogue and debate with propaganda. Mann's fictional debate between humanism and radicalism has been nullified by Nazi invective and the crews' burning of 'degenerate' art. Echoing *Pimpernel Smith* as well as Frances Myles' retort to von Aschenhausen, the critique of Nazi superiority in *49th Parallel* is intoned with mockery. Just as Smith lampoons von Graum's ignorance of British culture, so Scott asks Hirth if he read *The Magic Mountain* in German. The implication here is that the meaning of 'degenerate' is more appropriately aimed at the Nazis' use of German, which deleted the German humanist tradition, including Mann's reflexively critical debates. The self-consciously dialectical construction of these juxtaposed incidents, ideas and responses call attention to the film's exploration of propaganda as popular modern art.

49th Parallel intervenes in debates about the role of politics and propaganda in modern art by performing its own narrative experiments. Its cinematic and rhetorical forms coincide with modernist concerns about the viability of language as a medium of expression and a mode of critique. Combining spoken rhetoric with graphic imagery allows each iteration to complement the form of the other. A key example is the film's self-reflexive close-up of the burning of Scott's art, while he recites the artists' names and the art of the film restores their aesthetic and political significance. The film's polyphonic epic sweep through Canada and citations of modernist art embed references to the film's construction and its counterfactual warning; its internal debates reassign realist conventions of dialogue to oratorical arguments. Crowded with characters, none is a prototype or stereotype. Nor is there a singular protagonist. Instead, the film's authorial, focalising consciousness is played as a Canadian ensemble composed of characters' individual subjectivities. The rhetorical effect creates accessibility for its different audiences so that even Hirth's declamations inflect a portrait of Nazi villainy with credible passion.[46]

A compelling screen presence and the only character to appear and speak from beginning to end, Hirth unifies the film's disparate segments. Ironically, his tenaciously antagonistic presence also constitutes the film's epistemological link that allows the otherwise insular and separated Canadian communities to cohere. He is the catalyst that provokes them into articulating their democratic principles and activating resistance. Consolidating his roles as the film's *agent provocateur*, master spy, Nazi spokesman and locus of narrative and political disturbance, Hirth emerges as the film's focalising antagonist. A fusion of political and individual consciousness, his character is instrumentalised to embody and enact his Führer's *Mein Kampf* as though it is his book of life. In turn, his passion brings that book to life. As James Chapman proffers and the film demonstrates, representing Nazi ideology as a human voice is predicated on recognising significant ideological differences between the role of propaganda in democratic and totalitarian states:

> in closed political systems [. . .] propaganda can be seen relatively unproblematically as the expression of an official ideology. The expression of dissenting

points of view through the state-controlled media was impossible due to the stringent exercise of censorship; thus films like *The Battleship Potemkin* or *Triumph of the Will* can be read as presenting the 'party line' to the cinemagoing public. This was not the case in the democracies, where the media did not come under direct state control and where film-makers and other cultural providers were not always necessarily in line with official propaganda policy. In Britain, for example, Michael Powell and Emeric Pressburger made their film *The Life and Death of Colonel Blimp* (1943) in the face of intense hostility from the MOI, War Office and even Churchill himself. ('Power of Propaganda', 682)

The lines that Howard created for his role as Scott express his pride in the propaganda work of parody. Reading to Hirth and Lohrmann from his field notes, Scott's description of the Blackfoot war rituals parodies that of 'a modern European tribe': dressing up for battle with 'war paint, beating their drums loudly' and terrorising their victims before 'shooting them in the back'. The parodic analogy extends to the performative style of the Führer, who uses 'that most troubling of all public speakers' weapons – repetition'. One has only to recall Charlie Chaplin's parody of Hitler as Adenoid Hynkel in his 1940 film *The Great Dictator* to hear and see the reference enacted. Echoing Scott's mockery of Hitler's rhetorical bombast, the scene progresses with dramatic irony that dislodges the Nazis' construction of its dominant militarist masculinity. Hirth accuses the ethnographer of being 'soft and degenerate [. . .] not a man at all' because Scott prefers talk to punches or guns. With a skein of multiple references, including Peter's pacific speech and the exhibit of modernist art, Scott's talk rebels against the Nazi celebration of waging wars that 'go on forever'. Howard's son Ronald reports that Scott's 'long speech of considerable passion [was] directed principally at Josef Goebbels [who] would not easily forget when the occasion arose for punishment' and earned his father '"star-billing"' on the German black list. In fact, William Joyce, aka Lord Haw Haw, was to announce that '"this sarcastic British actor"' would be liquidated '"along with the Churchill clique"' (*In Search*, 102). Even when Hirth ties his adversary's arms to the teepee's support bars, not only can't he silence his adversary, but the visual allusion to crucifixion identifies masculinity as pacific, as victimised by an ideal of anti-humanist logic. Only with the attack by Nazi gunfire does the film allow Scott to combine defence and offence and beat Lohrmann, declaring victory on behalf of 'eleven million Canadians'.

The film's final episode, on a Canadian freight train bound for the United States, seals the exiled fate of the Nazi invaders. After the rest of the crew has been killed or arrested, Hirth is the last vestige of a

Figure 3.4 Michael Powell's 1941 film *49th Parallel*

Nazi invasion of North America. If he manages to cross the border, he will find safe harbour in the German Embassy, still operating in the neutral United States, where German rhetoric is on the offensive in its radio broadcasts, as we see in a juxtaposed image celebrating Hirth's Canadian adventure. In contrast to Scott's quietly ironic passion, elliptically echoing Howard's radio broadcasts, the bombastic voice of German radio recalls that of von Graum as both an assault on rationality and the object of mockery. The voice of Germany suffers its final blow when Hirth confronts Canadian resistance in the form of a plain-speaking ordinary Canadian. Like Hirth, Andy Brock is a soldier and a fugitive, but in opposition to Nazi Germany's demand for indisputable devotion, he celebrates his patriotism as the right to criticise his nation. If his tone is belligerent, his rhetoric is integral to the film's portrayal of Canada's cultural heterogeneity. In concert with the voices of the trapper Johnnie Barras, the Hutterites and Scott, and even Howard's radio voice, switching between 'I' and 'we', he proclaims the individual and collective freedoms mandated by Canadian democracy: 'I can grouse about anything I like [. . .] We own the right to be fed up with anything we damned please and say so out loud when we feel like it. That's more than your Gestapo and storm troopers can do. You can't even begin to understand democracy.' As the train moves inexorably towards the undefended border, it marks the acceleration of the plot's tensions; despite the film's polyphonic support, democratic principles remain threatened by Hirth. Having abandoned his ideological rants for a pragmatic plan to return home, he exposes Nazi Germany's relentless will to conquer. An embodiment of Nazi ideology and brutal practices, he has found no support on Canadian soil, only resistance.

Filmed in semi-darkness, the train scene employs Expressionist tropes that disturb any notion of social or political interaction or negotiation with an ominous claustrophobia. Even the beauty of Niagara Falls becomes sinister with the heightened sound of its unstoppable rushing waters. Dark shadows envelop the antagonists as the camera alternates close-ups of their two grimacing faces, each menacing the other. The freight car in which they travel provides no security, only the promise of war's brutality. Unlike the congenial interiors of the trappers or Scott's teepee, the train exudes hostility. Surrounded by crates and barrels, walled in, locked behind a gate, with bars silhouetted behind them, Brock and Hirth confront each other in a space that seems designed as a memory trace of World War I – a trench. As the train moves closer to the border, the meaning of this final confrontation lies in the implicit plea to the United States to abandon the scarred memory of the previous war and join Brock, a Canadian itching to fight his enemy face to face. After Brock convinces an American customs agent to reject the German's plea for entry, the train backs away from the border and returns to Canada, a metaphorical model of Canadian–American anti-Nazi resolve. As the train moves backwards but doesn't arrive anywhere, it also suggests that the Nazi agent invader is caught in perpetual exile – from the Fatherland that nurtured his supremacist beliefs and from the war those beliefs incited. Instead of proclaiming his cause as he had across Canada, he now sputters nonsense, the film's final critique of Nazi triumphalism. But before the screen blackens to proclaim victory over the Nazi leader, Brock punches Hirth in the face, silencing him beyond the film's ending.

The train can be read as an intertextual and intercontextual addendum to those in *Pimpernel Smith* and *Background to Danger* as well as those in Hitchcock's and Carol Reed's films of the period.[47] As British cultural artifacts, these fictional trains represent the urgency of travelling beyond Britain to bear witness to the escalating threat of Nazism to the self-determination of other nations and Hitler's victimised others. With persistent travel between Europe and Britain, and in *49th Parallel*, between Canada and the United States, these trains narrate a rejoinder to those writers who portray Britain as stuck, looking inward, and the imminent war cutting off outward bound possibilities for resistance, including activated concern for Europe's others. Amateur agents and civilians in Howard's broadcasts and films argue against both national insularity and Nazi Germany's *Lebensraum*, its ideology of expanding German space, by recognising its denial of the spatial sovereignty of others. Like other British writers, these films argue that the British home front must expand its horizons to include empathetic activism on behalf of deracinated others. In the light of official British and American neglect of Nazi victims, however, this argument may not be redemptive, but it remains a lasting hope and a plea.

Nowhere is this urgency figured more acutely by these writers and filmmakers than in their anxious representations of transporting stories of political oppression from Europe. Their fictional testimonies and warnings would be confirmed by the autumn of 1941 when reports began circulating in the British press about Nazi-perpetrated atrocities in Germany and Poland.[48] As a fighter and prisoner of Fascism during the Spanish Civil War, as an anti-Fascist, a Communist and then anti-Communist, as a perennial exile, Arthur Koestler reported from Europe throughout the 1930s up to the Cold War. As Anne Appelbaum notes, he 'illuminat[ed] some of the difficulties that France and other European countries still have in absorbing "foreigners" even today' (11). Writing as a Polish prisoner in an October 1943 essay, he narrated the fate of those undesirables as 'The Mixed Transport', those who would never emerge from suspicion or exile. As Koestler conveys, theirs was a journey to be murdered by the *Einsatzgruppen* (German mobile killing squad) in Poland in 1941 and as Tony Kushner reports, which 'received very little prominent coverage in the West' (*HLI*, 134):

> There are trains which are scheduled on no time-table. But they run all over Europe. Ten to twenty closed cattle-trucks, locked from outside, pulled by an old-fashioned locomotive. Few people see them because they start and arrive at night. ('The Mixed Transport', 244)

Koestler's description attests to the silence of those who chose not to see the trains that crisscrossed Europe, from France, Holland and Belgium in the West, from the Baltic States in the North and Ukraine, Belarus and Poland in the East. The locked cattle cars carried their prisoners to sites of mass incarceration and murder that were among the 30,000 labour and concentration camps constructed by Nazi Germany. Like the trains, the camps were omnipresent. Even in the dark of night, as the trains passed without stopping, the cries of prisoners carried across fields and towns. We have since learned that there were 'few people' on the continent who didn't see, who didn't know.[49]

The dead end of this travel was witnessed by Allied soldiers as they trudged eastward across Europe at the very end of the war and recorded in the 1946 British documentary, *Memory of the Camps*. The film exposes the costs of an inward turn, away from the fates of 'others'.[50] As they enter Dachau, Bergen-Belsen and other camps, the soldiers' speechless shock responds to the remains of a human cargo transported on sealed trains to destinations that were purpose-built to brutalise and exterminate Nazism's others. The trains in British espionage films and Ambler's novels, as well as witnesses in Helen MacInnes' and Ann Bridge's novels, construct a propaganda on behalf of recognising the humanity of their exiled and imperilled subjects.

Notes

1. 'Foreword', Eforgan, pp. xiii–xiv. I am deeply indebted to this masterful biography.
2. *Gone With the Wind* played to overflowing audiences throughout the war, becoming '*the* symbol of London's solidity', Gledhill and Swanson, p. 6.
3. Howard was returning to Britain from lecturing in Spain and Portugal when his civilian plane was shot down. The question of whether this was accidental was intensified when Nazi newspapers emphasised Howard's death. Ronald Howard analyses the plane crash in *In Search*.
4. McLaine notes that the MOI 'suffered from chronically low morale and [was] the object of general ridicule', p. 3.
5. See Nicholas Cull for a detailed study of British propaganda in relation to American responses.
6. Although an independent corporation, the BBC board of governors was appointed by the government, and 'was widely and correctly perceived in the United States as the voice of official London', Brewer, p. 69.
7. Mark Wollaeger argues that while perceived antithetically in earlier cultural history, the techniques of propaganda and modernist texts and films are 'constituted symbiotically', p. xiii. My study differs in exploring linkages between the content and forms of Howard's propaganda, the ideologies and practices of Nazism and Democracy, and the historical events he addresses.
8. For comparative study of British and Nazi war propaganda, see Jo Fox.
9. James Chapman considers '*The First of the Few* the most complex and technical film' Howard had ever worked on, combining 'a personal storyline with a background of real events [that was] closer to the documentary style', *The British*, pp. 119, 198.
10. From 1 September 1939 until Japan's attack on Pearl Harbor, in addition to diplomatic channels, the British government launched a propaganda campaign both in the United States and Britain to prod Americans into the war. For a comprehensive study, including efforts by American journalists such as Edward R. Murrow, see Nicholas Cull.

11. Brewer tracks Americans' resistance to war to the misguided propaganda campaigns, catastrophic losses, and 'failed peace' of World War I, p. 53.
12. Brewer reports that American critics judged the BBC broadcasts as too gracious and 'detached from the real war' while the BBC congratulated itself for its 'modesty and good will' and that J. B. Priestley's 'gritty versions of the war' and appeals to social progressivism were more effective than invocations of 'our cultural ancestors', pp. 102–3.
13. Reeves notes that once Hitler invaded Denmark in April 1940, in contrast to Chamberlain's 'deep regret' for another war, Churchill's 'defiant' voice, promising 'to lead the nation to victory', expressed 'popular emotions' and won him an 'extraordinary level of approval' that led the MOI's propaganda campaign to follow public opinion, pp. 142, 144. Janice Ho argues that Churchill's wartime invocations of such liberal values as '"freedom", "individual responsibility" and "tolerance"' denote a 'democratising myth' that is 'juxtaposed against the purported "totalitarian uniformity" of a fascist Germany', p. 92. The tendentious use of 'purported' along with Ho's elision of differences between British and German 'national characters' ignores documented contrasts between the Allies' and Nazi ideologies, political rhetoric and practices, such as Nazi Germany's slave labour and killing centres, p. 93. The research of historians Tony Kushner and Bernard Wasserstein would provide accurate historicity.
14. In its ethical and judicial frameworks, empathy has become a contested term, begging a particularly contentious question since World War II of who deserves it and under what circumstances.
15. According to Jewish law, Howard would not be considered Jewish because his mother was not born Jewish and had not converted. Such identity markers would not matter in antisemitic environments.
16. A similar scenario forms the plot of Storm Jameson's 1942 novel *And Then We Shall Hear Singing*, inspired by the Germans' destruction of the Czech city Lidice.
17. Jennifer Barker argues that Fascists viewed 'a multi-cultural society [as] a monstrous, unnatural, destructive and ridiculous idea [...] barbarism dressed up as civilization', p. 3.
18. Reeves concludes that despite official doubt, Britons' morale 'remained resolute' and they had proved to be 'the informed and reliable citizens that pre-war propaganda had assumed them to be', p. 144.
19. Jo Fox shows that early in the war, 'the MoI expressed little confidence in the British film industry's ability to produce entertainment features with propaganda value [and] escapist entertainment was to be left to the Hollywood dream factory'. The government believed that film entertainment was 'an unpredictable medium' for propaganda purposes, p. 33.
20. Early in the war, the MOI validated historical narratives that emphasised 'Britain's heritage [of] fair play', but by 1942 'realistic stories of everyday life' replaced 'fantasy [that] was thought to encourage jingoism: we may be the benefactors of the human race, but to rub it in can easily cause irritation', Harper, p. 195.
21. The MOI ideas committee organised discussions of film topics and propaganda among its members and directors and scriptwriters it chose from the Screenwriters' Association, Harper, p. 194.

22. See Aldgate and Richards for comprehensive information about Howard's wartime career and details of filming *Pimpernel Smith*.
23. Aldgate and Richards chart Howard's successes on radio and in film. For debates about the role of propaganda in British wartime film, see Cull and Harper, 'The Years of Total War'.
24. McLaine reports confusion about Britain's declaration of war over Germany's invasion of Poland since the government 'seemed to stand by while Poland was crushed by the Germans and as a consequence the public had little idea of what they were fighting for', p. 34.
25. Chapman's book *The British at War* cites the British spy movie cycle that developed in the 1930s and intensified between 1936 and 1939, emphasising the disruption of normality.
26. The film was certainly a hit with audiences, and only beaten in box office records by Howard's concurrent film *49th Parallel* and by Chaplin's *The Great Dictator*, Aldgate and Richards, p. 64. Murphy notes that British resistance films featured actors who became known for playing 'unostentatiously courageous, cultured' English gentlemen, including Howard, Rex Harrison, Clive Brook, Ralph Richardson and Robert Donat, p. 108. Antonia Lant argues that until its World War II film production, the success of British cinema had been overshadowed by Hollywood films, p. 4.
27. Chapman maintains that this film as well as Ealing Studio's *Ships With Wings* 'were criticized "because they present the war in absurdly romantic terms"', *British*, p. 52.
28. Murphy reports that wartime films dramatising resistance in Europe included the Boulting Brothers' *Pastor Hall*, Carol Reed's *Night Train to Munich*, Powell and Pressburger's *One of Our Aircraft Is Missing* and Anthony Asquith's *Freedom Radio*, p. 88.
29. See Richard Raskin for discussion of Wallenberg and the film.
30. For histories of refugees' internment or deportation as suspected enemy aliens, see Rachel Pistol and Cesarani and Kushner.
31. Phyllis Bottome's 1937 novel *The Mortal Storm* features a German Jewish scientist who denounces Nazi racial theory and is arrested and killed by the Nazis. His daughter Freya escapes to the United States, carrying his anti-Nazi message, and plans to complete her medical education.
32. While Rattigan notes the educated upper-class perspective in British wartime films and their contradictory representations of class, he finds emphasis on both a 'symbiotic' community and an organic hierarchy depicting the upper classes as leaders, p. 23.
33. Rattigan's point that British war films 'are profoundly inward-looking' is true but he does not include or discuss *Pimpernel Smith*, which as I argue, contests that view, p. 28.
34. For a survey of the experiences and effects on British culture of refugees from Nazi persecution, see Daniel Snowman.
35. Eforgan's research offers the strong possibility that the scientist is based on Ernest Chain, who escaped Germany in 1933 and later won the Nobel Prize for developing penicillin, p. 153. In the film, the scientist is working on a 'serum' to cure otherwise deadly diseases.
36. Aldgate and Richards interpret Howard's rhetoric as a 'blend of nation, empire, mysticism and war', p. 54.

37. Chaplin produced his anti-Hitler film *The Great Dictator* in 1940, and was his first speaking role as doubles: Adenoid Hynkel (Hitler) and a Jewish barber in a ghetto. The film, which was accused of warmongering, also jeopardised his enormous popularity.
38. Eforgan's interviews and archival research lead her to postulate that this incident was inspired by Paul Jacobsthal, a Jewish archaeologist at the University of Marburg, Germany, whose research, countering 'Nazi ideas of an early Aryan "master race"', led to his dismissal and escape to Oxford in 1936, p. xxiii.
39. Nicholas Cull argues that the 'script consisted of unrelenting propaganda' wherein 'Canadian innocents' are moved to renounce their 'personal neutrality' upon 'meeting the Nazis in the flesh', p. 84.
40. See Kevin Macdonald's biography of Pressburger.
41. Rebecca Margolis shows that at the beginning of the war, the Canadian army used civilian agencies to rally the nation's support, but in 1941 the National Film Board (NFB), led by John Grierson, produced films 'to galvanize a disunited Canada in the war effort', p. 125.
42. The 1926 Balfour Declaration declared the Dominions, including Canada, Australia, India, South Africa and others, as autonomous but part of the British Empire and Commonwealth and over the following fifty years, some, like Canada, became sovereign nations while others assumed the status of constitutional monarchies within the Commonwealth.
43. Although it never happened, Australia was particularly vulnerable because of the possibility of an invasion by Japan. See Geoffrey Bolton for historical explanation.
44. See Janet Epp Buckingham's study of the legal position of Hutterites in Canada.
45. Harper notes that the film's sexual politics are 'probably' attributable to MOI policy rather than Powell and Pressburger, 'The Years', p. 200.
46. Various reviewers registered concern that the 'hardships' endured by the Nazis might incline audiences to 'sympathise' with them, and that Eric Portman's 'brilliant performance [. . .] gains a certain warmth at times', but they also recognised the film's portrayal of the Nazis' brutality and Hirth's 'blind and fanatical loyalty', qtd in Aldgate and Richards, pp. 39–40.
47. Among the anti-Fascist films that feature European trains are Hitchcock's 1938 *The Lady Vanishes*, Carol Reed's 1939 *Night Train to Munich*, Powell and Pressburger's 1939 *The Spy in Black* and 1940 *Contraband*.
48. See Bernard Wasserstein and Louise London for comprehensive analyses of British knowledge and responses to these reports. Tony Kushner reports that the formation of the British Council of Christians and Jews in November 1941 was 'one of the first organizations [. . .] with the specific aim of helping the persecuted Jews of Europe', *Holocaust*, p. 147.
49. Knowledge of the Holocaust in Germany was extensive because, as historian Peter Hayes shows, 'ordinary Germans who did not carry out the killings directly witnessed the deportations, sometimes photographed them for local histories, frequently took over the possessions left behind, and received the rumors that abounded about the fate of not only Germany's Jews. In the East, awareness of the self-dug graves and shootings by the *Einsatzgruppen*, the Order Police, the foreign auxiliaries, and the German

Army was widespread, thanks to letters home and furloughs by German troops. Indeed, such information was sufficiently plentiful as time passed that more and more Germans spoke with open dread of the reprisals or retribution that they expected to experience once the tide of the war turned. A representative expression of this view, as well as of slightly more complete knowledge, is this diary entry by Curt Prüfer, a semi-retired diplomat and an antisemite who had purchased property formerly owned by Jews. On 22 November 1942, he wrote the following – mostly in French, as if to conceal what he was saying – "Men, women, and children have been slaughtered in large numbers by poison gas or by machine guns. The hatred that inevitably must arise from that will never be appeased. Today every child knows this in the smallest detail"', email 20 July 2015.

50. *Memory of the Camps* (Ministry of Information, 1945) is a documentary film that began in 1945 in the Psychological Warfare Division of Supreme Headquarters Allied Expeditionary Force as a visual testimony project involving Allied participants, but though it was never completed, parts were released in Germany in 1946 and as a whole, it has been shown on American and British TV, 'Film Viewing Notes No. 1', Department of Film, Imperial War Museum, 2001.

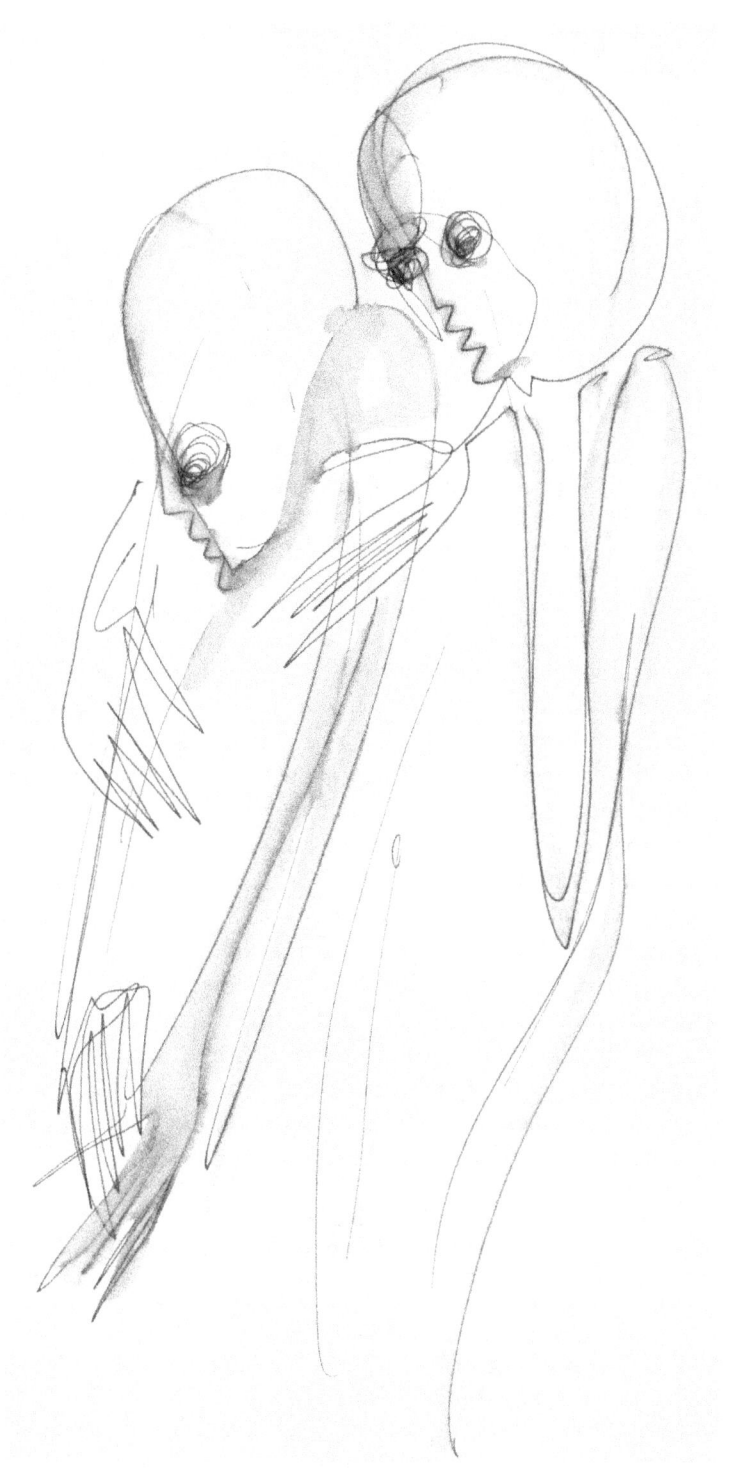

Chapter 4

John Le Carré's Never-ending War of Exile

> Once upon a time spies had motives. There was capitalism and there was communism. You could choose. And all right, there was the money and the sex and the blackmail [...] but in the end you either spied for a cause or against it. (le Carré, 'Glorious Technicolor', 1)

In John le Carré's fiction, spying for or against a cause dramatises a double-edged dystopian fantasy.[1] Regardless to which side his spies commit themselves, capitalist or liberal democracy or Communism, the 'cause' and those who work to achieve its goals are sacrificed to pragmatic, often brutal means. Critics have assumed that le Carré's grim Cold War spyscapes are based on his own experience in British Secret Intelligence and therefore must represent a critique of its ethically dubious policies and practices. Instead of responding directly, he refuses to discuss his own missions or the British intelligence agencies – MI5 and MI6 – for which he worked. He insists, however, that his fictional intelligence agencies and their plots and counterplots, treacheries and opportunism are purely imaginary. Nonetheless, beginning with his first novel, *Call for the Dead*, all his Cold War thrillers coalesce into a dystopian warning that the sacrifices demanded by political ideology erase historical memory. To countermand that erasure, his Cold War fiction dramatises the unhealed wounds of World War II suppurating in the grave ethical impact of the Cold War.[2] A recent documentary film reveals

> [t]he disbelief he felt as a young civil servant watching the construction of the Berlin Wall [which] drove le Carré to write his first novel, *A Call for the Dead* (1961). 'I saw the American and Russian tanks facing each other, waving their barrels at each other and the barbed wire being erected,' le Carré says. 'I think I really suffered. There was a serious sense of trauma. The barricades of the new Cold War were being built on the ashes of the old one.' (Bailey, np)

Le Carré's assertive repetitions of 'I' and impassioned language do not accord with the following interpretation of his response: 'We only see what le Carré wanted us to see: a man who has apparently dealt with the shadows of his past with good humour and determination' (Bailey, np). With his confessional voice, le Carré's statement is certainly crafted as eloquently and as cagily as his best imaginative writing. Rhetorically it creates the effect of overcoming cultural, social and stylistic differences and distances from his listeners and readers as though he speaks to them directly and candidly. The content of this revelation, however, is neither transparent nor unequivocal. To read it as a sign that le Carré has dealt with the shadows of his past with 'determination and humor' overlooks his bitterly sorrowful irony, the tenor of which echoes in his narrators' and characters' voices and that interweaves historical, allegorical and psychological images.

The diction and tone with which le Carré expresses Cold War memories indicate psychological and narrative urgency, both of which are apparent in his declaration that 'There was a serious sense of trauma.' The combination of historical distance in 'There was' and psychological state of 'trauma' accords with his narrative method in the Cold War novels where the modern history of Germany remains indelible and disorienting, staged as a Gothic Expressionist spyscape. For le Carré, the image of the Berlin Wall being built on 'ashes' suggests a monstrous mutation of the Phoenix rising.[3] Instead of connoting rebirth or a new and fruitful beginning, the image suggests a never-ending war. His memory of the wall, cloaked in barbed wire and behind which the East German Communist State (German Democratic Republic) rises, foretells the Cold War birthing a horrifying future.[4] In le Carré's nightmare vision, the possibility of a nuclear war might very well recapitulate the atrocities signified by the ashes produced by the Nazis' assembly line crematoria. Touring Germany in 1945, Stephen Spender also envisions unending horror: 'The whole world had seemed to be darkened with their darkness, and when they left the world, the threat of a still greater darkness, a total and everlasting one, rose up from their ashes' (*European Witness*, 245–6). While the image of ashes is redolent of the Holocaust, it occupies le Carré's Cold War in the form of exiled survivors who experience neither liberation nor victory, only ongoing deception and betrayal.

As an organising symbol of historical memory and presentiment, the image of ashes seeps into the consciousness of le Carré's narrators and spies. This does not, however, represent the wartime memory of a combatant or of nostalgia for Britain's heroic defeat of Nazism. As he has written, he disdains 'Britain's continuing self-perception as the victor in the '39–'45 war' (Foreword, *A Small Town in Germany*, x). By contrast, the affect of le Carré's Cold War novels is often that of despair for a victory that could not last and the loss of hope for a regenerative democratic sense of national purpose. The focalised perspective that projects this despair is that of an onlooker or belated witness whose 'sense of trauma' forms the plot of *Call for the Dead* and thereafter, the character of George Smiley, le Carré's haunted 'espiocrat' ('Spying [. . .] the Passion', 270). Le Carré links Smiley's character to the thematic trajectory of his novels – a '"*Comédie humaine*" of the cold war, told in terms of mutual espionage' (Garner, 20):

> I was young when I started writing about George Smiley – 28 – and Smiley was already old. But his journey through the novel is the journey of a young man's self-discovery. Underneath his inconspicuous exterior, he is a sensitive man still growing up, still looking for answers, and for the experience that delivers them. And Smiley's private journey – from this first novel, right through to his last – is a single Bildungsroman that leads him through disappointments, mistaken loves, failures and occasional successes, to some kind of ultimate maturity. ('Smiley's Secret', 7)

The representation of Smiley's embattled moral conscience may very well reflect le Carré's reflection on his own service where he was 'searching for moral certitudes that had so far eluded him – although, as he subsequently realized, "I had come to the wrong address"' (qtd in Sisman, 184).

While critics attribute Smiley's haplessness to his wife's serial infidelities, his existential malaise reaches far beyond this one relationship into the nightmares of Nazi Germany's power being recapitulated in the Cold War, and into his own actions and inaction. No smiley face there. This Holocaust memory and the images of successive, unrelenting wartime trauma create an epic cultural engagement with a history that, as historian Tony Kushner demonstrates, 'impinged [. . .] on the individual and collective histories of Allied nations' (*HLI*, 18).[5] In *Call for the Dead*, horrific history combines with le Carré's admiration of German literature to confront 'the unreconciled heritage of [Germany's] recent past' and his admission that 'Over time, Germany has never lost its lure for me' ('Smiley's Secret', 7).[6] That le Carré's ambivalence towards German culture and history remains haunted by the Holocaust is evident in his recollection of Bonn in the 1960s where 'Sometimes the very streets of the city seemed like a perilously thin surface laid hastily upon the recent dreadful past, like one of those nicely mown grass mounds at Belsen concentration camp, covering the mute agony of the innocent dead' (Foreword, *A Small Town in Germany*, viii).

A Cold War Anti-romance

The epic quality I attribute to le Carré's Cold War fiction does not disregard his varied narrative interests and forms. In fact his second novel, *A Murder of Quality* (1962), seems to retreat from Cold War plotting, with its confined setting and inward-looking plot evoking Agatha Christie's manor house murders. Here George Smiley is a detective, investigating a murder at the cloistered but deadly enclaves of Carne School, an elite, insidiously insular boarding school. The setting is inspired by Eton, where le Carré taught early in his career and which he described as giving him 'familiarity with crime, as well as an instinct for hypocrisy and both of them, in different ways, are not absolutely unknown in diplomacy' (qtd in Dean, 29). Carne's students appear to be children of the damned. Introduced as 'sad groups of black-coated boys', they look like 'black angels come for the burying' (*Murder*, 9). In addition to charting the death of their innocence, this novel also memorialises the demise of an English literary tradition, England as a green and pleasant land, the iconic setting for a boy's coming of age story. The novel's claustrophobic atmosphere, expressive of its internal cabals, is not an anomaly in le Carré's oeuvre. Like the social structure of Cambridge Circus, this is a secret, supremely masculine world. It is devoid of women and the emotional distraction, distress and romantic hope for comfort they represent in earlier espionage novels by John Buchan and Somerset Maugham and in the contemporary fiction of Ian Fleming and Robert Ludlum. In *A Murder of Quality*, the absence of women highlights the men's intensely ambivalent personal and professional relationships that erupt violently in eroticised vengeance. The novel's compressed, self-enclosed form indicates a Cold War anti-romance, reducing labyrinthine international intrigue to the curriculum of perpetual war. This is an underground war where the seductive power of intrigue begins among rivals for ideological and bureaucratic power. *A Murder of Quality* also mocks the treachery and romance readers expect in spy fiction by linking Smiley's passion for academic study to betrayal. Smiley's ratiocinative talents lead only to the revelation that in men's secret worlds, intellectual discourse and academic institutional integrity are, like the spies' bonds, mutually reinforcing deceptions.

Call for the Dead: Exile and the Question of History

> 'If I were asked to single out one specific group of men, one type [...] as being the most suspicious, unbelieving, unreasonable, petty, inhuman, sadistic, double-crossing set of bastards in any language, I would say without any hesitation the people who run counter-espionage departments' (Eric Ambler, qtd in Britton, 24)

In his review of John le Carré's 1965 novel *The Looking Glass War*, Eric Ambler offers an incisive contrast. On the one hand, there is 'the vicarious enjoyment of James Bond's license to kill and to pop into bed with his current heroine, while for those who require more subtle relief for the malaise there are the burnt-out cases of John le Carré's glum and gritty secret world' ('John le Carré Escapes', 8). Ambler's depiction of le Carré's Secret World, with its canny allusion to Graham Greene's 1961 novel *A Burnt-Out Case*, creates a nexus of literary historical relations that positions le Carré's fiction as cultural critique.[7] Unlike Ian Fleming's hyperkinetic action thrillers, but with resemblances to Greene's moral angst, le Carré's first novel, *Call for the Dead*, published the same year as *A Burnt-Out Case*, features a world of moral and psychological mayhem. Both novels are populated by protagonists and antagonists who are damaged souls, in states of inexorable exile, suffering beyond 'relief' from past and present wars.[8] In contrast to Fleming's James Bond, le Carré's spies are undoubtedly poor entertainment value. As the epigraph to *A Burnt-Out Case* suggests, Greene's allegorical leper colony could easily be home to le Carré's perennial outsiders:

> Within limits of normality, every individual loves himself. In cases where he has a deformity or abnormality or develops it later, his own aesthetic sense revolts and he develops a sort of disgust towards himself. Though with time, he becomes reconciled to his deformities, it is only at the conscious level. His sub-conscious mind, which continues to bear the mark of the injury, brings about certain changes in his whole personality, making him suspicious of society. (R.V. Wardekar in a pamphlet on leprosy, *A Burnt Out-Case*, np)

The alignment in this passage of disfigurement, self-loathing and alienation also characterises le Carré's anxiety-ridden spyscape, where British spies, their adversaries and victims share a state of chronic displacement, trapped in doomed isolation by fatalistic spy stories. Very near its conclusion, *Call for the Dead* diagnoses a lingering 'mark' of this 'injury' as 'the nausea of guilt', a symptom Greene's characters would recognise all too well (*CD*, 145). Exploited and betrayed by British Intelligence, spies like George Smiley and Alec Leamas become reconciled to their position as outliers, but their journeys through looking-glass wars also provide recognition that the aesthetic and ethical norms of their missions demand compliance with the Secret World's core values of deception, duplicity and treachery. This compliance, however, does not assimilate them into the nation they serve. Like an infinitely regressing mirror image, mutual espionage exposes each side's secrets until the very idea of secrecy dissipates and all that's left is the performance of spying without signifying content. When spies perform as double agents, loyalty to a nation recedes into absurdist comedy, rendering them suspect from the start. In either case, le Carré's 'espiocrats' live and die in the Cold, never invited to be insiders, to belong. Unlike voluntary exile, le Carré identifies with the spy's condition as cast-out even when he returns: 'I have been in exile for years on end, the enforced exile of being a foreign servant' (qtd in Dean, 32). No matter how well they perform or how loyal they prove to be, to a nation, an ideology or an agency, the spy's very nature and condition resembles that of a leper.

Ambler's mockery of James Bond also calls attention to the way le Carré's *comédies* and their spies question the gendered stability of Bond's hyper-masculinity. The first Bond novel, *Casino Royale* (1953), established Fleming's penchant for 'heroic spy fantasy', responding to the Cold War with a continuum of phantasmagoric wars in which his lone British superhero defends Britain and the world from a series of monomaniacal turbo-powered villains (Cawelti and Rosenberg, 52). Bond and his adversaries are clearly cartoon figures, especially as they perform their gender roles in extremis, equating their glamorous masculinity and femininity with moral righteousness and their monstrous opposition with depravity. Le Carré by contrast, creates a deceptively mimetic Cold War, featuring bureaucratic files instead of supersonic weapons, grim check-points, unsafe safe houses and moral pragmatism on all sides. As though mirroring his subject of espionage deception, his representation of the mundane is shadowed by an allegorical monstrousness that afflicts the exiled character and fate of his fallible spies on all sides. Unspectacular and unassimilated, these agents rarely save themselves and their worlds from treacherous masters and adversaries. Unlike Bond, the darling of his handlers, George Smiley suffers from declassed and skittish masculinity, indicating incompatibility with the public school arrogance that dominates the political and social culture of the British Secret World. The uncertain positions and psychologies of le Carré's displaced agents, and their lack of identification with the ideologies that justify their nations' goals and means, represent his critical perspective on the ethical and political relationship between his Secret World and the nation it serves.

In *Call for the Dead* Smiley is already a veteran agent of British Secret

Intelligence. But like the victims and villains he investigates, he is an outsider from beginning to end. In this novel his espionage and detective work combine in an investigation of the death of another agent, another intruder. Instead of achieving justice, the solution indicts the grim composition of British Secret Intelligence. That le Carré calls the agency the Circus attests to the tautological absurdity of the agency's goals and machinations. In effect, the Circus nurtures and harbours secret codes and conflicts that undermine its ability to decipher and expose the intrigues of its domestic and external enemies. The plot revolves around discovering whether Samuel Fennan, an agent working under Smiley, committed suicide or was murdered. The novel's title calls immediate attention to the multivalent meanings of the question, especially with the word 'call'. In addition to the phone call by Fennan's wife Elsa to report his death to the police, the word refers to his wake-up call from the local phone exchange. That the call comes through during Smiley's initial interview with Elsa provides the first clue erasing the diagnosis of suicide. Like the camera in Ambler's novels, the telephone is not a medium of communication or intelligence, but of misinformation. Samuel Fennan would not have requested a wake-up call for the morning after he intended to kill himself. Nonetheless the logic of this conclusion is dismissed by Smiley's superior, Maston, whose 'flexibility when formulating new commitments' petrifies the search for the truth (CD, 13). The truth would demystify the illusory stability and righteousness of his bureaucratic power.[9] Unlike Maston's insistence on a rigid, literal reading of the call, Smiley will interrogate the political, historical and ethical ambiguities encapsulated in the truth's multiple meanings. That the truth is manifold coincides with the indefinite word 'Call' in the title, without an article, neither 'A' nor 'The'. That the truth must be buried reverberates with the ashes of history that surface, despite efforts to deny its presence.

Fennan becomes suspect after an anonymous letter to British Intelligence claims that he was a double agent, spying for the Communists. He is then interviewed by Smiley who concludes, despite official disbelief, that his colleague is innocent and trustworthy. Whether Fennan took his own life is of grave importance as the answer affects the security, power structure and efficacy of British Intelligence as an arm of a democratic nation. The novel implies that after victory over Fascism and Nazism, and now embroiled in the indeterminacies of the Cold War, doubts emerged about Britain's future role in global politics. The pre-war and wartime 'inspired amateurism of a handful of highly qualified underpaid men' has been replaced by a new model of masculine conformity, a 'cumbersome machine of bureaucracy' ruled over by 'a man who could reduce any colour to grey' (*CD*, 12–13). The prevailing atmosphere of le Carré's Cold War novels and his nation is indeed gray, a dystopian Gothic Expressionist palate that illustrates the shadowy moral and gendered political qualms of the Secret World.

The question of Samuel Fennan's death also redefines the genre's construction of villain and victim, insider and outsider to the nation. Erin Carlston dissects the liminal and suspicious condition of the spy:

> In the case of spies, who by definition pass as something other than what they are, questions about loyalty become especially fraught with anxiety. Naturally, not all spies are traitors to their own nations, but in one sense all are treacherous; they are supposed to lie and deceive, to perform loyalties that they do not actually feel. So a spy's capacity for dissimulation, which makes him useful, also makes him irremediably dangerous, since his employer – his country, usually – can never be sure that even the most apparently patriotic and dependable spy is not really a double agent, working in the interests of a foreign power. Thus, while treason can take many forms besides spying, spies are particularly liable to fall under suspicion of treason. (4)

Even George Smiley, whose efforts all support his country, is suspect because his investigations threaten to expose the treachery of the Secret World towards its own mandate – protection of the nation's citizens.

Call for the Dead begins with 'A Brief History of George Smiley' that establishes his character as alien to the social culture of the Circus and to the romantic heroism on which so many spy thrillers depend for audience satisfaction:

> Short, fat, and of a quiet disposition, he appeared to spend a lot of money on really bad clothes, which hung about his squat frame like skin on a shrunken toad [. . .] Was he rich or poor, peasant or priest? (*CD*, 7)

A decidedly unromantic figure, Smiley also defies the model of Bond's irresistible masculinity by begging the question of why the beautiful Lady Ann Sercomb married '"a bull-frog in a sou'wester"', an inquiry soon vexed by her persistent leaving and then returning to him (*CD*, 7).[10] All the Cold War novels featuring Smiley explain him as lacking both the attributes of his colleagues in the Circus and more broadly, a position defined by class or heritage:

> And so Smiley, without school, parents, regiment or trade, without wealth or poverty, travelled without labels in the guard's van of the social express, and soon became lost luggage, destined, when the divorce had come and gone, to remain unclaimed on the dusty shelf of yesterday's news. (*CD*, 7)

The narrator's ironic tone expresses le Carré's mockery of the class-bound, public school tradition that begins among 'sad boys' and develops into the masculinist structure of his imagined British Secret Intelligence.[11] But mockery also targets the replacement model led by Maston – a sly combination of master and mastodon – 'with his expensive clothes and his knighthood [...] a man who [...] knew his masters and could walk among them' (*CD*, 13). Smiley fits neither mould. Neither upper-middle-class gentleman nor bureaucrat, Smiley, like his creator, is deeply suspicious of the qualities that Praseeda Gopinath analyses as 'bourgeois gentlemanliness: fair play, brotherhood, decency, honesty, forthrightness, and hardiness' (3).[12] As each of the Smiley novels unfolds, these traits are exposed as well rehearsed performances by gentlemen and bureaucrats posing as one another to prove they belong. Performance, however, both masks and reveals the inner sanctum of power as an evaporating illusion based on betrayal, duplicity and lies. While the word 'divorce' in the above quote clearly refers to Smiley and Ann, it also reflects the agent's marginal position in the agency where he must operate in a state resembling exile, typically in dingy, closeted rooms at Cambridge Circus. Constantly being retired, he is then recalled, albeit in begrudging and suspicious toleration, to unveil the internal treachery of the more gentlemanly agents and save British Intelligence from internal collapse – from itself. As le Carré assesses him, 'one of the functions of Smiley [...] is to act as a central intellect in whom the reader has so much confidence. When Smiley is becoming analytical and intuitive about things you more or less leave the reasoning to him' (qtd in Vaughan, 55).

The mirroring of Smiley's consciousness in the ambiguity of his official position raises questions about whether such reader confidence is viable, especially, as le Carré attests, 'Smiley changes very much from book to book' (qtd in Vaughan, 56). Such change is dramatically apparent in his shadowy role in *The Spy Who Came in from the Cold*. Professing to be Alec Leamas' trusted colleague at Cambridge Circus and offering his assistance to Liz Gold, Leamas' lover, aligns with the confidence invested in Smiley's intellect and integrity in the earlier novels. Yet at the end of *Spy*, even as Smiley helps Leamas over the Berlin Wall to safety, his role is ambiguous, as he calls out: '"The girl, where's the girl?"' (*Spy*, 221). Whether Smiley is concerned about Liz or worried that she knows too much and must be sacrificed to save the mission remains insoluble. James Buzard links 'the spy's enigmatic behavior' and unresolved 'question of motive' to the casting of Smiley as 'the Saint George of [...] a weakened nation in an uncertain age' (154). The allusion is apt, especially when read in tandem with Edward Elgar's lyrics for his ballad, *The Banner of Saint George*, a celebration of the Empire at Queen Victoria's Diamond Jubilee. Elgar's soaring music and libretto celebrate the nation's history as a myth, starring 'deathless heroes' whose 'glorious deeds of old [. . .] England ne'er forget'.[13] Armed with neither techno-weapons nor an athletic body, George Smiley is the anti-mythic, besieged and unheralded Cold warrior on behalf of a post-imperial nation struggling to revive faith in its significance.[14]

With the exception of *The Spy Who Came in from the Cold*, where Smiley's pivotal role occurs offstage, he is dramatically present as the unwanted, challenging and self-lacerating conscience of the Circus and by the end of his tenure, antithetical to his nation's struggle to remain globally relevant. The 'bloodless' emotional distance required of spies vies with his hatred and fear of 'the falseness of his life' as well as with his 'sentimental' and 'deep love of England', a romantic yearning and fidelity inscribed by Elgar that neither Smiley's mission nor his nation can satisfy (*CD*, 10). Whereas Ambler's novels of the 1930s position protagonists, villains and victims as suspicious, helpless and stateless aliens, and the 1940s novels of Helen MacInnes and Ann Bridge show the fragility of British identity, citizenship and power in Nazi-occupied Europe, the betrayals of George Smiley by his own system only reinforce his unabashed if antiquarian British identity and sense of justice. That his sense of justice will extend to the enemy only reinforces his status as outlier.

Despite his unprepossessing profile, Smiley is no ordinary man like Eric Ambler's amateur protagonists whose political and ethical consciousness is awakened, activated and proclaimed as their journeys transport them to challenge and escape the Fascist enemy. And despite Smiley's penchant for scholarship, he couldn't be more distinct from Leslie Howard's Horatio Smith, Cambridge don by day, rescuer by night. Smiley, by contrast, is unfit for inclusion in the canon of espionage heroes and amateurs. He even redefines the notion of anti-hero. In all the novels featuring him, he operates within the authority of the Secret World's power structure but as an irritant, not a rebel. His appearance and dress mark him as louche, like a refugee in his ill-fitting clothes and probing, infelicitous questions. Le Carré notes Smiley's status as 'socially rather a misfit' (qtd in Gross, 60). In no novel is he capable of disguise. Coupled with his inability to keep his wife, these qualities disqualify him as a model of manliness, which in so many spy thrillers and in the corridors of Cambridge Circus signifies authority and self-confident sexuality. Nonetheless, even though Smiley may lack the 'social express' of his colleagues and therefore seems an easy target of mockery and manipulation, his ruthless intellect and passions overwhelm his enemies, prove irresistible to his wife and redefine the masculinity of the spy. In interviews, le Carré sums up the complexities that make Smiley an intriguing character: 'Professionally he's illusionless, and yet in love he's the victim of self-deception' (qtd in Deindorfer, 15). He also explains the ironic apposition between Smiley's virtues and the classed nature of British masculinity: 'He stood for me [for] the decency which for better or for worse was believed to be the property of the English gentlemen' (qtd in Bailey).

Smiley remaps what it means to be an agent in the field. He neither manages a team nor goes undercover. Instead, he defines his professional work as that of a scholar, 'provid[ing] him with what he had once loved best in life: academic excursions into the mystery of human behavior, disciplined by the practical application of his own deductions' (*CD*, 8). Empirical and reflective, these heuristics threaten the unequivocal and pragmatic thinking that, in allowing no ambiguity, much less mystery, sustains the Circus and defines its goal-directed masculinity. Smiley's open enquiry, literally opening doors where he is unwanted, and then questioning and frustrating the duplicitous goals of the Circus, drives the novel's suspense and action. The plot traces his investigation through interviews cross-checked with lists of clues, all of which he reads as closely as he does German Baroque poetry. Eva Horn notes that he is like the 'melancholic' in German Baroque literature, poring 'over the mysterious debris of failed operations and destroyed lives' (271). The novel doubts whether Smiley's scholastic method is transferable to spycraft and whether the beauty of Germany's cultural past will yield clues to understanding Nazism's horrors and the nation's politically divided present. While his methods lead to solving the mystery of Fennan's character and fate, the academic approach produces only escalating irresolution, neither enriching enlightenment nor integration into Britain's Secret World.

Instead of the objective results of induction, Smiley's achievement necessitates baring his tortured subjectivity – 'the rising panic of frustration beyond endurance' (*CD*, 42). Integral to Smiley's ratiocinative talents are his emotional and ethical vulnerabilities, which defy the apolitical, ahistorical detachment that characterises the genre's prototypical masculinity.[15] By contrast, le Carré stages the emotional life of his characters within their historical positions. Smiley is made vulnerable by historical memory and consciousness. Like his creator, memories of the rise of Nazi power and later, the grafting of Fascism onto Communism produce 'disgust and terror' as well as 'total ideological disorientation' (Introduction, *Spy*, viii; Cameron, 20). Smiley's mission in *Call for the Dead* exposes how the terrors of Nazism did not end with defeat of the Third Reich in 1945, but linger in the make-up and machinations of East German Communism. In le Carré's post-war 1960s vision, refracted through Smiley's memory and responses, Fascist politics and practices re-emerge as endemic to Communism, producing an apotheosis of brutality.[16] From a post-war perspective, Stephen Spender reflects that 'the Stalinists now present the same threat to intellectual liberty as did the followers of Hitler in 1933. But at the time [...] this was not obvious' (*God that Failed*, 242).[17] If, in historical actuality, East Germany (GDR) was a satellite state, operating at the behest of the Soviet Union, le Carré's novels configure it as responsible for its own fascistic power and practices. Interestingly, except for Karla, the Soviet master spy in *Tinker, Tailor, Soldier, Spy* and *Smiley's People*, the face and identity of the enemy throughout le Carré's Cold War novels is East German. It is as though the Berlin Wall represents a dual political and cultural betrayal of the German Baroque literature so loved by le Carré and Smiley. Just as Nazi Germany declared its greatest writers and artists degenerate, so the GDR denounces them as bourgeois and therefore corrupt. In both cases, these pronouncements drove artists and writers into exile if they weren't arrested first.[18] The Berlin Wall thus represents the material symbol of cultural and historical repression. The novel's self-reflexive interweave of politics and art, Nazism and Communism, produces a skein of multiple human tragedies that emerge as the novel's case against the Fascist Communist State.

The argument against this lethal combination can be found in le Carré's plots, where in the form of double agents, Fascist Communism has either infiltrated British Secret Intelligence or been used by it. No matter who the enemy turns out to be, British, East German or Soviet, he – and the double agent is always male – represents a double-sided equivalence. Despite oppositional ideologies, callous exploitation is the preferred method of both the British and the Communists. Le Carré denounced this similarity in a letter to the *Moscow Literary Gazette*, published in the British periodical *The Spectator*: 'In espionage as I depicted it Western man sacrifices the individual to defend the individual's right against the collective. That is Western hypocrisy, and I condemned it because I felt it took us too far into the Communist camp' ('To Russia', 4).[19] In practical and political terms, this 'sacrifice' highlights the lack of protection for Britain's own agents. Despite the life-threatening risks their missions necessitate, British spies turn out to be less valuable than moles and traitors. Their humanity is not included in the British collective, the ordinary citizens British Intelligence is designed to defend.[20] Despite Smiley's love for England, his place within the nation is always being tested and endangered. Although he never leaves Britain in *Call for the Dead*, his own nation becomes enemy territory.

Combining his immersion into Baroque German culture, his espionage experience in 1930s Germany, intellectual acuity and political passion, Smiley becomes the British agent of historical and moral recognition. Whereas later, in the Karla trilogy, Smiley will sacrifice decency to his obsessive competition with his Communist counterpart, *Call for the Dead* marks the moment he recognises that the necessity of defending himself as an agent of democratic institutions means betrayal of democratic ideals.[21] Political and personal betrayal begins with the struggle to defeat Nazism, which despite Allied victory, can have no moral or historical resolution. The human costs of Burma, El Alamein and the final surge to defeat Nazi Germany have bled into an underground war of surveillance, deceit, emotional manipulation and assassination. The Allies' dependence on the Red Army to defeat Germany has led to agreements that allow Soviet hegemony throughout Central and Eastern Europe and the Baltic States.[22] In *Call for the Dead*, the plotting and perspective are driven by moments of recognition and memories of World War II and their intrusion on Cold War intrigue.

These memories invade Smiley's consciousness and shape both the novel's crucial back-story and le Carré's historical interpretation of the Cold War. Established in the very first chapter, le Carré's account of Smiley in 1937 relates the agent's love of England to his hatred of Hitler's 'new Germany, the stamping and shouting of uniformed students, the scarred arrogant faces' (*CD*, 11). With a rage undiminished by time, Smiley recalls that same defining event, encapsulated in *49th Parallel*, when he watched Nazi brown-shirts burning books by Thomas Mann, Heine, Lessing and so many others as degenerate culture, as 'hundreds of students cheered them on' (*CD*, 11). The scarred faces, conflating Germany's masculinist militaristic duelling tradition with Nazism's supremacist arrogance,[23] will question the nature of villainy and victimhood during the Cold War, when the promises of East German Communism for collective equality replay Nazism's oppression. No ideas even remotely suggesting political critique will survive the violence endemic to both ideologies. In practice, the murder of critical questioning will materialise in the novel's portrayals of Jewish victims of Fascist oppression. Also considered degenerate in Nazi policy and practices, the Jews embody feminine activities such as reading while accused of being sexual predators.[24] In critical relation to Nazi gender ideology, Smiley would be feminised by his reading and sexual failure, like a Jew, except that his reading becomes a lethal weapon.

One of the novel's Jewish characters, Smiley's police colleague Mendel, is a figure of resistance to political oppression in his role as Smiley's rescuer, sounding board, fellow traveller and Sancho Panza in the search for reality, truth and justice. That this resistance should take place in London, the seat of British power, chafes against the nation's claims for democratic justice, principles and institutions. For while Britain considers itself the exemplar of Enlightenment rationality and progress, the methods it uses to assert its moral and judicial superiority are questioned by the convergence of Smiley's memory of Nazi oppression with Mendel's search and the novel's range of Jewish characters. Each of the Jewish characters plays a critical role in the political drama at the centre of the novel and in the embattled political consciousness of the British agent. They reflect the 'ambivalent attitudes towards Jews' that constituted 'the norm [in] dominant liberal ideology' (Kushner, *HLI*, 42). Sharing contested ground with these Jewish characters, Smiley is le Carré's displaced witness.

In *Call for the Dead* the definition and place of protagonists, victims and villains is dislocation. Whether dead or alive, no one has a stable place anywhere. Even those who assume they belong, such as Maston, are mocked by the narrator and occupy only tenuous positions in the social, political and cultural time-place nexus of the novel. For those who are victimised by indeterminate positions, promises of protection and security by class, official status or ideological codes and rhetoric produce only betrayal and threats of expulsion or decimation. No ordinary victim, Samuel Fennan was an agent working for British Secret Intelligence and suspicion already reigns in his profile where

> The new world and the old met [. . .] The eternal Jew, cultured, cosmopolitan, self-determinate, industrious and perceptive. The child of his century; persecuted, like Elsa, and driven from his adopted Germany to University in England. By the sheer weight of his ability he had pushed aside disadvantage and prejudice, finally able to enter the Foreign Office. (*CD*, 68)

Only Smiley finds Fennan 'immensely attractive' (*CD*, 68). The stereotypical Jewish profile represented and critically historicised by the narrator above resonates with centuries of 'prejudice'. That antisemitism prevails even when the Jews are victimised anew is evinced by Ambler's witnesses, Frankau's Philip Meyer and MacInnes' Jew's alley. Portending no solution, antisemitism still finds a home in le Carré's England fifteen years after the liberation of the Nazi death camps. Whatever he assumed or wished for as a result of his service to Britain, Fennan did not find a home there. Branding his suspicious death as suicide erases his identity as a British victim of the nation's enemy. In turn, suicide absolves the Circus of any responsibility or sympathy for its own agent, detaining Fennan in a liminal political space, between citizenship and alien. Connoting the alternating statements of sympathy for the persecuted Jew and of iconic antisemitic stereotypes, the narrator's two-pronged voice in the above passage coheres in irony. Each statement questions the validity of the other to construct the Jew as mythic object and/or historical subject.[25] The Jew remains an involuntary migrant because his position is constructed as both eternally ossified and contingent. He may be equally useful to his host nation as a scapegoat or an agent, but in either case, he cannot escape suspicion. His position is stable only as a persona, not a person.[26]

What appear to be undeviating in *Call for the Dead* are the perceptions that construct the Jew's persona as unfit for British cultural and social integration. As Erin Carlston observes about the gendered and racialised position of the Jew, 'It was men who participated, and competed in the public institutions of national life; thus it is Jewish men, men who are perceived as feminine but are not women, who are the focus of anxiety about the nation' (38). The Jew is 'cosmopolitan' by decree, not by choice. In his historical time, crossing borders is a life-threatening enterprise, not a pathway to self-determination as theoretically conceived today.[27] The German Jewish émigré has no subjectivity to call his own. Unlike Ambler's Sachs/Borovansky, Fennan's Jewish identity and story are verified, but they coincide with a political profile that reinforces his 'disadvantage' through racist rhetoric. Interestingly, both men are murdered, and at the very start of the fictions in which they feature. Ambler and le Carré foreground the Jew as necessary to their historically centred espionage fictions, but then the Jew must be shown as expendable as well. Unforgiven, their Jewish characters and stories are also not to be forgotten.

Le Carré's narrator provides a back-story for Fennan that aligns him with a political persona which could win him both sympathy and antipathy, a story that could be used both to understand and vilify him:

> It had been natural enough that Fennan should join the Left at Oxford. It was the great honeymoon period of University Communism, and its causes, heaven knows, lay close enough to his heart. The rise of Fascism in Germany and Italy, the Japanese invasion of Manchuria, the Franco rebellion in Spain, the slump in America, and above all the wave of anti-Semitism that was sweeping across Europe: it was inevitable that Fennan should seek an outlet for his anger and revulsion. Besides, the Party was respectable then; the failure of the Labour Party and the Coalition Government had convinced many intellectuals that the Communists alone could provide an effective alternative to Capitalism and Fascism. There was the excitement, an air of conspiracy and comradeship which must have appealed to the flamboyance in Fennan's character and given him comfort in his loneliness. (*CD*, 68–9)

The narrator's survey of British intellectuals' support for Communism in the 1930s recalls a history to which Ambler's narrators and characters also attest. In the early 1930s Stalinism had not yet extended its insistence on total conformity to the Communist Parties of other nations. The concerns registered in this quotation remind us that liberal thinking shared economic and moral consciousness with Communism.[28] In an era when writers were asked what it meant to take sides, Ambler's contemporary and le Carré's analeptic dissection of 1930s political vacillations share critical terrain. Deploying polemical speeches on behalf of those persecuted by Communism and Fascism, both novelists dramatise the consolidation of Stalinist power in the late 1930s throughout the European Communist Parties and its resemblance to Fascist oppression. In *Call for the Dead* support for Communism is acceptable and even endowed with cachet, but only within the cloisters of the élite: 'Half the Cabinet were in the party in the thirties', asserts Smiley (CD, 20).[29] By contrast, Communist affiliation confirms suspicions about Samuel Fennan. For those like Maston, 'wearing the cloak for masters and preserving the dagger for his servants', Communist sympathies are an indelible sign of the undesirable, expungable alien (CD, 13). Regardless of historical contingencies, Communist sympathies link Fennan to an inherent Jewish duplicity.

This characterisation is so central to this novel that it becomes a guide to the hostile relations around which the plot is constructed. The figure of the Jew is mediated through antisemitic stereotypes, including those that permeate spy thrillers of the early twentieth century, as in John Buchan's 'Jew-Anarchists' (*The Thirty-Nine Steps*, 37). In turn, the tragic fates of the historic and constructed Jewish characters anatomise the conventions of spy thrillers that use historical context as a backdrop, but as with the Bond and Bourne franchises, do not construct characters as historically conditional. For le Carré, Jewish characters are neither objects to be used nor shorthand for villainy. His writing about post-Holocaust British and East German espionage dramatises the necessity for a revisionary approach. Like Ambler's novels of the 1930s, le Carré's Cold War novels address epistemological and political relationships between responses to Fascism and fiction. In particular, they depict how Fascist violence would require narrative methods that reflect the nature and breadth of its villainy, its victims and Britain's responses.

Return of the Survivor

tell me did I really come back
from the other world?
As far as I'm concerned

> I'm still there
> dying there
> a little more each day
> dying over again
> the death of those who died (Charlotte Delbo, *Auschwitz and After*, 224)

The primary subject of Smiley's interviews, Fennan's widow, Elsa, embodies a story that insists on the presence of the World War II and Holocaust past in the Cold War present. Like her husband, she is a German Jewish refugee who 'suffered badly in the war', a factor that for Maston only 'adds to the embarrassment' of Samuel Fennan's suspicious identity and allegiance and subtracts sympathy (*CD*, 21). The narrator and Smiley offer a different, but mutually reinforcing description of Elsa, one that might very well have been inspired by le Carré's postwar assignment, 'trolling through the displaced-persons camps, looking for people who were fake refugees, or for people whose circumstances were so attractive to us from an intelligence point of view [. . .]' (qtd in Plimpton, 147).

> She must have been older than Fennan. A slight, fierce woman in her fifties with hair cut very short and dyed to the color of nicotine. Although frail, she conveyed an impression of endurance and courage, and the brown eyes that shone from her crooked little face were of an astonishing intensity. It was a worn face, racked and ravaged long ago, the face of a child grown old on starving and exhaustion, the eternal refugee face, the prison-camp face, thought Smiley. (*CD*, 25)[30]

The only clue Elsa's body yields signifies an indelible memory trace of the Holocaust. The typical suspense of the spy thriller's chase has been obliterated by an extreme horror from which the historicised victim cannot escape, thus stonewalling the reader's complacent expectations of the genre. In effect, as this epic is written on the body of a Holocaust survivor, it conflates Hepburn's distinction between reading the codes of spy fiction allegorically and the clues of detective fiction that 'require literal reading' (25). The survivor's body can be deciphered as a realistic story of physical and emotional decimation resulting from her concentration camp experience.[31] Smiley remembers that Elsa was bedridden for three years after the war. The entire description quoted above recalls Nazi gender policies and practices for women who were racially targeted as diseased and poisonous. The bodies of all women prisoners were robbed of their sexuality and, with Nazi logic, aptly punished for being sexually threatening. Their 'vampiric power to control the male's rationality' earned them a sexually abusive initiation into the Nazi camp universe (Gilman, 109).[32] Elsa's 'very short hair' is a reminder that women were forcibly shaved from head to toe, starved into submission, and subject to crippling medical experiments. The 'nicotine' colour of Elsa's dyed hair, a sign of the abject condition of survival, suggests an indelible stain, the lasting effect of continuous and various forms of torture, all working as a lethal poison, destroying basic capacities for restoration and regeneration. Holocaust survivor Jean Améry (Hans Mayer), who committed suicide years after liberation from Auschwitz, testifies: 'Whoever was tortured, stays tortured' (34).

To mark such suffering as unremitting, Elsa confesses that while she 'should' be crying for her dead husband, 'I've no more tears, Mr Smiley – I'm barren; the children of my grief are dead' (*CD*, 27). Smiley's 'vision' of her as a child forms his diagnosis of her remaining a 'half woman [. . .] ruthless in her fight for self-preservation [. . .] like George Sand's "Petite Fadette"', the girl so abused and fiercely defensive, she is a witch in the eyes of her townspeople (*CD*, 38). Co-ordinating individual and collective abuse, the novel positions Elsa as isolated from human development and devoid of family, community and belief in continuity with which she can identify or be identified.[33]

Le Carré creates an indefinite timeline – 'long ago' – that ironically alludes to fairy tales, for the context and substance of Elsa's depredations contravenes any suggestion of a happy ending for her. 'Long ago' only reminds us that for the Holocaust survivor, the passage of time cannot produce healing. Combined with no reference to a specific camp, Elsa is a Nazi victim, survivor and refugee, writ large. A disquieting, uncanny presence in the bifurcated Secret World of Britain and its enemy, the suffering Elsa allows no respite for herself and for readers. Her words and the narrator's offer no narrative or epistemological distance from World War II, the Cold War and the Holocaust. She remains both totally alienated and an intractable presence in the British historical consciousness of the novel. That she is murdered in a theatre attests to the unreality, the artificiality of her quest for justice. As she reminds Smiley of the liminal historical and narrative space that separates them, but which they share, 'sometimes the division between your world and ours is incomplete' (*CD*, 26). Tony Kushner analyses the ideological and historical connection between these worlds: 'the liberal democracies became directly connected to the antisemitic policies of the Third Reich through the reception or rejection of Jewish refugees' (*HLI*, 23). A spectre of the camps, the survivor unsettles the spy thriller's myth of the nation's righteous heroism and the genre's ethical realism. As Allan Hepburn observes, 'As a recurrent trope in spy narratives, ghosts signify ethical dilemmas that have no resolution [and] reintroduce unresolvable complexities. They represent nodes of unassimilable traumatic matter' (84).

Elsa's character disrupts the world of the Cold War spy thriller because her Holocaust story both limits and expands the genre's conventional and imaginative parameters.[34] With its specific references to concentration camp suffering and lingering aftereffects, the survivor's story enters debates about the limits of fictional Holocaust representation and critical interpretation. A major concern of these debates is that no matter how realistic its narrative style, fictional representation of the Shoah encourages historical revisionists who deny the veracity of its events. For example, Sara Horowitz cogently argues that 'the literary text – in avowing its own artifice, rhetoricity, and contingent symbol-making – threatens to shift and ultimately destroy the ground by which one measures one set of truth claims or one historical interpretation against another' (20).[35] While there is no remedy for Holocaust denial, many scholars accept representation and interpretation only if historical accuracy is maintained in the interest of providing consistent, verified versions of the event's actual occurrence. Elsa's story also embeds the problem of readers' empathy towards the suffering Holocaust subject. Scholars of Holocaust representation worry about readers inserting or substituting their own feelings and erasing the specific historical distances and distinctions between reader and representative victim.[36] Readers may feel pity and fear for the suffering Holocaust survivor, but contrary to Aristotle's claims for a resulting catharsis, Elsa's story fails to produce closure, resolution or exemplary lessons about citizenship or history. In this sense le Carré engages debates about whether the Holocaust has taught any lessons at all, when pleas for 'Never Again' have been silenced by continuing genocides.[37]

The survivor's story also extends le Carré's immersion in twentieth-century political history to question discrepancies between democratic ideologies of individual rights and pluralistic inclusion and the practices of nation-states that curtail membership. This discrepancy plays out in Elsa's impact on Smiley, who from their first interview, is haunted by her as 'a mystery and a power', imagining in her 'smile the light of her early innocence, and a steeled weapon in her fight for survival' (CD, 100, 38). By the end of the novel, when we learn that it was Elsa who was spying for the GDR and that she helped betray Samuel, her character unsettles the opposition between victim and villain that World War II had confirmed. She is both. A tortured survivor of Nazi Germany, she suffers once again in turning to Communism as the safeguard against the resurgence of oppressive German power:

> It was not a pretty sight for us, the new Germany. Old names had come back, names that had frightened us as children. The dreadful, plump pride returned,

you could see it even in the photographs in the papers, they marched with the old rhythm. (*CD*, 106)

Confirming her observations, le Carré's Introduction to his 1968 novel *A Small Town in Germany* provides a list of those old names working in the West German government of Konrad Adenauer:

> Herr Globke, who had had a hand in drafting Hitler's Nuremberg laws discriminating against the Jews, or [. . .] Herr Achenbach, who helped organise the deportation of French Jews from Paris, or the ebullient Herr Zegelmann, who [. . .] had been a high-ranking figure in the Hitler Youth. In the West German police, the judiciary, the intelligence fraternity, and the armed services, in industry and science and the teaching professions and, most particularly, in the bureaucracy, old Nazis abounded, either because they had done nothing for which they could be purged or because they had been deemed indispensable to West Germany's reconstruction. But most often because their cases had laid gathering dust in someone's drawer, filed and forgotten as part of a tacit agreement between partners to put the past behind us. (7–8)[38]

In *A Small Town in Germany* le Carré characterises the suspected double agent, Leo Harting, as a 'ghost', in part because he is only seen once, and as a distorted image through a telegraphic lens, but primarily because his survivor-refugee Jewish identity denies him subjectivity in a political climate of resurgent 'nationalist passions' (xii, xi). In le Carré's Cold War the Nazi past has not been forgotten by those who find its brutality a useful model. Mundt, an ex-Nazi who enjoys beating Jews, wields his sadistic skills serving East German Secret Intelligence in *Call for the Dead* and then reappears as a double agent working for Britain in *The Spy Who Came in from the Cold*. That this historical memory serves up a haunting lesson is only too apparent in a newspaper story Smiley reads, about 'the lynching of a Jewish shopkeeper in Düsseldorf', in the new West Germany (*CD*, 116). In either case for le Carré, in the GDR and Third Reich, state authorised barbarity is the norm, a foundational feature of their civilisations, a sign neither of exceptional nor compromised ethics.

In turning to Communism as a bulwark against a revival of Fascism, Elsa's reward is to be exploited and then murdered for her desperate idealism. Constitutive of her character, fate and story, the meanings of these oppositions lie in their fusion which negates the desirability or possibility of her redemption. Her story, in life and in murder, signifies the failure of redemption as an idea in the face of character being reduced to a tortured object. She never has an opportunity, nor do we know if she desired one, to explain her allegiance to a system that despite its oppositional promises, is as oppressive as Nazism. Smiley speculates:

> I think she dreamed of a world without conflict, ordered and preserved by the new doctrine. I once angered her, you see, and she shouted at me: 'I'm the wandering Jewess,' she said, 'the no-man's land, the battlefield of your toy soldiers.' As she saw the new Germany rebuilt in the image of the old, saw the plump pride return, as she put it, I think it was just too much for her; I think she looked at the futility of her suffering and the prosperity of her persecutors and rebelled. Five years ago [. . .] the re-establishment of Germany as a prominent western power was well under way. (*CD*, 155–6)

The opposition here between the desire for order and preservation and the uncanny figure of 'the wandering Jewess' summarises the significant role of the Jewish character in British spy fiction of the 1930s through to World War II, the Cold War and beyond. As depicted in novels by Eric Ambler, Frankau, Helen MacInnes and le Carré, the Jew ruptures the stable narrative of citizenship. In Storm Jameson's 1947 novel *The Black Laurel*, Heinrich Kalb, a German Jewish survivor, returns to Germany only to find himself reinstated in 'the depths of an exile covering centuries' (191). Suspected of having spied for Germany, his real crime is that 'every refugee is a traitor and the Jews doubly so' (*BL*, 146). Elizabeth Maslen notes Jameson's ironic portrayal of Kalb's illusory trust in British democracy: 'He has been a refugee in England, and has a touching faith in British fairness and compassion' (342). Showing that rescue from the Reich was most often in doubt, Maslen cites

> the case of a group of Jewish writers and academics who had fled to Prague from Germany and Austria, and who were now in danger of being trapped there. One of these was Max Hermann Jellinek, who had been a Jewish professor at the University of Vienna, one of at least thirteen, among them so valuable a writer as Bernhard Menne whose book 'Krupp' not long ago has found a warm appreciation in this country. (244)

In her searing essay, 'We Refugees', Hannah Arendt reminds us that 'being a Jew does not give any legal status in this world [. . .] I can hardly imagine an attitude more dangerous, since we actually live in a world in which [. . .] society has discovered discrimination as the great social weapon by which one may kill men without any bloodshed' (273). Arendt's generalised word choices, 'society' and 'social weapon', remind us that in 1943, when her essay was written, all efforts to rescue the Jews, from the Evian conference in July 1938 onwards, had disintegrated as a result of social indifference and complicity.[39] In perpetual exile, over the course of history and legend, the Jews' wandering questions the ideologies and structures that preserve political, cultural and social order, whether in Central European, British societies or in modernist fiction and conventional spy thrillers. Regardless of historical documentation, Jews are judged as lacking national loyalty and are therefore suspect as citizens. They are all too often considered diseased, deformed, abnormal – in short, 'lepers'.[40] Hannah Arendt depicts the double bind that entraps European Jews in 1943:

> If patriotism were a matter of routine or practice, we should be the most patriotic people in the world [. . .] But since patriotism is not yet believed to be a matter of practice, it is hard to convince people of the sincerity of our repeated transformations [. . .] The natives, confronted with such strange beings as we are, become suspicious; from their point of view, as a rule, only a loyalty to our old countries is understandable. That makes life very bitter for us [. . .] Our so frequently suspected loyalty of today has a long history. It is the history of 150 years of assimilated Jewry who performed an unprecedented feat: though proving all the time their non-Jewishness, they succeeded in remaining Jews all the same.[41] ('We Refugees', 272–3)

Arendt's bitterly ironic voice, pitting 'we' against 'The natives', addresses both as rhetorically and politically irreconcilable. Mocking the mystifying perception of Jews as 'strange' discloses that in both historical and cultural constructs, assimilation does not mean acceptance of Jews as 'human beings' in any unqualified and integrated sense of legal, social or economic invitation to belong wherever they reside for however long or short ('WR', 265).[42] Rather assimilation is only another form of wandering, from one disorienting, unacceptable symbolic, mythic and political position to another. No longer different but never the same, Jews remain threatening in their fluid, inconstant relation to the nation and its dominant culture. In the cutting words of Arendt's good friend Mary McCarthy, 'the 'Wandering Jew [. . .] is the archetypal exile, sentenced to trail about the earth until the second coming' (qtd in Gluzman, 235). Whether by choice or expulsion, Jewish wandering is attributed to an ontological condition. In turn, this displacement both supports and questions what it means for Jews to be human in thrillers from the run-up to Nazi domination, through the Holocaust and on through the Cold War.

In le Carré's fiction, Jewish refugees are like spies. Simultaneously visible and invisible in their places of origin and those to which they migrate, they are endangered if they are recognised and threatening if undetectable. In their efforts to integrate anywhere, in their disguises as citizens, their nature becomes manifold, constituting an excess of categories of being. Protean creatures, they are therefore mysterious. They occupy a no man's land between humanity and monstrousness. Valued for their talents, they are reviled for being profligate and craven in their utility. Constructed as essentially suspect, duplicitous in their use of false, forged or changing identity papers, appearances and national identities, they can expect no protection from any State. Historically, response to the Jews' positions as stateless refugees 'was essentially ambivalent as humanitarian sympathy and economic self-interest, international solidarity and ethnic prejudice all intertwined' (Kushner, *HLI*, 46). Perennial outliers, le Carré's Jews and espionage agents question the nature of liberal ideologies as well as citizenship and its stability as documentary evidence of belonging, integration, State legitimacy and protection.

We feel the effects of duplicitous ideologies in the historical representation of Elsa's fury at Britain's hypocrisies and at Germany's resurgent power. That she was born in Dresden is no narrative coincidence, for it represents dual betrayals. It was fire-bombed by the Allies, when an estimated 135,000 people and the city's core were destroyed, and became part of East Germany in the post-war period.[43] Whatever their ideological differences, Britain and all of Germany, from West to East, deceive her. Her life and her character cannot escape alienation, as we witness it, from Maston's antisemitic slurs to the treachery of Dieter Frey, her Jewish GDR handler. As critiqued by Ambler, when Jews appear only as antisemitic caricatures and in comments by characters of significance, slurs are endowed with authority, as though the truths they are assumed to contain can therefore be taken at face value. In effect, for these writers, stories of the endangered Jew reveal a moral vacuity on the part of those who ignore, dismiss or remain indifferent to Jewish persecution. But whether in silence or expressed, this moral void is not merely rhetorical. From the trains crisscrossing Central Europe to the alleyways of Nuremberg and Berlin and dead-ending in London, the normative consequence for the wandering Jew is exploitation, displacement, torture, abandonment and murder.[44] Extending this representation and its consequences, it is no wonder that any and all of the diverse forms of Jewish life and culture are absent from these narratives. Reading this absence in relation to le Carré's dystopian topography inscribes a memory trace of Jewish decimation that strains to be represented in the timorous and haunting character of Elsa Fennan. Beginning with Ambler, the inclusion of wandering Jews and their stories as subject to historical catastrophe unsettles the restoration of faith in a well-ordered, homogeneous society and a satisfying conclusion in spy fiction.

The wandering Jew and stories about Jewish persecution also extend to the gendered political terrain and historical memory of British spy thrillers. If, as Elsa laments, she is 'the no-man's land, the battlefield of your toy soldiers', then, as her generalised metaphors indicate, she is also, like women civilians in all wars, the unacknowledged victim of men's continuous battle for supremacy.[45] Her identity as a Jewish survivor of the Holocaust and an East German spy marks her as a perpetual refugee who remains unwanted and abandoned, without official or unofficial protection from any European state or in Britain. There is no plotting in spy thrillers that can save her. Allan Hepburn's point about spies' essential abjection applies to Elsa: they 'express ambivalence about whether death prowls the world or lurks in the body. Fear of death and fear of being caught motivate spies' actions' (xvi). Despite having survived the Holocaust, Elsa embodies death. She contravenes interpretations that, in Eva Hoffman's analysis, idealise exile, that consider it 'morally heroic, even glamorous' (57) or as Guy Stern proffers, 'signal[s] the triumph of life over threatened death or confinement' (368). Subject to her dreams of peace at a time when 'Peace is a dirty word', as Smiley remarks, and subject to the men she believes will activate a peaceful future, she becomes their expendable weapon of war (CD, 156). She possesses no power of her own; except, like Freud's 'uncanny', her presence defamiliarises that which is taken for granted as ordinary in the Secret World. What we see of her in Smiley's descriptions and therefore in his reactions, is a discarded shell of a woman, one of the living dead. She metonymically represents the throbbing, unhealed historical memory, not only of World War II but of its precursor, in the iconic 'no-man's land', World War I. Like so many of the ghost women in Elizabeth Bowen's World War II fiction, Elsa is an example of a dispossessed victim of twentieth-century wars that leave these women haunting the very ideas of home and homeland and their traditional promises of protection. Mocking male militarism as 'toy soldiers' recalls Virginia Woolf's satire of war, in *Three Guineas*, as a cavalcade of male power embellished with medals of heroic victory.

One of the bitter ironies embedded in Elsa's enraged indictment is that the men who have interrogated, exploited, abused and murdered her operate in secret, as unquestioning, unselfconscious and unrecognisable soldiers. They battle underground, with deception their weapon and adorned only with the drab uniform of disguise. Lethal 'toy soldiers' nonetheless. Smiley's work and by extension, that of the novel and its readers, is to try to 'understand her suffering and her frightened lies', but also to recognise that what we can ultimately 'know of her' is 'Nothing' (CD, 40). Within, and despite the focus on Samuel Fennan's death, Elsa's elusiveness is the novel's core mystery and therefore refutes the notion that the war waged by both sides 'is nothing but a self-referential game [. . .] revealing the emptiness at the core of the Cold War' (Horn, 262). Instead, in this novel, the core of the Cold War is filled with World War II and the Holocaust, both of which have emptied Elsa of self-definition. This is why her repeated interviews produce only oblique responses and ghostly, dystopian atmospherics, obliterating any resemblance to a 'game'. Yet her uncanny presence becomes a powerful force, haunting and determining the novel's historical consciousness as an object of never-ending mourning for the lost.

Dystopian Homeland

Ghost meets ghost in Smiley's encounter with Elsa Fennan. When he feels 'safe and warm' in his London taxi it is because safety is 'unreal' and he wanders his city as a 'ghost' (*CD*, 15). Although Elsa lives in suburban Surrey, this is no green and pleasant land. Nor is the Home County any sort of home for this stateless phantom. Instead, as we learn from two pages of description, efforts to win 'a relentless battle against the stigma of suburbia' and create 'an appearance of weathered antiquity' have only produced the look of dystopian decay (*CD*, 23). While the commercial opportunism of estate agents may be the nominal culprit in this enterprise, the path to Elsa's adopted home reeks with an organic compost of the dead decaying in an abandoned battleground: the meaning of home in Home Counties 'degenerates into a sad little mud track' at the centre of which 'is a cannibal hut with a thatched roof called '"The War Memorial Shelter", erected in 1951 in grateful memory to the fallen of two wars, as a haven for the weary and old' (*CD*, 23–4). This is a desiccated monument that cannot shelter anyone, dead or alive, victims or survivors, from the wars that feed upon each other. In bleak concert, the Fennans' home is described in Gothic Expressionist tropes: 'an air of neglect, even disuse [a] dark, restless house', as though it shivers with fright (*CD*, 24, 29). The house personifies the war Elsa still suffers and that has bled into another, as she admonishes Smiley: 'You dropped a bomb from the sky: don't come down here and look at the blood, or hear the scream' (*CD*, 27). Elsa Fennan is the undead embodied memory and key witness to the atrocities that cannot be acknowledged and inscribed in the nation's war memorials.[46] For Elsa, there was no Allied victory over Fascism. Her direct address to Smiley, in a voice of desperation, resonates with 'Much of the original exile literature [that] is structured by a quest: to bear testimony to Nazi horror, to arouse rescuers, and in later texts, to alert the world to the possibility of its recurrence' (Stern, 330). Elsa must be discarded, however, to erase the failure of historical memory and commemorations as tributes to a nation's heroism, now lost, along with its soldiers. More broadly, her spectral figure suggests the failure of the idea that urban renewal or the new home for the post-war domesticated woman can reflect the lessons of wars past and present and be regenerative.

Le Carré paints London as a ruin, a Gothic Expressionist battleground darkened by memories of two World Wars, the ghostliness of which pervades the underground machinations of Cold War intrigue. The home front has been destroyed as are its corollaries like homeland. In 1961, the characters respond to the mystery of Samuel Fennan's death as though they are under siege, one could say *entrenched* in an endless and boundless war, expanding the idea of 'no-man's land' to include the ghosts of World War II and the Holocaust. Throughout the novel every danger that confronts Smiley and from which he cannot protect himself is accompanied by rain and darkness, even in the light of day. Needless to say, upon Smiley's arrival at Elsa's house, 'It was raining heavily, driving cold rain, so cold it felt hard upon the face' (CD, 24). Raindrops recall bullets. All of London, from upmarket Chelsea where Smiley lives to Whitehall's seats of power and beyond, is represented as a war-torn dystopia twenty years after the Blitz. One investigation takes Smiley and Mendel to a scrap yard in Battersea which is situated

> between two dilapidated pre-fabs in an uncertain row of hutments erected on the bomb site. Rubble, clinker, and refuse lay everywhere. Bits of asbestos, timber, and old iron, presumably acquired by [the suspicious] Mr Scarr for resale or adaptation, were piled in a corner, dimly lit by the pale glow which came from the farther pre-fab [...] three or four pre-war cars in various stages of dilapidation became dimly discernible. (CD, 54)

Inhering in the novel's overall dystopian atmosphere, adaptation here suggests entropy, not renewal. This is an ashen site of devolution. The shards that litter the yard are irreconcilable, at odds with each other, in anxious juxtaposition. It is as though these broken objects express the characters' isolation from each other and from acquiring recognition from the State. They all exist in ubiquitous loneliness. Nothing here can be salvaged or combined to build anything resembling a productive future, including the owner of the scrap yard, aptly named Adam Scarr. Dressed in army boots and 'threadbare' clothing, as though permanently damaged by a state of expulsion into the ravages of continuing warfare, this Adam is the opposite of generative humanity (CD, 55). As the asbestos residue indicates, danger lurks in his yard: the fire retardant is a carcinogen. Because the material signs of war are everywhere, signalling the spilling over of one war into another, the unspecified 'pre-war' is so long ago and far away that its fairytale setting is self-mocking; it has become a ruin like the scarred warscape. This is the site where Smiley is attacked, 'broken like rock; cracked and split into fragments', a human shard, the victim of a war that will not end (CD, 58).

Even Smiley's house loses its promise of safe harbour when it is invaded by premonitory menace. Early in the novel when Smiley returns home, an interloper appears in the window as 'a shadow', recognisable as a 'human form' but unidentifiable (*CD*, 46). Sharply honed spycraft is no protection against this ineffable peril. That villainy should appear on the inside of Smiley's house indicates that for a spy, the traditional meaning of home is an oxymoron. It represents neither physical nor emotional refuge; it is always subject to the determination of externally produced and disguised imperatives. Home becomes a battleground where Smiley, like Elsa, is caught in a no-man's land between the intrigues of both the foreign enemy and home-grown betrayal. The boundaries between private and public domains are erased. The stranger within mirrors Smiley's estrangement from home and the protective guarantees of his British loyalties and citizenship. Smiley can't even claim his home as his. Frozen in fear, on his own doorstep, the seasoned agent must turn to primal, unschooled instincts of self-preservation to free himself from the dangerous delay of deliberation. As Allan Hepburn maintains, 'the spy dwells in the cleavage between rationality and corporeality' (14). In Smiley's case, danger necessitates that body and mind combine forces to produce a visceral, overwhelming mistrust of any bifurcated sense of self. Not that combining mind and body produces coherence, but rather a reminder that each owes allegiance to the other, sending signals to recognise and respond to menace. Otherwise, he is stuck on the threshold between his romantic belief in the authority of personal conscience and the political self-interest that erases guarantees of individual freedom. While seemingly opposing goals, self-preservation and the search for truth cohere in producing a state of gendered, political and narrative disorientation for the spy. The villain inside Smiley's house casts a shadow of doubt over all conventional expectations of British stability, including moral, ideological and patriotic certainty. In particular, the scene creates an existential doubt from which Smiley's otherwise doggedly righteous character cannot escape, foreshadowing his excruciatingly ambivalent response to defeating his nemesis.

All this uncertainty should come as no surprise. This is the house he has shared with his wayward wife Ann; it is haunted by betrayal, offering neither respite nor rejuvenation. Instead the house suggestively aligns her with the deceptions of his antagonists. Like the 'human form' in the window, she exists as a shadowy presence, but a powerfully determining one. Present only fleetingly, she contributes to the narrative's refusal to offer a consoling emotional and ethical resolution. Filtered through Smiley's memories of her charms, nightmares of her perfidy and romantic hopes for reconciliation, her absent presence agitates the male-ordered Secret World. A rebellious angel of the hearth, she is adrift from domesticity and its marital norms, a revisionary role confirmed by le Carré's assessment: 'where others might simply leer or lust [...] she acts, and that is a more honest way to behave than to live a repressive and voyeuristic sort of life' (qtd in Vaughan, 58). Although Ann returns intermittently to Smiley, there is never any indication that she values the home they share or that it could represent stability or self-determination for her. Home has neither meaning nor utility for Ann. Unlike Evelyn Waugh's Brideshead or Daphne du Maurier's Manderley, Ann's decaying ancestral home (in Cornwall, like Manderley) and aristocratic heritage will yield neither lyrical nostalgia nor Gothic melodrama; it can't even produce a ghost, much less an heir. As though suffering from an overdose of entropy, Sercomb Manor is on the verge of total collapse: 'The house stood on a hill, in a coppice of bare elms still waiting for the blight. It was granite and very big, and crumbling,' with 'acres of smashed greenhouses' and 'collapsed stables' (*Smiley's People*, 333). Such description buries the idea that the ancestral manor represents a viable English cultural tradition. The Sercomb estate has no more coherence or value than the ashen junk yard where Smiley is attacked or the War Memorial near the Fennan home. As the heir to an ancestral heap, and as she floats in and out of all the Smiley novels, Ann's position in the novel suggests that the place for women in the gendered literary culture of spy fiction is narrative discontinuity and displacement.

If Ann possesses all the fatal attractions of the genre's femme fatale, her character is not drawn as villainous in itself. Instead, her elusiveness signals uncontained and demanding desire, an autonomous wilfulness related to her aristocratic status and style. Sue Harper argues that since 'the Regency' and extending to 'Second World War film culture [...] the exiled aristocrat has been a potent symbol of marginality and energy' ('Years', 206). The aristocratic woman in wartime British film, like Ann during the Cold War, 'engages her own destiny' ('Years', 206). Christine Gledhill's analysis of transgressive women in wartime costume melodrama applies to Ann's refusal 'to sink her individuality within the collective. She is a home breaker not a home stabilizer [...]' ('An Abundance', 223). Ann's free-floating lifestyle signals a rejection of national loyalty as well as ideology at a time when national identity was associated with opposing political systems. She also signals the danger encompassing the entire narrative and which, like her character, cannot be constrained. While Ann's presence remains obscured, the apprehension it suggests emerges in full force as embodied by Elsa Fennan. Equally elusive in many ways, but robbed of any heritage or space of belonging, not to mention sex appeal or sexuality, Elsa materialises as the subject and object of political and personal terror from which no home is safe. Both stability and self-determination are voided in Elsa's experience. She has been made homeless by Nazism, the Holocaust and her Cold War work for the GDR. Exiled from the Edenic promises of East German Communism, she is killed by Dieter Frey, a stand-in for the snake who tempted her with the forbidden knowledge transmitted by espionage. She belongs nowhere, a state that defines her as a threat both to the British and to East German historical memory. In Elsa's case as in Ann's, the combination of enforced and chosen elusiveness and untamed inconstancy constitutes their femininity, gendering political danger. Smiley's responses to both women reflect back on his own gendered vulnerabilities against which he struggles in his search for the truth but without which there is no truth, as multivalent and entrapping as that may be.[47]

With both women betraying their secret agent spouses, Elsa and Ann expose the home as an anomaly in espionage fiction. Instead of support, the home harbours suspicion, betrayal and alienation. This novel questions 'the belief that the sense of home was ever an immediate experience of being there', but rather, as Benjamin Robinson argues, 'is mediated by relations of power, gender, and race' (179). The home's mythic, psychological and cultural associations with maternal fecundity and nurture are subverted by the depiction of both women as childless. The world of espionage is no place for regeneration. A microcosm of the British Secret World, the Fennan and Smiley households are fertile grounds for only self-deluded trust in both the language and behaviour attributed to loyalty, decency and the greater good. There is no hierarchy among these betrayals, only interchanges of mutual deception that in intensifying persistence, form the essential core of le Carré's fiction. Where hierarchy does appear, and to critical effect, is in the comparative political and class positions of Elsa and Ann. Despite her despoiled home, Ann's privileged position as upper-class Englishwoman allows her to choose transience. The only choice Elsa's refugee identity and position offer her is to recapitulate the betrayal to which she is subjected.

Exiled into the Fog of War

> If you caught an enemy spy, your conscience was clear; you were entitled to hang the wretch on the nearest tree. But what about the spies you employed? Was your association with them compatible with the spirit of the code [of honour]?' (Eric Ambler, 'Introduction', *To Catch a Spy*, 8–9)

That betrayal may be integral to the search for truth and its nature brings the novel to its climactic confrontation between Smiley and his nemesis, Dieter Frey. A charismatic figure, Byronesque with his dark good looks and 'deformed' leg, Dieter had been Smiley's student and then anti-Nazi recruit (*CD*, 92). At first, however, Smiley doubts that Dieter can be a trusted agent: 'There was a fierce independence, a ruthlessness about him', expressing a 'defensiveness [that] derived not only from his deformity, but his race, which was Jewish' (*CD*, 92). Smiley's initial reservations include Dieter's 'firebrand' socialism which, combined with his Jewish identity at a time of 'intolerance run mad', made him an obvious Nazi target and therefore a security risk for British Intelligence (*CD*, 95, 91). But referring to Jewish identity as a 'race' also alludes to the more general antisemitic designation from which the Jew cannot escape in any of le Carré's locales. In this sense, Dieter's representation also leans towards the critical problem that Jews represent an alterity that transcends time and place, as French Jewish scholar Alain Finkielkraut poses:

> The foreignness of Jews is a kind of difference unlike others. They are 'those people' whom no label fits, whether assigned by the Gaze, the Concept or the State [. . .] It's an insubstantial difference that resists definition [. . .] are they a people? A religion? A nation? All these categories apply, but none is adequate in itself. (164)

The novel situates its critical response to this conundrum as erupting in 1938, in response to Dieter's condemnation of Nazism.

A crucial year in the consolidation of Nazi antisemitism, it was on 9 November that Hitler launched *Kristallnacht*, the pogrom that previewed the decimation of Europe's Jewish population and culture. It is in that year that Smiley finds himself caught between personal conviction and performing as dispassionate teacher and recruiter, 'an enlightened man', unwilling and unable to reveal his own politics (*CD*, 93). Although the scene takes place in summer 1938, le Carré's 1961 perspective embeds the troubling memory of *Kristallnacht*. Smiley's necessary and pragmatic evasions support Britain's contradictory claims to uphold enlightenment and democratic principles while concealing condemnation of Nazism behind the liberal rhetoric of 'artistic freedom' (*CD*, 93). For Dieter, this academic cliché obfuscates the Nazis' destruction of political freedom, as dramatised the next time Smiley sees him – a prisoner of the Gestapo:

> He had not changed. He was the same improbable romantic with the magic of a charlatan; the same unforgettable figure which had struggled over the ruins of Germany, implacable of purpose, satanic in fulfillment, dark and swift like the Gods of the North [. . .] Dieter *was* out of proportion, his cunning, his conceit, his strength and his dream – all were larger than life, undiminished by the moderating influence of experience. He was a man who thought and acted in absolute terms, without patience or compromise. (*CD*, 131)

The language through which Smiley's response is focalised represents Dieter as a monstrously monumental embodiment of Nazi racial and gendered ideology. The persecuted Jew has metamorphosed from despised racialised pariah to its revered opposite: from *untermensch* or subhuman into the apotheosis of Nazism's Nordic mythic hero. Despite his physical and emotional resemblance, however, Dieter defies the romantic darkness of another vengeful outsider, Emily Brontë's Heathcliff.[48] In dialectical terms, the oppositions between Nazism's dreams of a Master Race and its victimised enemy have synthesised into an uncanny and hideous mongrel – the Jewish *ubermensch* or Superman who defies and defeats his enemy by becoming him. With his crippled leg, suggestive of the devil's cloven foot, and in his turn to Communism, Dieter's character reflects a corrosive Faustian bargain. Oppressor and oppressed have merged, begging the question, what is a Jew in this post-Holocaust Cold War spyscape?[49] The template of Freudian defence mechanisms is helpful here: Dieter Frey wreaks revenge on Nazi brutality by incorporating the masculinist militarism of the aggressor and escaping into Nazism's enemy system – Communism. Communism, however, only exploits his aggression; instead of safe harbour, it becomes another form of exile from history. The Holocaust victim expresses the Holocaust past that East Germany never acknowledges.[50] In London, Dieter is in exile, but in East Germany he is displaced from the Holocaust. Dieter represents how the opposition between Nazism and Communism collapses into a crucible of destruction.

Smiley's vision does not reject Dieter; revulsion co-exists with reverie and empathy: 'Memories returned to Smiley [. . .] memories of dangers shared, of mutual trust when each had held in his hand the life of the other [. . .]' (*CD*, 131). Sharing contested ideological ground, theirs is the most emotionally intense relationship in the novel and the one that ends with the greatest sense of personal and political betrayal.[51] Like le Carré's quote with which this chapter begins, Smiley's impassioned response to Dieter shelves detachment as a viable response to the enmeshing of personal and political desire. Instead, as the conclusion reveals, this entanglement forecloses resolution, reconciliation and victory. Enveloped in a 'thick and yellow' fog, the final chase to capture Dieter Frey questions the moral high ground to be claimed by British Secret Intelligence for the defeat of the East German spymaster (*CD*, 135).[52] Although there is never any doubt about Dieter's villainy, especially after he murders Elsa and is about to 'hit Mendel a [second] hard, brutal blow with the pistol', Smiley's response exposes a passionate attachment to the assassin more determining than calculated spy craft:

Smiley ran at him blindly, forgetting what little skill he had ever possessed, swinging with his short arms, striking with his open hands. His head was against Dieter's chest and he pushed forward, punching Dieter's back and sides. He was mad and, discovering in himself the energy of madness [...] was shouting at Dieter; 'Swine, swine!' [...] Smiley beat frantically at his arms, and then [...] Dieter was falling, falling into the swirling fog beneath the bridge, and there was silence. No shout, no splash. He was gone; offered like a human sacrifice to the London fog and the foul black river lying beneath it. (CD, 141)

The zeal with which Smiley beats Dieter complicates a verdict of justifiable self-defence. Shouting 'Swine' translates the German *Schwein* into English, casting doubt on British liberal tolerance. In both languages the epithet degrades Jewish identity and culture by conflating their presumed filthy and bestial nature and the animal their dietary laws forbid. With overdetermined suggestiveness, 'Swine' also recalls Orwell's 1945 depiction in *Animal Farm*, of the villainous and victimised pigs, an opposition that coalesces in a satire of the descent of Marxist idealism into Stalinist Fascism. The attraction and revulsion of this political trajectory are embodied by Smiley's relationship with Dieter. At the same time that Smiley batters Dieter to save himself and Mendel, he also embraces him. Entangling his body with his adversary's reveals Smiley's irreconcilable political and emotional ambivalence towards his agent-enemy. What has been sacrificed is a double-sided fantasy. From one perspective, personal loyalty would transcend the *realpolitik* of political betrayal. The mirror image of this perspective is the political fantasy that the protection of Britain's democratic ideals justifies the sacrifice of personal loyalty.

Like the bonded antipathy between Matthew Gilroy and Blessington, the divide between Smiley's and Dieter's political positions remains inviolable but entwined with a history of war that overwhelms all other relationships in the novel. Like Robert Louis Stevenson's James and Henry Durie in *The Master of Ballantrae*, Feraud and D'Hubert in Conrad's 1908 story *The Duel* and Alexander Dumas' Corsican brothers, the everlasting battle between two male protagonists performs an erotically charged love–hate relationship that transcends time and place and their conflict. I term the men's bond homo-political, adapting Eve K. Sedgwick's theory of 'homosocial desire' or the erotically charged triangular rivalry between persons of the same sex for another. For Sedgwick, the bond between rivals in an erotic triangle is far more determining than that between either of the lovers and the beloved.[53] The novel, however, does not construct this bond as identifying homo-political desire with a particular political system in the way that homosexuality is sometimes fictionally tethered to Fascism as the expression of a narcissistic combination of sadism and self-loathing.[54] The political antipathies between Smiley and Dieter entwine to produce a deadly symbiosis. Homo-political bonding transfigures the gritty, mean streets of Gothic Expressionist wars into political allegory. All of these duellists fight a never-ending war that ultimately engulfs them and which, in its peripatetic battles, exiles them from the very idea of national causes and allegiances.

Le Carré, however, is not content to stay the course of political ambiguity. The combination of rage and despair with which Smiley beats Dieter registers a profound sense of betrayal compared to which the ongoing pain of Ann's serial infidelities pales. The marriage that was always more mirage than reality is superseded by a series of homo-political relationships in le Carré's fiction whose main attraction and the core of the Secret World may very well be the inevitability of betrayal. As Holly Beth King notes, le Carré's spy's world produces 'paranoia' as 'the appropriate reaction to all external signs [...] There seems no longer any chance for security, for trust, anywhere' (87).[55] Ann's presence is persistently overshadowed by the treacherous relationships formed and deformed in the boys' public school codes, as they determine the protected class hierarchies of the Circus and the nature of British citizenship and belonging.[56] The insularity of this power structure exposes the rot that links the Circus to the decaying status of the Sercomb aristocratic pile and the war monument near the Fennans' home. Le Carré dissected the treacherous hold of class mythologies on British nationhood in his Introduction to a study of the British double agent, Kim Philby:

> SIS would not merely *defend* the traditional decencies of our society; it would embody them. Within its own walls, its clubs and country houses, in whispered luncheons with its secular contacts, it would enshrine the mystical entity of a vanishing England. Here at least, whatever went on in the big world outside, England's flower would be cherished. *'The Empire may be crumbling; but within our secret élite, the clean-limbed tradition of English power would survive. We believe in nothing but ourselves.'* (15)

Contrary to the theme of Elgar's triumphant *Banner of St George*, George Smiley discovers that instead of saving his nation and its citizens, his missions are designed to protect the borders of a mythic, self-enclosed England. The threat consists of what Hannah Arendt described as stories of 'real experiences that make [the] flesh creep', stories embodied by the likes of Elsa Fennan, survivors of Europe's recent cataclysms who must be kept at bay so that the fabled nationality of the English survives for its chosen few ('We Refugees', 266). As le Carré's Smiley novels reveal, the 'cherished' myth of inherited tradition and citizenship would marginalise the very agent of the nation's survival – the wandering spy, George Smiley. As a focalising subject, Smiley resembles a reader of traditional spy thrillers, but one who becomes disoriented by the intrusion of historical contingency into the mythic structures of righteous victory and national heroism. In this novel and as we shall see in *The Spy Who Came in from the Cold*, Holocaust experience and memory produce Jewish villains who are victimised by their reliance for justice on betraying political myths, both British and Communist.

Like Dieter Frey and Elsa Fennan, many Jews and intellectuals, according to Stephen Spender, were attracted to Communism when '[t]heir assumption that they were living in a world where intolerance was decreasing was shattered by the triumph of Hitlerism' (*God*, 243). In the work that proved to be 'one of the Cold War's most audacious cultural interventions', Arthur Koestler analyses his commitment to Communism as 'clinging to the last shred of the torn illusion [of] the Soviet myth' (James Smith, 144; *The God that Failed*, 74).[57]

> [T]he only thing that mattered was to fight against Nazism and the threatening war. I did not know that it was a shadow fight in which *we* were the shadows [. . .]But we never tired of telling each other – and ourselves – that [. . .] the Communist Party was [. . .] the vanguard of the Proletariat, the incarnation of the will of History itself [. . .] The only dialectically correct attitude was to remain inside, shut your mouth tight, swallow your bile and wait for the day when after the defeat of the enemy and the victory of the World Revolution, Russia and the Comintern were ready to become democratic institutions. (Koestler, *God*, 65–6)[58]

In his contribution to *The God that Failed*, journalist Louis Fischer testifies how his attraction to Communism as a bulwark against Nazism turned to 'disenchantment' with the Moscow trials of 1936–1938 when 'ubiquitous fear [. . .] had killed revolt, silenced protest, and destroyed civil courage. In place of dedication [and] living spirit, dead conformism, bureaucratic formalism, and the parroting of false clichés' (Fischer, 211, 217).[59] Taking sides, but with a sly touch of hesitation, le Carré admits: 'I do believe, reluctantly, that we must combat communism. Very decisively'; his Cold War novels never hesitate to highlight its villainy (qtd in Gross, 33). Aligned with this condemnation, *Call for the Dead* shows total contempt for the hypocritical governance in Cambridge Circus that endangers the democratic principles and institutions it is designed to protect. Because of bureaucratic self-interest and self-deception, the nation's defensive postures and strategies become part of the pervasive peril it faces. The nation is entrapped in its own duplicities.

The inevitability of political iniquity applies to the contradictory relationship between the spy's moral consciousness and the necessary but problematic place of the Jew in the Secret World. The bonding of Smiley and Dieter disturbs fictional categories of the spy and the Jew. Dieter's malevolence and Jewishness and Smiley's judiciousness and marginalisation serve as critical interventions that trouble any generic or conventional depiction of villain and victim. Just as Dieter Frey collapses distinctions between oppressed and oppressor, so the righteous Smiley has absorbed the very ideology he loathes, sharing racialist constitutions of self and other, citizen and stateless exile. His violent outburst at Dieter erases the analytical logic and study of causality to which he has committed his service. Instead it reverberates with collusion, as unwilling as this might be, with the self-deception necessary to construct an enemy to destroy. Anti-Communism leads to moral obfuscation, where the good man is forced to do evil on behalf of another ghostly dream. At the end, there is no defence against Smiley's shock and the mystery of his own behaviour, his complicity in implementing violent justice.[60]

The blinding fog that envelops the scene of Smiley's battle with Dieter, combined with the foul river into which Dieter's body falls, proclaims a revisionary narrative. The spy thriller fantasy has morphed into a narrative critique that destabilises conventional antecedents of hero and villain in order to represent a secret nation threatened by the betrayal inherent in its ambivalences. Erin Carlston shows how such ambivalence is expressed in Cold War rhetoric that represents Jews, Communists and homosexuals as linked in their physiological, social and political threat to the health of the nation:

> Secretive, conspiratorial, physically and psychically unhealthy, exotic, intellectual, and well educated, urban, individually weak but collectively powerful, alien, deviant and treacherous; this is the idiom of several centuries' worth of antisemitism, operating in the 1950s to 'Jewify' Communists and homosexuals while largely ignoring, or even explicitly exempting, Jews themselves. (218)[61]

Trapped in a double bind – as victim of Fascist and liberal antisemitism and as villainous agent of Fascist Communism – the Jew in *Call for the Dead* rhetorically manifests the Englishman's moral and political anguish. After all, what we know of Dieter Frey's character is filtered through George Smiley's responses. From beginning to end, there is no narrative access to the Jew's interiority. Whatever his moral and political consciousness might consist of, however complicated it is likely to be, is shrouded in his disappearance, as when he kills Elsa, or in an attack so sudden and terrifying, the narrator's language retreats into a dehumanising simile: 'bursting [...] out of the night fog [...] like a massive wild beast' (CD, 140). It is as though there is no precise language through which to represent the Jewish Holocaust survivor as both villain and victim. The only time we hear Dieter speak is in Smiley's recollection of his rant against political detachment. Animated by Smiley's self-doubt, the memory constructs Dieter's political commitment as an impassioned and monolithic mind-set that opposes his mentor's ambivalent detachment. He is silent but, despite his death, a menacing survivor. In this sense, Jews are not victims but participate in the Holocaust survivor's drama of bearing witness as an agent of narrative violence. In turn, this agency tests Smiley's moral position and decentralises that of the novel. Because Smiley's reactions are presented in the form of free indirect discourse, entwining the spy's representations with those of the narrator, a multifaceted critical perspective emerges, mediating between antisemitic suspicion and sympathetic doubt. The rhetorical effect is to confirm the Jew's liminal position in British spy fiction.

That the representation of the Jew is a compelling issue in le Carre's fiction is confirmed by his response to the charge of antisemitism:

> All my life, ever since I started writing, because of the extraordinary childhood I had – the early introduction to the refugee problem in central Europe and what not – I have been fascinated, enchanted, drawn to and horrified by the plight of middle European Jews. It has infected my writing – book number one, book number three, *The Spy Who Came in from the Cold*, I could go on. It is the one issue in my own life on which I may say I have a clean record. (qtd in Plimpton, 157)

In *Call for the Dead* and elsewhere in le Carre's fiction, Jews are necessary to the Cold War espionage plot, but as unassimilable, permanent exiles and ghostly survivors, they remain constant in questioning the viability of narrative and moral resolution in spy fiction from the 1930s throughout World War II and the Cold War. Although their wandering over time and place lends itself to mythmaking, Jewish experiences of exile create a historical template for reading twentieth-century fiction.

Espionage as Exile: *The Spy Who Came in from the Cold*

> 'I equally detest the notion that our spies are uniformly immaculate, omniscient, and beyond the vulgar criticism of those who not only pay for their existence, but on occasion are taken to war on the strength of concocted intelligence.' (John le Carré, qtd in Copping, Farmer and Dixon)

> 'Certainly when I saw the Berlin Wall going up [...] I conceived that story, *The Spy Who Came in from the Cold* [...] I was determined that [Alec Leamas and Liz Gold] would be killed at the wall [...] It's the Gothic gloom that takes over in me at some point.' (qtd in Plimpton, 159)

Painted with 'Gothic gloom', the Berlin Wall in *The Spy Who Came in from the Cold* portends dystopian doom. Although London is also depicted as a threatening spyscape in *Call for the Dead*, it is a site of moral epiphany and ambiguous rescue for its British agent, George Smiley. No such luck for Alec Leamas and Liz Gold. By the time they decipher the ethical entanglements of their entrapping missions, it is too late and too far. Their fates represent the dead end of exile from Britain's promises to protect its citizens. Trapped in East Germany, they are stateless, with no protection; their British citizenship is a liability. Despite the defeat of Fascism two decades earlier, they resemble Ambler's 1930s refugee protagonist, Vadassy, in *Epitaph for a Spy*, caught between exploitation by the West and a doomed fate at the hands of Fascist Central Europe. In the logic of le Carré's dystopian geography, the victimisation of Leamas and Liz can only occur on the Fascist Communist side of the wall to highlight the West's duplicity. As the unfolding narrative builds its arguments, it underscores Control's contradictory rationalisation as the cover for the West's abandonment of its democratic ideals:

> 'Of course, we occasionally do very wicked things'; he grinned like a schoolboy [. . .] 'I would say that since the war, our methods – ours and those of the opposition – have become much the same. I mean you can't be less ruthless than the opposition simply because your government's *policy* is benevolent, can you now?' (*Spy*, 19)

Because, as le Carré maintains, the West 'sacrifices the individual to defend the individual's right against the collective', it represents betrayal of the very idea of redemption ('To Russia', 5).

> I have equated, in hypothetical terms, the conduct of East and West in the espionage war. I have suggested that they use the same weapons – deceit – and even the same spies [. . .] I have posed this question: for how long can we defend ourselves – you and we – by methods of this kind, and still remain the kind of society that is worth defending? ('To Russia', 5)

The duplicating duplicity of East and West also undermines the historically justified opposition that led to the Allies' war to defeat Fascism. Images of Nazi Germany's slaughter of the innocent flash through Leamas' consciousness to contrast with questionable operations on both sides of the Cold War: 'Leamas saw. He saw the long road outside Rotterdam [. . .] the stream of refugees moving along it [. . .] and the plane coming in, neatly over the dunes; saw the chaos, the meaningless hell, as the bombs hit the road' (*Spy*, 19).

Although so many Cold War spy thrillers characterise the Berlin Wall as a monument to the division between the Fascist practices of East German Communism and the democratic principles of the West, *The Spy Who Came in from the Cold* questions the stability of these oppositions by examining the ruthless ideological pragmatism of espionage on both sides. In his Introduction to the novel's 2001 reprint, le Carré reflects: 'the wall was perfect theatre as well as a perfect symbol of the monstrosity of ideology gone mad' (*Spy*, viii). Leamas' oft quoted rant at the novel's end bitterly parodies the ideologies on both sides as lethal slogans: '"One sacrificed for many. It's not pretty, I know, choosing who it'll be – turning the plan into people [. . .] I can't see it in black and white. People who play this game take risks [. . .] It was a foul, foul operation. But it's paid off, and that's the only rule"' (*Spy*, 212, 213). Merging oppositional ideologies and practices in this novel intensifies the meaning of treachery in reflexive forms of doubling. Unbeknownst to Leamas, to be successful, his mission as a double agent is designed to deceive him. He is sent to East Germany to bring down Mundt, who in addition to his infamies in *Call for the Dead*, has assassinated Leamas' field agents. Only at the end, however, does Leamas learn that Mundt works for the British and is to be saved. With a double dose of villainy, Mundt's second appearance replays his brutal Nazi background and antisemitism as the agent of political and ethical violence. An enemy twice over, representing mutually supportive duplicity and self-deception on both sides of the wall, the double agent animates support for le Carré's condemnation of 'Western hypocrisy' ('To Russia', 5). He explained his condemnation as it related to the novel:

> No wonder then if Alec Leamas found himself rubbing shoulders with some pretty unsavoury colleagues in the ranks of western intelligence. Former Nazis with attractive qualifications weren't just tolerated by the Allies; they were positively mollycoddled for their anti-communist credentials. ('Afterword', 62)

Double Duplicities

Both sides of the wall are dystopian homes to the villains and victims of state-sponsored betrayal. Purpose-built to locate villainy as the other side, the wall rises as a Gothic Expressionist paean to the violence that awaits whomever is marked as outsider, as unassimilable to the double duplicity of espionage:

> Leamas went to the window and waited, in front of him the road and to either side the Wall, a dirty, ugly thing of breeze blocks and strands of barbed

wire, lit with cheap yellow light, like the backdrop for a concentration camp. East and west of the Wall lay the unrestored part of Berlin, a half-world of ruin, drawn in two dimensions, crags of war. (*Spy*, 9–10)

The image of a concentration camp into which the Wall is enfolded evinces le Carré's prevailing linkages of World War II, the Holocaust and the Cold War with his fears for Western democracy. The Wall is an unmovable, untraversable stronghold. Leamas and Liz are ordered to cross over through a gap cut into the barbed wire, but of course the gap is a trap.[62] There is no crossing to safety or belonging for them. The space of the gap may be constricted, but it figures expansively as a battleground and a weapon. Suggesting a war that transcends time and place, the description of the Wall recalls that of Scarr's junk yard in *Call for the Dead*, as though the detritus of World War II and the treachery of Cold War espionage drift back and forth between London and East Berlin. Resonant with Gothic Expressionist tropes of terror, of inexorably entrapping forces on either side, le Carré's sinister Wall recalls Edgar Allan Poe's 1842 story 'The Pit and the Pendulum', with its crushing walls and threat of torture and death at the hands of another secret world of state security, the Spanish Inquisition. The Tribunal of the Holy Office of the Inquisition could be a model for le Carré's East German Tribunal where guilt for transgressing state-sponsored orthodoxy is presumed and torture is designed to confirm it.[63] It is noteworthy that a primary target of the Spanish Inquisition were Jewish converts to Catholicism who were suspected of practising their Judaism in secret. As *conversos*, they could be cast as duplicitous double agents.

Embodied Identities

Duplicitous identity is an ideologically and epistemologically vexed cornerstone of spy thrillers. Le Carré's double-sided wall threatens self-defined identity on both sides because individuality is perceived as inherently perfidious, a sign of treason, and must therefore be eliminated. The only way individual identity can be tolerated is if it is doubled to serve as a useful instrument for the two States' intelligence systems. Mundt survives because his double identity serves both sides well. Leamas' double agency fails because it coheres at the end into recognition of the individual's value. Liz and Fiedler are killed because they are doubly dangerous as critically questioning Jews. That critical questioning and identity remain dangerous instruments in spy thrillers is apparent in Robert Ludlum's 1980 novel, *The Bourne Identity*. The plot revolves around US agent-assassin and amnesiac Jason Bourne who searches for his real identity. His personal mission marks him as a rogue spy to his handlers who decree anonymity and masquerade as a loyal agent's identity and ideology. No sequel, however (and the series appears to be ongoing), produces a trustworthy answer, as though the genre depends on maintaining the instability of individual subjectivity as the goal of all intelligence seeking. In contrast, the James Bond franchise depends on his inimitable and evident persona as an emblem of Britain's iconic superiority, the only ideology the nation seems to need.

Alec Leamas' character seems split between the spy propelled by his missions and the man who succumbs to impulse. Yet the spy and the man are also so thoroughly entangled as to be inseparable. Years of managing agents in the field, of charting danger zones, dead drops and escape routes, and of weighing intelligence and balancing his relationship with Cambridge Circus demonstrate the acuity of his espionage skills. This expertise, however, may also be a liability. Leamas may not be able to come in from the cold because the cold is who he is, because to be a spy means to remain remorselessly detached, friendless and loveless. He is not, however, lacking in temperament or emotion. His persistent irritability overwhelms the sang froid needed to assess the gradations of a spy's decisive action. Instead, he trusts his body to obliterate reflection and drive him to action, as when his left hand strikes the grocer with 'phenomenally rapid movement' as though on automatic pilot or when he retaliates against his prison mates' punitive crowding (*Spy*, 42). Because his espionage skills are perpetually at war with his instincts, he suffers from a form of character disfigurement that obviates integration into the political and literary cultures the novel dissects. Instead of producing the dynamism of agency, the result of incorporating spy and man is to question the relationship between meanings of the human and the State and between belonging and expulsion. In this sense the cold also represents a state of limbo to which the spy is consigned, recalling our first glimpse of him waiting interminably at the East/West German checkpoint and at the end, his body falling both into and out of the cold. Regardless of his actions and the plots swirling about him, Leamas exists on a threshold to nowhere, in a never-ending state of not knowing, of not being able to give or get protection or security. As le Carré assesses his character, "'Leamas is destructive out of weakness, out of a spirit of revenge. But above all because he's a man of action in a world of confused ideologies'" (qtd in Volmane, 5). Despite his combativeness, stasis is his exile until the very end, when for the first and last time, he deciphers the duplicities of Cambridge Circus and articulates their relationship to Britain's stewardship of its citizens.

Leamas' character and identity can be defined as the embodiment of unromantic espionage. Unlike the invincible bodies of Bond and Bourne, Leamas' physicality enunciates recognition of his fallibility, ultimately steering him to death, as forecast in his introductory description: 'He met failure as one day he would probably meet death, with cynical resentment and the courage of a solitary. He'd lasted longer than most; now he was beaten. It is said a dog lives as long as its teeth; metaphorically, Leamas' teeth had been drawn [. . .]' (*Spy*, 13). In addition to expressing himself through his body, as Hepburn persuasively argues, Leamas' individuality, like so many of Dickens' characters, is written on his body and predicts his fate (181). His feigned drunkenness is both a cause and sign of vulnerability, morphing into actual illness; to be restored to physical and mental strength, he must succumb to Liz's loving care of his body. In turn, whether or not he really loves her, he cannot extricate himself from her enveloping love, which is both nurturing and treacherous. There is neither passion nor romantic love in this novel; all verbal expressions of love are Liz's and silenced. Leamas never responds except to dismiss the very idea: 'he said he didn't believe in fairy tales' (*Spy*, 41). His derision encapsulates the novel's critique of conventional narratives of the spy's righteously insuperable body and the adventurous romance of espionage. Instead, the novel debunks the genre's conventional promises of resolution as illusory. If Leamas' cynicism is supported by the novel, it is also characterised as ceding the power of critique to his body. Even when restrained, his body becomes a weapon to prove his mastery over dangerously seductive fictions. Instead of connoting a romantic union of bodies, sexual passion is a strike against political impotence: 'sometimes he would put his thick fingers in her hair, holding it quite tight, and Liz laughed and said it hurt' (*Spy*, 41). His fleeting memories of their intimacy focus on 'the soft-hard touch of her long body' (*Spy*, 43). Only at the end, on their ill-fated drive to the Wall, when Leamas and Liz become sparring partners in their search for political meaning, do the sparks of spontaneous and reciprocal passion fly. Critical questioning rescues love from betrayal.

Outsiders Together

Despite its duplicity and immutability, identity in le Carré's historical citations of villainy and victimisation is a reliable testing ground for the genre's self-critical capability. Nowhere is this more apparent than in representing the durability of Fascism, as evidenced in the characters of Mundt and his victims. In addition to his brutality in *Call for the Dead*, the inveterate Fascist has 'Fiedler beaten up, and all the time [. . .] baited and jeered at him for being a Jew' (*Spy*, 198). Karden, Mundt's defence counsel, learned his craft at Buchenwald (*Spy*, 157). The exposition of antisemitism as having flowed uninterrupted from Nazism to East German ideology and practice is voiced by the woman Commissar in charge of Liz's imprisonment: '"Jews are all the same," the woman commented [. . .] If they join the Party they think it belongs to them. If they stay out, they think it is conspiring against them"' (*Spy*, 203). Charged with the crime of inherent hypocrisy, Jews can neither be rescued nor redeemed, only marginalised, expelled and eliminated. Their only stability across le Carré's dystopian spyscapes is as a test case for the survival of humanistic principles and practices to which he subscribes, stating that his '"aversion to Soviet Communism was humanist, for it did terrible things to people in the name of an ideology. It was for this reason that I considered it to be an abominable doctrine"' (qtd in *Der Spiegel*, 118). As defined by Rachel Brenner in her study of Polish Holocaust diaries, humanism endorses the 'universals of human dignity and the sanctity of human life, a world in which the capacity for empathy, which enables human beings to recognize each other's mental and emotional sameness' is either achieved or betrayed (3–4). As in *Call for the Dead*, the victim of political oppression is the European Jew, imperilled on either side of the wall, whether at the hands of Fascist Communism or the British Circus. Le Carré testifies: 'I used Jewish people because I felt that after Stalin and Hitler they should particularly engage our protective instincts' ('To Russia', 5).

Allan Hepburn argues that memory is allegorised in spy fiction as either an excess or erasure, and 'the willful eradication of memory in *The Spy Who Came in from the Cold*' results in dehumanisation until too late when recognition of self-deceit leads to tragedy (169). I would add the historical memory of World War II that haunts le Carré's Cold War fiction. Those whose Cold War fate replicates that of World War II's victims can therefore be read as 'tragic ghosts, the unfallen dead of the last war' ('To Russia', 6). The historical, emotional and moral complications that relate the characters and fates of the British agent to the Jew in *Call for the Dead* coalesce in *The Spy Who Came in from the Cold*. With multiple skeins of reference, Leamas, Liz Gold, the British Jewish Communist and Jens Fiedler, an East German Jewish security official, are trapped in 'fascist treachery' as each side of the Wall duplicates the treachery of the other (*Spy*, 177). Both Fiedler and Leamas are seasoned field agents, carrying out their missions with unquestioning devotion; both are exploited for their considerable talents and betrayed by their respective nations. Liz Gold, entrapped in her love for the burnt-out

British spy, a British citizen but romantic believer in Communist ideology, is sacrificed as a result of both allegiances.[64] As Fiedler tells Leamas, '"We're all the same, you know, that's the joke"' (*Spy* 159).

This suggestion of equivalence does not, however, extend to assuming that le Carré approves of any aspect of Communism. Indeed, he has rejected the ideology repeatedly as commingled with organised State terror which at its most treacherous, exploits and punishes its most loyal agents. Le Carré's interest in these victims resulted from having 'placed myself intellectually in the shoes of those on one side of the Curtain who took the short walk to the other; and that rationally and imaginatively I had understood the magnetic pull of such a step, and empathized with it' (qtd. in Lyall 9). Empathy resounds in his characterisation of Fiedler:

> Fiedler was a rarity in the Abteilung – he took no part in its intrigues, seemed content to live in Mundt's shadow without prospect of promotion. He could not be labelled as a member of this or that clique; even those who had worked close to him in the Abteilung could not say where he stood in its power complex. Fiedler was a solitary; feared, disliked and mistrusted. Whatever motives he had were concealed beneath a cloak of destructive sarcasm. (*Spy* 109)

An ideological and pragmatic loner, Fiedler is both a Communist idealist and an outsider; his position in East German secret intelligence is liminal – stamped with suspicion. Although he executes his work brilliantly, creating a sympathetic bond with Leamas even as he interrogates him with ruthless precision, he is ultimately unassimilable to East Germany's despotic social and political culture. His 'sarcasm' is a sign of dissent, and therefore attests to political promiscuity. Like Fiedler's proclivity for demonstrating 'the discrepancy between evidence and perfective truth', his sarcasm is 'destructive' to the Abteilung because it is an instrument of irony, a rhetorical weapon that distances Fiedler from the double messages and double binds that constitute the agency's mandate and praxis (*Spy* 122). Such critical distance leads Fiedler, 'the clever little Jew', to 'suspect the truth' (*Spy* 209). Fiedler is also tainted by having spent the war in Canada with his German Jewish Marxist parents who brought him back to East Germany in 1946, 'anxious to take part, whatever the personal cost, in the construction of Stalin's Germany' (*Spy* 111).

The locus of meaning in Fiedler's displacement lies in his Jewish identity and history, both of which are encapsulated in the narrator's sympathetic but ironic account and in Mundt's activist antisemitism.[65] Dramatising these perspectives elucidates le Carré's intervention in the cultural history of representing the spy in relation to the imagined and historical Jew. In critical relation to stereotypical representations, le Carré depicts his Jewish characters with the subjectivity of questioning self-consciousness. In effect, he humanises them with even more complexity by expressing both their romantic quest for ideological integrity and integration and its doomed historical outcome.[66] Despite subjecting his Jewish characters to perpetual exile, le Carré's depictions do not isolate them politically or epistemologically. Instead, he anatomises their isolation as originating within political and cultural ideologies that presume their characters to be unassimilable to any collective humanity worth protecting or preserving. In critical response to the Jews' displacement, he integrates them into an imagined community of critical outsiders, Jewish and non-Jewish, in the East and West. With critical support, each of his Jewish characters is alienated from the deceitful language of ideological righteousness. Included in this community of critical outsiders is the narrator whose ironic phrase 'Stalin's Germany' echoes Leamas' sardonic anti-Communist diatribe as well as the tone of Fiedler's prosecution of Mundt. At the end, although the narrator can neither intervene nor comment, his account of Fiedler's death and the impassioned exchange between Leamas and Liz brings them out of the cold of indifference. Although Liz Gold is often neglected in studies of the novel, her critical questions at the end are crucial to Leamas' political and ethical understanding and that of readers.

Altogether, Liz Gold's voice and those of Fiedler, Leamas and the narrator suggest reciprocal affirmation, creating a bond of historical and ethical testimony in their combined roles of victim and displaced witness. For each of them, critical questioning is always inserted too late to crack the systemic encoding of perfidy that constitutes the structural foundations of the novel's Secret Worlds. Simultaneously, as with Elsa Fennan, their powerlessness manifests a countervailing epistemological power. Speaking out in opposition to the romantic promises of ideological rhetoric and its deadly silencing, they change the political and historical composition of the spy thriller and intervene in the political complexion of twentieth-century British fiction.

Notes

1. John le Carré is the nom de plume of David Cornwell, but to avoid confusion, I'll use le Carré.
2. Andrew Hammond situates British 'literary fiction of the 1945–89 period' as 'expressly Cold War', responding to the Soviet threat and 'nuclear annihilation', powerful secret services, a waning British socialist movement and British Empire and emerging 'US global supremacy', p. 1. He excludes

'popular fiction' because its critics 'overemphasise' its source material', p. 217.
3. Tony Judt figures Europe's 'miracle' post-war recovery as the 'Phoenix' rising 'from the ashes of its murderous – suicidal – past', *Postwar*, p. 5.
4. Michael F. Hopkins, Michael D. Kandiah and Gillian Staerck maintain that by 1962 'A preoccupation with the Cold War pervaded the thinking of all policy-makers and politicians' so that Britain's 'commitment to fighting the Cold War internationally and domestically was unreserved. British decision-makers were in general agreement that communism and collectivism posed the most serious danger to both Western security and civilisation', pp. 2, 4.
5. Kushner calls for interdisciplinary study of the Holocaust, including 'gender studies, labour history, social history, cultural studies and even immigrant and minority studies', *HLI*, p. 18. Glenn Everett observes that le Carré's depiction of Britain's espionage establishment contrasts with writers who highlight adventurous individualism, p. 496. Fintan O'Toole concludes that 'pushing bureaucratic grayness to such an extreme turns it into an expression of the individualism that le Carré upholds', p. 20.
6. Tony Judt shows that Gemany 'was not crushed in the war or the post-war settlement', but that because it 'didn't pay its First World War debts the cost of victory to the Allies exceeded the cost of defeat to Germany [. . .] The "German problem" that had surfaced in Europe with the rise of Prussia a generation before remained unsolved', p. 4.
7. In his Afterword to the fiftieth anniversary reissue of *The Spy Who Came in from the Cold,* le Carré expresses umbrage 'that now and forevermore I was to be branded as the spy turned writer, rather than as a writer who, like scores of his kind, had done a stint in the secret world and written about it', p. 61.
8. Critics agree that the moral and psychological complexities of le Carré's novels distinguish them from conventional spy thrillers that accord with John Gardner's template. Umberto Eco contrasts Ian Fleming's and le Carré's novels ('Narrative Structures').
9. John Atkins notes that evidence of 'sordidness' in espionage is the lack of authorities' responsibility for their agents: 'He is on his own,' p. 149.
10. David Monaghan views Lady Ann and other corrupt elites of the Secret World as evidence of Britain's 'moral decay', spurning such values 'as loyalty, duty, and concern for others' and justified 'by glib and self-seeking epigrams such as "there is no loyalty without betrayal"', 'John le Carré and England', p. 569.
11. As Dwight Garner notes, le Carré 'has long been an acid critic of the British class system', '"find[ing] our obsessions with class to be absurd [. . .] I have a right to these feelings, because I have pretended to be a gentleman for so long"', p. 23.
12. Gopinath traces gentlemanly qualities to 'the abstract ideals' espoused by George Orwell 'in the name of socialism and Englishness', but taught in late-nineteenth-century public schools, p. 3.
13. With bitter irony, Arthur Koestler casts Hitler as St George battling 'the first composite super-dragon called the Judeo-Liberal-Stalin-Rothschild-World Conspiracy', *Scum of the Earth*, p. 99.

14. John Sutherland notes: 'The English [. . .] revere their monarch not because he or she is lovable [. . .] but because it affirms that "there'll always be an England"', p. 20.
15. This includes the enormous popularity of the Jason Bourne franchise. Bourne is both an agent and a victim of CIA rogue cadres, but like Bond, his personal politics are neither revealed nor of any consequence. These novels overall express anxieties about the emergence of unprecedented terror.
16. Hannah Arendt analyses this amalgam in *The Origins of Totalitarianism*, recalling the 1938 pact between the Soviet Union and the Third Reich. David Seed reports that in 1979, when le Carré accused Graham Greene of 'perpetuating a thirties perspective on political commitment [. . .]', Greene rejected le Carré's ironic view of the intelligence service, retorting: '"the confrontation between Communism and Catholicism is still very powerful"', p. 123.
17. James Smith notes that Spender's disenchantment with Communism began during the Spanish Civil War when he experienced 'the ruthlessness of the Party', and yet for Special Branch, he remained 'in the convoluted category of a "supporter of communistic theories"', pp. 40–1. In the 1940s and 1950s Spender became 'well integrated with the British Cold War propaganda effort', p. 75.
18. Artists who fled Nazi Germany include Thomas Mann, Max Beckmann, Eric von Stroheim and Billy Wilder. In the GDR, Wolf Biermann, renowned poet and singer, was expelled for his dissent, creating a scandal. He escaped to West Germany where he criticised the West safely, as did Jurek Becker, exiled author of *Jacob the Liar*. Arthur M. Schlesinger's *The Vital Center* (1949), an early Cold War defence of liberal ideology, provides context for le Carré's critique. Schlesinger emphasises free expression, especially in the arts and education: 'Direct political control [. . .] either throttles the serious artist or makes him slick and false', p. 6. Schlesinger criticises modernist artists who 'reflect and incite anxieties which are incompatible with the monolithic character of "the Soviet person"', p. 79.
19. Eva Horn interprets the letter as condemning the West's 'lip service to individual rights and freedom' while exploiting 'humaneness' as 'the worst of all weapons deployed by the netherworld of espionage', p. 258.
20. Given le Carré's complex, humanising portraits of spies, I disagree with Horn's argument that in the Cold War 'humans do not count – unless as a site of unreliability, manipulability, or weakness', p. 251.
21. Monaghan argues that Smiley's ability to balance 'his duty to the Circus and his obligation to be human' is threatened in *Smiley's People* when he manipulates Karla's devotion to his daughter and coerces him into defecting to the West, p. 581.
22. See Tony Judt for incisive analysis of these events.
23. Klaus Theweleit's psychoanalytic study of the German Freikorps applies to the masculinist ideology of Nazi militarism.
24. Sander Gilman analyses the history of modern European antisemitism and its scientific and cultural discourses.
25. I base my analysis on David Bathrick's study of Holocaust representations of the Jew: 'As opposed to the indexical, iconic signs often express an aura of timelessness and a lack of spatial specificity' while they 'claim implicitly to tell the whole story', p. 3.

26. Harry Pendel in le Carré's *The Tailor of Panama* represents a multi-cultural Jew: half Jewish, half Irish, from London's East End immigrant community, combining Jewish chutzpah with Irish blarney and whose Jewish uncle Benny reminds him to '*drucken* himself [. . .] to go small', to not 'be anybody', pp. 82, 43.
27. Karen Remmler analyses current theories of cosmopolitanism as revealing 'a noticeable silence about the intersection of European nationalism and the vilification of Jews as "cosmopolites"', p. 17.
28. I thank Elizabeth Maslen for noting this crucial relationship.
29. Karen Horn explains Kim Philby's successful deception: 'despite all suspicions [he] had been protected by a network of friends in the British establishment', p. 263.
30. Adam Sisman notes that Elsa was inspired by le Carré's memory of meeting a Frenchwoman resistance fighter who with 'insouciant humour' worried that her hair would never grow back after being shaved at a concentration camp where she spent a year, p. 96.
31. My reading of Elsa's embodied story fits into ongoing debates about representing Holocaust experience, whether and in what discursive forms the unprecedented suffering perpetrated by Nazi Germany can be expressed, dramatised, transmitted and comprehended. See James E. Young, Sara R. Horowitz and Michael Rothberg.
32. For historical analysis of this victimisation, see Dalia Ofer and Lenore J. Weitzman; Elizabeth Baer and Myrna Goldenberg; and Sonja Hedgepeth and Rochelle Seidel.
33. Rosie White views the representation of older women in spy fiction as devoid of or mocked for their sexuality, but that asexuality can also serve as a cover for women spies, rendering them invisible.
34. Henry Gonshak discusses the importance of the Holocaust in American and British spy thrillers, questioning whether these serve as 'genuine historical argument[s]' or 'lively potboiler[s]' and concludes that those tales 'set after the war are better' because their critical distance prevents attempts to recreate the atrocities, p. 16.
35. See also Saul Friedlander, *Probing the Limits of Representation*.
36. For critique of 'the perilous effects of empathetic substitution' for audiences of Holocaust representation, see Elke Heckner. Other affective dangers include vicarious titillation through images of extreme brutality and sentimentalising stories of suffering with platitudes of hope and heroism when as so many testify, survival was primarily a matter of luck.
37. Holocaust philosopher Beryl Lang discusses this issue.
38. Adam Sisman records that while working as a field security agent in Austria in 1951, Cornwell (le Carré) became aware 'that almost every official he dealt with had previously worked for the Nazi regime. This was a period of extraordinary reversals, when former foes became friends, and former friends foes', p.100.
39. On the Evian conference and other failed efforts, see the US Holocaust Memorial Museum site: http://www.ushmm.org/outreach/en/article.php?ModuleId=10007698 Tony Kushner reports that by the end of 1942 the West knew that 'Polish Jews were being killed in the hundreds of thousands', but that in January 1943 less than half the Americans polled believed

'that up to 2 million Jews had been killed. Over one-quarter believed the story was just a "rumour"', *HLI*, pp. 173, 137. Facing powerful opposition in the British government, publisher Victor Gollancz and MP Eleanor Rathbone spearheaded rescue efforts in Britain, but with little effect.
40. Arthur Koestler reports that in the French concentration camp Le Vernet, the 'remnants of the International Brigades' were incarcerated in 'the Leper Barrack [. . .] infested with vermin and disease', *Scum of the Earth*, p. 127. As a rhetorical trope, irony does not necessarily distance today's positive usage from yesterday's antisemitism. For discussion of Arendt's ironic voice in *The Origins of Totalitarianism* and *Eichmann in Jerusalem*, see Lyndsey Stonebridge's distinction between 'refugee and cosmopolitan style', p. 110.
41. Noting that Jewish survivors represented a distinct problem of resettlement, Tony Judt contrasts 'displaced persons (assumed to have, somewhere, a home to go to) and refugees (who were classified as homeless)', whether they were 'nationals of a wartime ally (Czechoslovakia, Poland, Belgium, etc.) or a former enemy state (Germany, Romania, Hungary, Bulgaria, etc.)', p. 29.
42. Julia Kristeva responds to Hannah Arendt's critique of the abstract language of the 1789 *Declaration of the Rights of Man and Citizen* by insisting that its 'universality, of a symbolic dignity for the whole of humankind, appears to me as a rampart against a nationalist, regionalist, and religious fragmentation', but it must also integrate 'that portion of conflict, hatred, violence, and destructiveness that [. . .] has ceaselessly been unloaded upon the realities of wars and fratricidal closeness', p. 27.
43. The firebombing of Dresden lasted from 13 to 15 February 1945, and remains controversial because the city had no wartime industry, the victims were primarily civilians and Allied victory was already predictable. See Richard Overy.
44. Kushner notes that few in the liberal democracies 'devoted themselves in an unreservedly positive way to the fate of the Jews' while others 'remained uncritical of the Nazi regime, including its antisemitic policies', *HLI*, p. 32. Scepticism about Nazi persecution of the Jews in liberal democracies was motivated by 'a more general distrust of the Jews', *HLI*, p. 55.
45. Scholars on women and war in the twentieth century include Karen Schneider, Gill Plain, Jenny Hartley and Phyllis Lassner.
46. The Imperial War Museum Holocaust Exhibition opened in 2000, occupying an entire floor, separated from other World War II exhibits. Le Carré's dystopian scene registers with moral fallout of the war, as described by Tony Judt: 'For most Europeans World War Two was experienced not as a war of movement and battle but as a daily degradation, in the course of which men and women were betrayed and humiliated, forced into daily acts of petty crime and self-abasement, in which everyone lost something and many lost everything', p. 41.
47. In le Carré's 1974 novel *Tinker, Tailor, Soldier, Spy*, Ann betrays Smiley with Bill Haydon, her cousin and double agent, calling attention to the insidiously insular relations in le Carré's Secret World.
48. Terry Eagleton has argued that Heathcliff's origin is Irish, viewed in the nineteenth century as an alien, inferior race.

49. For discussion of the Jew as a monstrous figure see Lester Friedman, Carol Davison, Judith Halberstam, and Andrew Smith and Jeff Wallace.
50. Tony Judt observes that the GDR held 'Hitler's West German heirs' responsible for Nazism and 'commemorated not Germany's victims but eleven million dead "fighters against Hitler fascism"', p. 822. David Shneer shows that by the time of the Cold War, the Russians were depicting Nazi atrocity photos as a meditation on war tragedy.
51. Unlike Buzard, I don't find the 'strong element of closure' and 'readerly gratification' in this ending, p. 164.
52. Laura Tracey argues that le Carré's villains question idealism by showing how its activation 'emerges as a danger finally eliminated', p. 25.
53. Brenda Silver notes that le Carré's women characters 'function solely as the third term in a triangle that is predicated on male rivalry and male bonding', p. 1.
54. See Alberto Moravia's dissection of Italian Fascism in *The Conformist*.
55. Jost Hindersmann argues that le Carré's agents don't realise 'they have been betrayed by their leaders' until their missions are well under way, p. 26.
56. In both *Tinker, Tailor, Soldier, Spy* and its sequel, *Smiley's People*, a crucial source of the Secret World's memory is a woman, Connie Sachs, but her active role in the past is absent in the present where she is exiled to an isolated farmhouse, situated perhaps happily beyond the secret world of men in a lesbian relationship.
57. Koestler recalls his initial attraction to Communism at the age of twenty-six as 'the intoxicating effect of a sudden liberation from the rusty chains with which a pre-1914 middle-class childhood had cluttered one's mind' and his denunciation when Communism became 'twisted round into its opposite', *The God that Failed*, p. 20.
58. James Smith reports that Koestler's MI5 files reveal a complicated history of 'witting Comintern asset', his later status as a fanatical anti-communist', and self-serving 'canny manipulator of the British secret state', pp. 124–5.
59. Louis Fischer was an international journalist who covered the Spanish Civil War and wrote books on Gandhi and Stalin.
60. Robert Snyder contends that le Carré 'sides with the person who can lay claim to a new beginning regardless of past compromises', p. 143. I maintain that Smiley's grief infuses all his later appearances, reflecting the omnipresence of World War II.
61. Allan Hepburn proffers that 'to create a definition of citizenship that might include foreigners, defectors, refugees, dissidents, Jews, homosexuals, traitors – the spy thriller postulates absolute [. . .] allegiance to country or ideology, an allegiance that few citizens of the twentieth-century world could endorse', p. 25.
62. Hepburn interprets the Wall incisively as an allegory of reading and misreading of death and violence, and the betrayal of literary romance, pp. 166–86.
63. For a critical history of the Spanish Inquisition, see Henry Kamen.
64. Aronoff describes Liz as 'the paradigmatic naïve victim', p. 117, and Beene maligns her as stupid, p. 56, but while her commitment to Communism may be untested idealism, it resembles that of Fiedler. Moreover, her incisive responses to Leamas at the end parallel the author's. Le Carré charac-

terises her as significant to '"a very romantic story: two people fall in love and one has to betray the other and both of them, in a sense, perish in a mental institution; both of them, in the same breath, make a statement in favour of humanity"', qtd in Dean, p. 30.
65. Asserting the importance of studying representations of Jews in spy fiction, Hepburn posits that 'all spies are always already Jewish in the sense of having multiple perspectives on identity, allegiance, and commitment', pp. 295–6, n1. I find that such multiplicity targets fictional Jews for opprobrium rather than being valued as complexity when depicting non-Jewish characters.
66. Le Carré defended himself against charges of antisemitism on several occasions, which to his credit, he has taken very seriously and to which he has responded persuasively with full exposition of his writing. See 'Nervous Times' and his interview with Plimpton.

Conclusion

The narrative and heuristic bridge connecting espionage fiction and exile is built on suspicion. Suspicion drives characters and plots and reigns as an over-determined metaphor, designating nations, organisations, ideologies and individuals as agents as well as objects of distrust. Espionage is driven by the anxiety that, institutionally or individually, the suspect contains secret knowledge portending danger to the subject. Because, however, secret intelligence invariably turns out to be only partially detectable at best and most often contradictory or distorted, it almost never leads to any conclusion other than to confirm the elusiveness of information or that of the suspect. This outcome intensifies mutual wariness, setting in motion a vicious cycle of espionage and counterespionage plots, each of which draws attention to the dubious value of the other. Distrust applies to protagonists and antagonists alike, including Ambler's Vadassy who will be a suspicious alien wherever he goes, or Frankau's Blessington whose identity and villainy remain mythically double-sided.

When suspicion is activated and becomes operative as espionage, it threatens violence – assassination, corporate conspiracy or among nations, war. But despite the historical and narrative power of armed conflict, military wars are not presented in spy thrillers directly, but as nightmares from the past or as ghosts bleeding into the future; they are absent in the fictional present. In these haunting espionage wars, victory is stalemated; nations and spies neither win nor lose. Instead, like secret intelligence, espionage violence and its outcome remain ambiguous and therefore unconfirmed, narrated between the lines, offstage or fleetingly. It also remains unclear whether espionage is even a primary or definitive action or subsidiary to suspicion. Which comes first – espionage or suspicion?

Suspicion occupies an unsettling narrative space where the home front is experienced as no less dangerous than the battlefield, as in Matthew

Gilroy's Yorkshire home and garden in *Colonel Blessington* or Smiley's home in *Call for the Dead*. Symbolising that threat, settings in espionage fiction are enacted in claustrophobic spaces, such as the Nuremberg streets and alleys in *Above Suspicion*. In the same novel, even the vast range of the Dolomites closes in on the protagonists, metonymically reflecting Nazi oppression. These Gothic Expressionist figurations indicate that fictional espionage wars are fought outside the mimetic conventions through which real politics are historically recorded and represented. But neither are these espionage wars related to romantic adventure or science fiction. Instead of deploying megalomaniacs and their weapons of cosmic destruction, Ambler's aptly titled novel *The Dark Frontier* lampoons such plotting and in effect highlights the atavistic nature of espionage conflict. In le Carré's novels espionage wars explode soundlessly in darkness, burrowing deep into the unacknowledged seamy side of state security. Whether agents are professionals or amateurs, when they attack each other, as with Dimitrios and Peters, Kenton and Mailler or Smiley and Dieter, the results and collateral damage remain uncontained by the Expressionist secret world.[1] As the phrase suggests, this Secret World lies beyond realism. It is answerable only to itself, and even when called to account for its methods, promises to persist for another mission, another underground war. Although these fictions embed ethical questions, their non-realist forms challenge those listed by J. J. Macintosh as typical of the genre: whether actions are morally justifiable, including distinctions 'between good and bad crimes' (178). All too often the narrative space between good and bad crushes the difference.

The ethical no-man's land of espionage fiction extends to the fate of spies. Whether they occupy an official or civilian position, secret agents are suspect, in the office and in the field; they have no access to protection, negotiating power or to the rights of citizenship. Regardless of their motivation for becoming spies or how well they perform, they must fend for themselves. Neither spycraft nor instincts for survival ameliorate their perilous condition. Isolated from families, professional and social communities, when they are injured, 'disappeared' or killed, they leave no mark on the nations and agencies for which they work or on the conflicts that engage them. They occupy a narrative space that needs them, but as fictional spies they are suspended between the desire to matter and the probability that they don't.

What does matter is the critical intervention made by tethering the exiled condition that defines the spy's place in the fictional secret world to that of the stateless refugee in twentieth-century history. In both cases, the issue of human rights or in Hannah Arendt's words, the right to have rights, does not apply. The lives and fates of spies and refugees are not inscribed in the laws and civil expectations that govern those of ordinary citizens. When plotted together, spies and refugees are also outliers in the sphere of conventional characterisation. In what I call espionage romance, the twin qualities of great looks and audacity define spies like James Bond, Jason Bourne or Stella Rimington's Liz Carlyle. Regardless of the constraints or perils they face, these celebrity spies are preserved for another sequel. Unlike le Carré, whose espionage career led him to question the spy's character and the ethics of espionage, Rimington's contested position as first woman director of MI5 is transformed into the romance of belonging, surviving and succeeding.

The protagonists, bystanders and victims studied in this book are not so lucky. Whether they die or live beyond their novel's ending, they remain threatening to all sides of all conflicts. In *The Dark Frontier* the character of Professor Barstow is contained in a sanitorium but not safely resolved; any intelligence about his identity and purpose remains ominously ambiguous. Though innocent, Liz Gold is killed because she is suspected of knowing too much. Hope Kirkland is cocooned in wealth, privilege and romance, but the novel's ending leaves her open to suspicion if she should recount her story of the Moranskis. The Myleses fulfil their mission about the missing British agent, but the story of the Jew's cry in the Nuremberg alley will, as the historical record confirms, remain unheard. Although these characters and plotting are clearly imagined, aligning them with actual conditions of exile and the fate of refugees produces spy fiction that serves as historical testimony, propaganda and criticism, whether contemporaneous with the novel's plot or retrospectively.

Witnesses to Dystopian History

As the writers under discussion attest, from the mid-1930s throughout World War II and the Cold War there were British artists reaching beyond their own culture and history to create spy fictions that bear witness to totalitarian oppression and question the liberal mandates of the democratic West. Storm Jameson presented the case against turning inward in her essay 'Writing in the Margin – 1939':

> [The writer] cannot think in terms of destroying Hitlerism in one country, but only of saving the Europe of which England is a part [. . .] He must not, in conscience, be turned from pursuing his imagination of this Europe to its bounds, and from thrusting it on people's notice. Even the griefs of the war must not turn him from this, which is half of his clear task. The rest is to

experience despair as a stage in courage, pain as inescapable but a source of strength, the thought of defeat as a reminder that no Dark Age has outlasted, or can outlast, the unquenchable energy and curiosity of the mind. (200)

Written only a month after Nazi Germany invaded Poland and Britain declared war on Germany, Jameson's assertion that England is part of Europe responds to widespread feeling that the opposite was true.[2] Although war is always on Jameson's mind, still grieving the loss of her brother in World War I and sharing the anxieties of other Britons about an even greater conflagration, she argues for a necessary relationship between the preservation of her own nation's democratic principles and the fate of Europe.[3]

Ever on the move, crisscrossing Europe and the Canada of *49th Parallel*, the writers in this book dramatise the urgency of looking beyond the British horizon to narrate the fragmented and often unimaginable stories of persecuted Europeans. Images of Ambler's and Howard's trains hurtling across Fascist Europe, of Philip Meyer's ship embarking for Nazi Germany or of Alec Leamas' car racing to the Berlin Wall integrate Europe's fate into the plotting of British cultural production. These journeys become mobile forms of propaganda to combat the menacing designs of Fascism, Nazism and Communism.

All of the novels and films discussed in this book are filled with suspect spies and refugees. Representing a broad swathe of Central, Southern and Eastern Europe, a test case emerges as the exiled condition of Jewish characters, who epitomise racial, political and cultural persecution. In *Call for the Dead*, two are Holocaust survivors. In *The Spy Who Came in from the Cold* two Jewish characters are victims of the entanglements of British political pragmatism with Communist and Fascist inhumanity. The key presence of Jewish characters and their references acknowledge an underlying racialist ideology that encourages official and popular indifference to the fate of Europe and its exiled Others – antisemitism.[4] In effect, the wide spread of racialised persecution exposes the transnational and transpolitical forces that estrange all suspicious and undesirable Others from the rights of belonging and citizenship. In their various guises, these forces represent permutations of Fascism as they take hold throughout Central Europe in the 1930s and remain a haunting presence in Cold War British fiction, perpetrating political and existential forms of exile. Streaming across time and place, the political and imaginative power of Fascism coalesces in Gothic Expressionist imagery and atmospherics. For example, le Carre's Gothic Expressionist sites of exile link London to East Germany as places where damaged survivors of World War II represent the unresolved threat of Fascism. This infiltration of political oppression is all the more insidious because the espionage and counter-espionage plots that oppose Fascism also exploit the vulnerability of spies and refugees – a political and humanitarian double-cross.

If Fascist oppression seemed to belong to the long-buried past as the Cold War took hold, its haunting of le Carré's fiction carries forward the political concerns of other writers studied in this book. A large share of the narrative tension in all their thrillers derives from the worry that as dramatically entertaining and popular as their novels proved to be, who would heed their warnings and pleas to help the targeted victims of Fascism, Nazism and Communism? Who would even notice that the vulnerability of stateless refugees like Vadassy, the dissidents in *Pimpernel Smith* or the Moranskis matter more than plot devices, that Ambler's hapless Sachs/Borovansky is more than a throwaway corpse, or that Liz Gold is more than a failed romance? Who would sympathise with those exiled several times over, within the Nazi state or sacrificed to the promises of Communism, or by misguided political choices, like Elsa Fennan and Dieter Frey?

These British fictions express the urge to provide counter-narratives to the casual prejudices, wilful ignorance and silences that constituted official and general responses to political and racialised victims of exile in their times and that reverberate today. For example, Ambler's Sachs/Borovansky, and le Carré's portraits of Elsa Fennan and Jens Fiedler complicate the social and cultural suspicions that create oppositions between victim and villain, between self and Other. These suspicions also challenge critical assumptions about the formation of fictional character in spy fiction as primarily action-based. Instead, the writers studied in this book expand the depth of individual psychological complexity and ambiguity to include historical and political contingency. For example, the elusive characters of Dimitrios and Blessington are both shaped and decentred by historical contingency and crisis, which in turn become the novels' primary agent. Read together, these characters, their stories and their round trip or one-way transports revise the plotting of espionage fiction by showing how suspense emerges from historical crisis and functions as a political and polemical narrative instrument.

The stories embodied by Elsa Fennan and Philip Meyer, those carried by Desmond Kenton, Frances Myles and Hope Kirkland, by the rescue train of Leslie Howard and the resistance of Canadians, may be wishful fantasies, but as they made their way to mass audiences on both sides of the Atlantic, they achieved a coherent reality in the form of revisionary political thrillers. Stories of exile, refugees, spies, double agents and secret intelligence encode suspicion of a target that lies beyond the genre's conventions – the absence or disinformation about the victims of political oppression. Recovering their stories of exile and espionage reveals the evasions, elisions and distortions that perpetuate oppression in the form of silence. Because the spy's story is an old one, its familiarity lends accessibility to those silenced stories. They share the narrative of betrayal, deception, social and psychological isolation and compromised humanity and loyalty. Viewing espionage stories as entangled with the historical conditions that create exile activates their political work as a critical response to unwritten wars on others.

Notes

1. J. J. Macintosh notes that defences of '*good* spy fiction' include the lack of 'much' violence, its symbolic relief and entertainment value, p. 59.
2. That this opposition prevails today, in 2015, reflects unresolved debates about Britain's relations with the European Union.
3. For analysis of the trajectory of Jameson's views about World War II, see Elizabeth Maslen's biography.
4. Hepburn questions Liz's Jewish identity but le Carré is aware that many Jews were affiliated with Communism from the 1930s onwards or were assimilated and would have foregone Jewish practices, p. 297.

Bibliography

Primary Sources

Aciman, André (ed.), *Letters of Transit: Reflections on Exile, Identity Language, and Loss* (New York: The New York Public Library, 1999).
Ambler, Eric, *The Dark Frontier* [1936] (New York: Vintage Crime, 2012).
—, *Epitaph for a Spy* [1938] (New York: Vintage Crime, 2002).
—, *Cause for Alarm* [1939] (New York: Vintage Crime, 2002).
—, *A Coffin for Dimitrios* [1939] (New York: Knopf/Galahad, 1992).
—, *Journey into Fear* [1940] (New York: Vintage Crime, 2002).
—, 'Footnote' [1951], *Epitaph for a Spy* (New York: Vintage Crime, 2002), pp. 261–3.
—, 'Epitaph for an Espione', *Lilliput*, January–February 1953, np.
—, 'John Le Carré Escapes the Follow-up Jinx'. Review of *The Looking Glass War*. *Life Magazine*, 30 July 1965, p. 8.
— (ed.), 'Introduction', *To Catch a Spy* (London: Four Square, 1966), pp. 7–21.
—, 'A Better Sort of Rubbish: An Inquiry into the State of the Thriller', *London Times*, 30 November 1974, pp. 1–7.
—, *Here Lies: An Autobiography* (London: Weidenfeld and Nicolson, 1985).
—, 'Preface', *The Dark Frontier* (New York: Warner-Mysterious, 1990), pp. x–xvi.
—, *Waiting for Orders: The Complete Short Stories of Eric Ambler* (New York: Mysterious Press, 1991).
—, *The Story So Far: Memories and Other Fictions* (London: Weidenfeld and Nicolson, 1993).
—, *The Mask of Dimitrios* [1939] (London: Penguin, 2009).
Améry, Jean (Hans Meyer), *At the Mind's Limits: Contemplations by a Survivor of Auschwitz and its Realities*, trans. Sidney Rosenfeld and Stella P. Rosenfeld (Bloomington: Indiana University Press, 1980).
Andreas-Friedrich, Ruth, *Berlin Underground 1938–1945*, trans. Barrows Mussey (New York: Henry Holt, 1947).
Arendt, Hannah, *The Origins of Totalitarianism* (New York: Harcourt, Brace, 1968).
—, 'The Perplexities of the Rights of Man', *The Origins of Totalitarianism* (New York: Harcourt, Brace, 1968), pp. 31–45.

—, 'We Refugees', in Jerome Kohn and Ron Feldman (eds), *Hannah Arendt: Jewish Writings* (New York: Schocken Books, 2007), pp. 264–74.
Atwood, Margaret, *The Handmaid's Tale* (Toronto: McClelland and Stewart, 1985).
Banville, John, *The Untouchable* (New York: Vintage International, 1998).
Borinsky, Alicia, *One-Way Tickets: Writers and the Culture of Exile* (San Antonio: Trinity University Press, 2011).
Boyd, William, *Restless* (New York: Bloomsbury, 2006).
Bridge, Ann, *A Place to Stand* (New York: Macmillan, 1953).
—, *The Tightening String* (London: Chatto and Windus, 1961).
—, *Facts and Fictions: Some Literary Recollections* (New York: McGraw-Hill, 1968).
Buchan, John, *The Thirty-Nine Steps* (Oxford: Oxford University Press, 2007).
Burdekin, Katharine, *Swastika Night* [1937] (New York: The Feminist Press, 1985).
Childers, Erskine, *Riddle of the Sands* [1903] (New York: Barnes and Noble, 2005).
Christie, Agatha, *Passenger to Frankfurt* [1970] (London: HarperCollins, 2003).
Conrad, Joseph, 'The Duel: A Military Story', *A Set of Six* [1908] (New York: Garden City Publishing, 1924).
Delbo, Charlotte, untitled poem. *Auschwitz and After*, trans. Rosette C. Lamont (New Haven, CT: Yale University Press, 1995), p. 224.
Dumas Alexander, *The Corsican Brothers*, trans. Andrew Brown (London: Hesperus Classics, 2007).
Du Maurier, Daphne, *Rebecca* (New York: Doubleday, 1953).
Eco, Umbert, 'Ur-Fascism', *The New York Review of Books*, 22 June 1995, pp. 12–15.
Elgar, Edward, 'Epilogue', *The Banner of Saint George*, Op. 33, 1897. Reprinted in concert programme notes, 2014.
Engelmann, Bernt, *In Hitler's Germany: Daily Life in the Third Reich*, trans. Krishna Winston (New York: Pantheon, 1986).
Fischer, Louis, *The God that Failed*, ed. Richard Crossman (Washington, DC: Regnery Gateway, 1983), pp. 196–228.
Frankau, Pamela, *I Find Four People* (London: Nicholson and Watson, 1935).
—, *The Devil We Know* (London: Heinemann, 1939).
—, *Pen to Paper* (New York: Doubleday, 1962).
—, *Colonel Blessington* (London: The Bodley Head, 1968).
—, *The Willow Cabin* (London: Virago, 1988).
Gellhorn, Martha, *A Stricken Field* (London: Virago, 1986).
Greene, Graham, *The Confidential Agent* (New York: Viking, 1939).
—, *The Third Man and The Fallen Idol* (London: Heinemann, 1950).
—, *A Burnt-Out Case* (New York: Viking, 1961).
Haffner, Sebastian, *Defying Hitler: A Memoir*, trans. Oliver Pretzel (London: Weidenfeld and Nicolson, 2001).
Harris, Robert, *Fatherland* (London: Hutchinson, 1992).
Henry V, film, dir. Laurence Olivier (UK: Eagle Lion Films, November 1944).
Howard, Leslie, 'English Films and the War', 26–7 July 1940, in *Trivial Fond Records*, 156.

—, 'First Fortnight of the Battle of London', *Britain Speaks*, 23–4 September 1940, pp. 1–4.
—, 'The Tree of Liberty', *Britain Speaks*, 30 September 1940, pp. 1–5.
—, 'Shopkeepers and Poets', *Britain Speaks*, 14–15 October 1940, pp. 1–5.
—, 'That Unspeakable Word', *Britain Speaks*, 12 December 1940, np.
—, *Trivial Fond Records*, ed. Ronald Howard (London: W. Kimber, 1982).
James, P. D. *The Children of Men* (New York: Knopf, 1992).
Jameson, Storm, *And Then We Shall Hear Singing* (London: Macmillan, 1942).
—, *The Black Laurel* (London: Macmillan, 1947).
—, 'Writing in the Margin – 1939', *The Writer's Situation* (London: Macmillan, 1950), pp. 189–200.
—, *A Ulysses Too Many* (London: Macmillan, 1958).
Koestler, Arthur, *Scum of the Earth* [1941] (New York: Macmillan, 1968).
—, 'The Mixed Transport', *Horizon* 8.46, October 1943, pp. 244–52.
—, *The God that Failed*, ed. Richard Crossman (Washington, DC: Gateway, 1991), pp. 15–75.
Le Carré, John, *Call for the Dead* [1961] (New York: Walker and Co., 1962).
—, *A Murder of Quality* [1962] (London: Penguin, 1982).
—, *The Spy Who Came in from the Cold* [1963] (London: Penguin, 2012).
—, *The Looking Glass War* [1965] (New York: Pocket Books, 2002).
—, To Russia with Greetings: An Open Letter to the *Moscow Literary Gazette*, *Encounter*, 26, 1966, pp. 3–6.
—, *A Small Town in Germany* [1968] (New York: Pocket Books, 2002).
—, *Tinker, Tailor, Soldier, Spy* [1974] (New York: Simon and Schuster Pocket Books, 2000).
—, 'Introduction, in B. Page, D. Leitch and P. Knightley, *Philby: The Spy Who Betrayed a Generation* (London: Sphere, 1977), pp. 9–24.
—, *Smiley's People* [1979] (New York: Simon and Schuster Pocket Books, 2000).
—, 'Spying [. . .] the Passion of My Time', *Queen's Quarterly*, 100.2, Summer 1993, pp. 269–72.
—, *The Tailor of Panama* (New York: Knopf, 1996).
—, 'Nervous Times', An Address at the Annual Dinner of the Anglo-Israel Association, November 1997 (London: The Anglo-Israel Association, 1998), pp. 5–22.
—, 'Introduction', *The Spy Who Came in from the Cold* (New York: Simon and Schuster Pocket Books, 2001), pp. v–x.
—, 'We See, in Glorious Technicolor, the Spy Swap of the Century', *The Guardian*, 10 July 2010, p. 1.
—, 'Smiley's Secret: He Wants Us to Love Germany', *The Sunday Times*, 11 July 2010, p. 7.
—, 'Afterword', *The Spy Who Came in from the Cold. Harpers*, April 2013, pp. 61–3.
Ludlum, Robert, *The Bourne Identity* (New York: Random House, 1980).
MacInnes, Helen, *Above Suspicion* (Boston: Little, Brown, 1941).
—, *Assignment in Brittany* (Boston: Little, Brown, 1942).
—, *While Still We Live* [1944] (New York: Crest Books/Fawcett World Library, 1964).
—, *Horizon* [1945] (London: Fontana Collins, 1981).

—, *The Double Image* [1965] (New York: Ballantine, 1985).
—, *The Salzburg Connection* [1968] (London: Titan Books, 2012).
Mann, Thomas, *The Magic Mountain*, trans. H. T. Lowe-Porter (New York: Limited Editions, 1962).
—, 'Germany and the Germans: Address to the Library of Congress, 5 May 1945' (Washington, DC: Library of Congress, 1963), np.
Memory of the Camps, film, prod. Sidney Bernstein (UK, 1945).
—, 'Film Viewing Notes No. 1', Imperial War Museum Department of Film, np.
Metropolis, film, dir. Fritz Lang (Germany: Babelberg Studios, UFA, 1927).
Milosz, Czeslaw, *The Captive Mind*, trans. Jane Zielonko (New York: Vintage Books, 1955).
Moravia, Alberto, *The Conformist*, trans. Tami Calliope (S. Royalton, VT: Publishers Group West, 1999).
Nabokov, Vladimir, *Pale Fire* (New York: Putnam, 1962).
Night Train to Munich, film, dir. Carol Reed (US: Twentieth Century Fox, 1940).
Nosferatu, film, dir. F. W. Murnau (Germany: Film Arts Guild, 1922).
Orwell, George, *Animal Farm* (New York: Harcourt Brace, 1946).
—, 'Antisemitism in Britain', in Sonia Orwell and I. Angus (eds), *The Collected Essays, Journalism and Letters of George Orwell. Volume 3: As I Please, 1943–1945* (Harmondsworth: Penguin, 1970), pp. 378–88.
Poe, Edgar Allan, 'The Pit and the Pendulum' (Charlottesville: University of Virginia Netlibrary, 1993).
Priestley, J. R., *Britain Speaks* (New York: Harper, 1940).
Rimington, Stella, *Open Secret* (London: Hutchinson, 2001).
—, *At Risk* (New York: Vintage Crime, 2006).
Scarlet Pimpernel, film, dir. Howard Young (US: United Artists, 1934).
Schlesinger, Arthur M., *The Vital Center* (Cambridge, MA: Riverside, 1949).
Spender, Steven, *European Witness* (New York: Reynall and Hitchcock, 1946).
—, *The God that Failed*, ed. Richard Crossman (New York: Harper, 1949), pp. 229–73.
Stevenson, Robert Louis, *The Master of Ballantrae, A Winter's Tale* (London: Cassell, 1889).
The Americans, TV series, writer, creator, prod. Joe Weisberg (US: FX Television Productions, 2012–).
The Great Dictator, film, dir. Charles Chaplin (US: United Artists, 1940).
The Lady Vanishes, film, dir. Alfred Hitchcock (UK: Gainsborough/Gaumont Productions, 1938).
Waugh, Evelyn, *Brideshead Revisited* (New York: Dell, 1959).
West, Rebecca, 'Preface', in Pamela Frankau, *Colonel Blessington*. Unpublished typescript, pp. 1–10.
Woolf, Leonard, *Barbarians at the Gate* (London: Victor Gollancz, 1939).
Woolf, Virginia, 'Thoughts on Peace in an Air Raid', *The Death of the Moth and Other Essays* (London: Hogarth Press, 1942), pp. 154–7.
—, *Three Guineas* (New York: Harcourt, 2006).

Interviews and Biographies

Amory, Malcolm, 'The Ambler Way, an Interview with Eric Ambler', *The Sunday Times Magazine*, 5 January 1975, pp. 30–2.

Bailey, Patricia, 'Secrets and Spies: A New Documentary Explores the Life of Reclusive Novelist John le Carré', a report on the film by filmmakers Werner Köhne and André Schäfer. http://www.cbc.ca/'/arts/film/story/2010/03/18/f-john-le-carre-documentary.html (accessed 10 July 2014).

Bruccoli, Matthew and Judith S. Baughman (eds), *Conversations with John Le Carré* (Jackson: University Press of Mississippi, 2004).

Cameron, James, 'Schoolmaster Who Came in from the Cold', in Bruccoli and Baughman (eds), pp. 18–26.

Dean, Michael, 'John le Carré: The Writer Who Came in from the Cold', in Bruccoli and Baughman (eds), pp. 27–32.

Deindorfer, Robert G., 'A Conversation with John le Carré', in Bruccoli and Baughman (eds), pp. 15–17.

Der Spiegel, 'What Would I Be Like If I Were He?', in Bruccoli and Baughman (eds), pp. 112–21.

Eforgan, Estel, *Leslie Howard: The Lost Actor* (London: Valentine Mitchell, 2013).

Garner, Dwight, '"I Have Pretended to be a Gentleman for So Long"', interview with John le Carré, *The New York Times Magazine*, 21 April 2013, pp. 18–23.

Gross, Miriam, 'The Secret World of John le Carré', in Bruccoli and Baughman (eds), pp. 60–71.

Hopkins, Joel, 'An Interview with Eric Ambler', *Journal of Popular Culture*, 9, 1975, pp. 285–93.

Howard, Leslie Ruth, *A Quite Remarkable Father* (New York: Harcourt, 1959).

Howard, Ronald (ed.), *Leslie Howard: Trivial Fond Records* (London: Wm Kimber, 1982).

—, *In Search of My Father: A Portrait of Leslie Howard* (New York: St Martin's Press, 1982).

Le Carré, John, 'Master of the Secret World', interview, 21 October, 1996. http://salon.com/weekly/lecarre961021.html (accessed 12 July 2014).

Maslen, Elizabeth, *Storm Jameson: A Life in Writing* (Evanston: Northwestern University Press, 2014).

'Miss Helen MacInnes', Obituary, *The Times*, 2 October 1985, p. 12.

Plimpton, George, 'Interview, The Art of Fiction', *The Paris Review*, Summer 1997. http://www.theparisreview.org/interviews/1250/the-art-of-fiction-no-149/johnlecarré (accessed 12 December 2014).

Sisman, Adam, *John le Carré: The Biography* (New York: HarperCollins, 2015).

Van Gelder, Peter, 'Miss MacInnes on the Pleasures of Writing: A Natural Story-Teller', *New York Times* 1923– Current file: 26 July 1942; ProQuest Historical Newspapers, p. BR2.

Vaughan, Paul, 'Le Carré's Circus: Lamplighters, Moles and Others of That Ilk', in Bruccoli and Baughman (eds), pp. 53–9.

Volmane, Véra, 'John le Carré: The Writer, like the Spy, is an Illusionist', in Bruccoli and Baughman (eds), pp. 3 5.

Historical and Critical Scholarship

Alderman, Geoffrey, *Modern British Jewry* (Oxford: Clarendon Press, 1992).
Aldgate, Anthony and Jeffrey Richards, *Britain Can Take It: The British Cinema in the Second World War* (Edinburgh: Basil Blackwell, 1994).
Ambrosetti, Ronald, *Eric Ambler* (New York: Twayne, 1994).
Anon., 'Recent Reprints: Review of Helen Macinnes, *Above Suspicion*', *New York Times* 1923–Current file, 12 September 1943, ProQuest Historical Newspapers, BR22 (accessed 10 April 2014).
Appelbaum, Anne, 'Yesterday's Man?' *The New York Review of Books*, 11 February 2010, pp. 10–11.
Aronoff, Myron J., *The Spy Novels of John Le Carré* (New York: St Martin's, 1999).
Atkins, John, *The British Spy Novel: Styles in Treachery* (London: John Calder, 1984).
Baer, Elizabeth and Myrna Goldenberg (eds), *Experience and Expression: Women, the Nazis, and the Holocaust* (Detroit: Wayne State University Press, 2003).
Bakhtin, Mikhail, *The Dialogic Imagination*, trans. Caryl Emerson and Michael Holquist (Austin: University of Texas Press, 1981).
Barker, Jennifer L. *The Aesthetics of Antifascist Film* (New York: Routledge, 2013).
Barron, James, 'Curiosities Emerge about Suspected Russian Agents', *The New York Times*, 29 June 2010. http://www.nytimes.com/2010/06/30/nyregion/30suspects.html?_r=0 (accessed 5 July 2015).
Baruma, Ian, *Year Zero: A History of 1945* (New York: Penguin, 2013).
Bathrick, David, 'Introduction', in David Bathrick, Brad Prager and Michel D. Richardson (eds), *Visualizing the Holocaust: Documents, Aesthetics, Memory* (Rochester, NY: Camden House, 2008), pp. 1-18.
Bauman, Zygmunt, *Modernity and Ambivalence* (Ithaca, NY: Cornell University Press, 1991).
Beene, Lynn D., 'John Le Carré', in Robin W. Corrigan (ed.), *Mystery and Suspense Writers: The Literature of Crime, Detection, and Espionage*, vols 1–2 (New York: Scribner's; 1998), pp. 569–87.
Bergen, Doris, *War and Genocide* (New York: Roman and Littlefield, 2003).
Bloom, Clive, *Spy Thrillers: From Buchan to le Carré* (New York: St Martins, 1990).
Bloom, Harold (ed.), *The Magic Mountain: Modern Critical Interpretations* (New York: Chelsea House, 2002).
Bluemel, Kristin (ed.), *Intermodernism: Literary Culture in Mid-Twentieth-Century Britain* (Edinburgh: Edinburgh University Press, 2009).
Bold, Christine, 'Domestic Intelligence: Marriage and Espionage in Helen MacInnes's Fiction', *Paradoxa*, 24, 2012, pp. 31–53.
Bolton, Geoffrey, *The Oxford History of Australia 1942–1988: The Middle Way* (Oxford: Oxford University Press, 1990).
Bond, Alice Dixon, 'A MacInnes Masterpiece', *Boston Herald Traveler*, 22 September 1968, np.

Breitman, Richard and Allan Lichtman, *FDR and the Jews* (Cambridge, MA: Harvard University Press, 2013).
Brenner, Rachel Feldhay, *The Ethics of Witnessing: The Holocaust in Polish Writers' Diaries from Warsaw, 1939–1945* (Evanston: Northwestern University Press, 2014).
Brewer, Susan A., *To Win the Peace: British Propaganda in the United States during World War II* (Ithaca, NY: Cornell University Press, 1997).
Britton, Wesley, *Beyond Bond: Spies in Fiction and Film* (Westport, CT: Praeger, 2005).
Broe, Mary Lynn and Angela Ingram, *Women's Writing in Exile* (Chapel Hill: University of North Carolina Press, 1989).
Brown, Erica and Mary Grover (eds), *Middlebrow Literary Cultures: The Battle of the Brows, 1920–1960* (Basingstoke: Palgrave, 2012).
Buckingham, Janet Epp, *Fighting over God: A Legal and Political History of Religious Freedom in Canada* (Montreal: McGill Queens University Press, 2014).
Buzard, James, 'Faces, Photos, Mirrors: Image and Ideology in the Novels of John le Carré', in David B. Downing and Susan Bazargan (eds), *Image and Ideology in Modern/Postmodern Discourse* (Albany, NY: SUNY Press, 1991), pp. 153–80.
Byron, John, *Cain and Abel in Text and Tradition: Jewish and Christian Interpretations of the First Sibling Rivalry* (Leiden: Brill, 2011).
Carlston, Erin, *Double Agents: Espionage, Literature, and Liminal Citizens* (New York: Columbia University Press, 2013).
Carroll, Rachel, *Rereading Heterosexuality: Feminism, Queer Theory and Contemporary Fiction* (Edinburgh: Edinburgh University Press, 2012).
Cawelti, John and Bruce A. Rosenberg, *The Spy Story* (Chicago: University of Chicago Press, 1987).
Cesarani, David (ed.), *The Making of Modern Anglo-Jewry* (Oxford: Basil Blackwell, 1990).
Cesarani, David and Tony Kushner (eds), *The Internment of Aliens in Twentieth Century Britain* (London: Routledge, 1993).
Chace, William M, 'Spies and God's Spies: Green's Espionage Fiction', in Bryan Cheyette and Laura Marcus (eds), *Modernity, Culture, and the Jew* (Cambridge: Polity Press, 1998), pp. 156–80.
Chapman, James, *The British at War: Cinema, State and Propaganda 1939–1945* (London: I.B. Tauris, 1998).
—, 'The Power of Propaganda', *Journal of Contemporary History*, 35.4, October 2000, pp. 679–88.
Cheldelin, Sandra, Daniel Druckman and Larissa Fast (eds), *Conflict: From Analysis to Interpretation* (New York: Continuum, 2008).
Cheyette, Bryan and Laura Marcus (eds), *Modernity, Culture, and the Jew* (Cambridge: Polity Press, 1998).
Cobbs, John L., *Understanding John le Carré* (Columbia: University of South Carolina Press, 1998).
Cohen, Deborah, 'Who Was Who? Race and Jews in Turn-of-the-Century Britain', *Journal of British Studies*, 41, 2002, pp. 460–84.
Commire, Anne, 'Helen MacInnes', *Something about the Author*, vol. 22 (Detroit: Gale Research, 1981), p. 181.

Confino, Alon, *A World Without Jews: The Nazi Imagination from Persecution to Genocide* (New Haven, CT: Yale University Press, 2014).
Copping, Jasper, Ben Farmer and Hayley Dixon, 'John le Carré on the Inspiration for George Smiley'. *The Telegraph Bookshop*, http://www.telegraph.co.uk/culture/books/10676670/John-le-Carre-on-the-inspiration-for-George-Smiley.html (accessed 19 December 2014).
Coulson, Anthony (ed.), *Exiles and Migrants* (Brighton: Sussex Academic Press, 1997).
Creed, Barbara, 'Horror and the Carnivalesque: The Body-monstrous', *Fields of Vision: Essays in Film Studies, Visual Anthropology, and Photography* (Berkeley: University of California Press, 1995), pp. 127–59.
Cull, Nicholas J., *Selling War: The British Propaganda Campaign against American Neutrality in World War II* (Oxford: Oxford University Press, 1995).
Cull, Nicholas J. and Sue Harper, 'The Years of Total War: Propaganda and Entertainment', in Gledhill and Swanson (eds), pp. 193–212.
Davison, Carol, *Anti-Semitism and British Gothic Literature* (New York: Palgrave, 2004).
'Deadly Medicine: Creating the Master Race', http://www.ushmm.org/information/exhibitions/traveling-exhibitions/deadly-medicine (accessed 20 September 2014).
Denning, Michael, *Cover Stories: Narrative and Ideology in the British Spy Thriller* (London: Routledge and Kegan Paul, 1987).
Deutelbaum, Marshall and Leland A. Poague (eds), *A Hitchcock Reader* (London: Wiley, 2009).
Diethe, Carol, 'Anxious Space in German Expressionist Films', in Myrto Constantarakos (ed.), *Spaces in European Cinema* (Portland: Intellect, 2000), pp. 52–62.
Doak, Robert, 'Am I My Nation's Keeper: The Cain and Abel Myth and the Reluctant Spy', *Clues*, 20.2, Fall–Winter 1999, pp. 13–25.
Eagleton, Terry, *Myths of Power: A Marxist Study of the Brontës* (Basingstoke: Palgrave, 2005).
Eco, Umberto, 'Narrative Structures in Fleming', *The Role of the Reader: Explorations in the Semiotics of Texts* (Bloomington: Indiana University Press, 1984), pp. 144–65.
—, 'Ur-Fascism', *New York Review of Books*, 22 June 1995, pp. 12–15.
Elsaesser, Thomas, 'Time, Space and Causality: Joe May, Fritz Lang and the Modernism of German Detective Film', *Modernist Cultures*, 5.1, 2010, pp. 79–105.
Endelman, Todd, *Radical Assimilation in English Jewish History, 1656–1945* (Bloomington: Indiana University Press, 1990).
—, 'Jews, Aliens, and other Outsiders in British History', *Historical Journal*, 37, 1994, pp. 959–69.
—, 'The Frankaus of London: A Study in Radical Assimilation', *Jewish History*, 8.1–2, 1994, pp. 117–54.
Esty, Jed, *A Shrinking Island: Modernism and National Culture in England* (Princeton: Princeton University Press, 2004).
Everett, Glenn, 'Smiley's Fallen Camelot: Allusions to Tennyson in John le

Carré's Cambridge Circus Novels', *Papers on Language and Literature*, 27, 1991, pp. 496–513.
Finkielkraut, Alain, *The Imaginary Jew*, trans. David Suchoff (Lincoln: University of Nebraska Press, 1994).
Fox, Jo, *Film Propaganda in Britain and Nazi Germany: World War II Cinema* (Oxford: Berg, 2007).
Freud, Sigmund, 'The Uncanny', in Anna Freud, Alix Strachey and Alan Tyson (eds), *The Standard Edition of the Complete Psychological Works of Sigmund Freud*, trans. James Strachey, vol. 17 (London: Hogarth Press, 1955–73), pp. 217–56.
Friedlander, Henry, *The Origins of Nazi Genocide: From Euthanasia to the Final Solution* (Chapel Hill: University of North Carolina Press, 1995).
Friedlander, Saul, *Probing the Limits of Representation* (Cambridge, MA: Harvard University Press, 1992).
Friedman, Lester, 'The Edge of Knowledge: Jews as Monsters/Jews as Victims', *Melus*, 11. 3, Autumn 1984, pp. 49–62.
Fyrth, Jim, *Britain, Fascism and the Popular Front* (London: Lawrence and Wishart, 1985).
Galchinsky, Michael, '"Permanently Blacked": Julia Frankau's Jewish Race', *Victorian Literature and Culture*, 27.1, 1999, pp. 171–83.
Gardner, John, 'The Espionage Novel', in H. J. R. Keating (ed.), *Whodunit? A Guide to Crime, Suspense and Spy Fiction* (New York: Van Nostrand Reinhold, 1982), pp. 70–80.
Geraghty, Christine, 'Disguises and Betrayals: Negotiating Nationality and Femininity in Three Wartime Films', in Gledhill and Swanson (eds), pp. 230–7.
Gilman, Sander, *The Jew's Body* (New York: Routledge, 1991).
Ginzberg, Louis, *The Legends of the Jews, Vol. 1, Bible Times and Characters from the Creation to Jacob* (Philadelphia: The Jewish Publication Society of America, 1968).
Gledhill, Christine, '"An Abundance of Understatement": Documentary, Melodrama and Romance', in Gledhill and Swanson (eds), pp. 213–29.
Gledhill, Christine and Gillian Swanson, *Nationalising Femininity: Culture, Sexuality and British Cinema in the Second World War* (Manchester: Manchester University Press, 1996).
Gluzman, Michael, 'Modernism and Exile: A View from the Margins', in David Biale, Michael Galchinsky and Susan Heschel (eds), *Insider/Outsider: American Jews and Multiculturalism* (Berkeley: University of California Press, 1998), pp. 231–53.
Goldstein, Philip, 'Telling the Ugly Truth: Communism, Theory, Spies, Art', in Philip Goldstein (ed.), *Styles of Cultural Activism: From Theory and Pedagogy to Women, Indians, and Communism* (Newark: University of Delaware Press, 1994) pp. 233–55.
Goldsworthy, Vesna, *Inventing Ruritania: The Imperialism of the Imagination* (New Haven, CT: Yale University Press, 1997).
Gonshak, Henry, 'The Holocaust in Mystery, Thriller, and Espionage Fiction', *American Jewish Congress Monthly*, May/June 2001, pp. 15–17.
Gopinath, Praseeda, *Scarecrows of Chivalry: English Masculinities after Empire* (Charlottesville: University of Virginia Press, 2013).

Gracome, Sarah, 'Imperial Englishness in Julia Frankau's "Book of the Jew"', *Prooftexts*, 30. 2, Spring 2010, pp. 147–79.
Grenville, Anthony, 'Thomas Mann and the "inner emigration"', *The Association of Jewish Refugees Journal*, August 2012. http://www.ajr.org.uk/index.cfm/section.journalissue.Aug.12/article=10802 (accessed 10 October 2014).
Grenville, Anthony and Andrea Reiter, *Political Exile and Exile Politics in Britain after 1933* (Amsterdam: Rodopi, 2011).
Griffin, Roger (ed.), *Modernism and Fascism* (Basingstoke: Palgrave, 2007).
Gross, Miriam, 'The Secret World of John le Carré', *Observer*, 3 February 1980, p. 33.
Halberstam, Judith, *Skin Shows: Gothic Horror and the Technology of Monsters* (Durham, NC: Duke University Press, 1995).
Haltof, Marek, 'From Gothicism to Demonism: A Literary Transition to German Expressionist Film', *European Journal for Semiotic Studies*, 4.3, 1992, pp. 441–58.
Hammel, Andrea, 'The Kaleidoscope of Elsewhereness in Women's Exile Writing', in Alexander Stephan (ed.), pp. 199–226.
Hammond, Andrew, *British Fiction and the Cold War* (Basingstoke: Palgrave, 2013).
Hansen, Miriam Bratu, 'The Mass Production of the Senses: Classical Cinema as Vernacular Modernism', in Christine Gledhill and Linda Williams (eds), *Reinventing Film Studies* (London: Arnold, 2000), pp. 332–50.
Hark, Ina Rae, 'Keeping your Amateur Standing: Audience Participation in and Good Citizenship in Hitchcock's Political Films', *Cinema Journal*, 29.2, 1990, pp. 12–13.
Harper, Sue, 'The Years of Total War: Propaganda and Entertainment', in Gledhill and Swanson (eds), pp. 193–212.
Harrisson, Tom, *Living Through the Blitz* (London: Penguin, 1990).
Heckner, Elke, 'Whose Trauma Is It? Identification and Secondary Witnessing in the Age of Postmemory', in David Bathrick, Brad Prager and Michael D. Richardson (eds), *Visualizing the Holocaust: Documents, Aesthetics, Memory* (Rochester, NY: Camden House, 2008), pp. 62–85.
Hedgepeth, Sonja and Rochelle Seidel (eds), *Sexual Violence against Jewish Women during the Holocaust* (Waltham, MA: Brandeis University Press, 2010).
Hepburn, Allan, *Intrigue: Espionage and Culture* (New Haven, CT: Yale University Press, 2005).
Hindersmann, Jost, '"The Right Side Lost but the Wrong Side Won": John le Carré's Spy Novels Before and After the End of the Cold War', *Clues*, 23. 4, 2005, pp. 25–37.
Ho, Janice, *Nation and Citizenship in the Twentieth Century British Novel* (Cambridge: Cambridge University Press, 2015).
Hoffman, Eva, 'Out of Exile: Some Thoughts on Exile as a Dynamic Condition', *European Judaism*, 46.2, Autumn 2013, pp. 55–60.
Homberger, Eric, 'English Spy Thrillers in the Age of Appeasement', in Wesley Wark (ed.), pp. 80–91.
Hopkins, Chris, 'Leftists and Thrillers: The Politics of a Thirties Sub-Genre', in

Antony Shuttleworth (ed.), *Time: Vision, Revision, and British Writing of the 1930s* (Lewisburg: Bucknell University Press, 2003), pp. 147–62.

Hopkins, Michael F., Michael D. Kandiah and Gillian Staerck (eds), *Cold War Britain, 1945–1964* (Basingstoke: Palgrave, 2003).

Horn, Eva, *The Secret War: Treason, Espionage, and Modern Fiction* (Evanston: Northwestern University Press, 2013).

Horowitz, Sara R, *Voicing the Void: Muteness and Memory in Holocaust Fiction* (Albany: State University of New York Press, 1997).

'Host', *Oxford English Dictionary Compact Edition*, vol. 1 (Oxford: Oxford University Press, 1985), pp. 1336.

Humble, Nicola, *The Feminine Middlebrow Novel, 1920s to 1950s* (Oxford: Oxford University Press, 2001).

Hüppauf, Bernd, 'Modernism and the Photographic Representation of War and Destruction', in Leslie Devereaux and Roger Hillman (eds), *Fields of Vision: Essays in Film Studies, Visual Anthropology, and Photography* (Berkeley: University of California Press, 1995), pp. 94–126.

Hynes, Samuel, *The Auden Generation* (London: Bodley Head, 1976).

Iordachi, Constantin (ed.), *Comparative Fascist Studies* (New York: Routledge, 2010).

Jowett, Garth S. and Victoria O'Donnell (eds), *Propaganda and Persuasion* (Beverly Hills: Sage Publications, 1986).

Judt, Tony, *Postwar: A History of Europe since 1945* (New York: Penguin, 2005).

Kaes, Anton, *Shell Shock Cinema: Weimar Culture and the Wounds of War* (Princeton: Princeton University Press, 2009).

Kamen, Henry, *Imagining Spain: Historical Myth and National Identity* (New Haven, CT: Yale University Press, 2008).

King, Holly Beth, 'Child's Play in *Tinker, Tailor, Soldier, Spy*', *Clues: A Journal of Detection*, 3.2, 1982, pp. 87–92.

Kingra, Mahindra, 'In from the Cold: Review Ambler Omnibus', *City Paper*. http://www2.citypaper.com/arts/review.asp?rid=5119 (accessed 11 December 2012).

Konuk, Kader, 'Jewish-German Philologists in Turkish Exile: Leo Spitzer and Erich Auerbach', in Alexander Stephan (ed.), pp. 31–47.

Krefetz, Gerald, *Jews and Money: The Myths and the Reality* (New Haven, CT: Ticknor and Fields, 1982).

Kristeva, Julia, *Nations without Nationalism* (New York: Columbia University Press, 1993).

Kushner, Tony, 'Beyond the Pale? British Reactions to Nazi Anti-Semitism, 1933–39', *Immigrants and Minorities*, 8, 1989, pp. 143–60.

—, *The Holocaust and the Liberal Imagination* (Oxford: Blackwell, 1994).

Lang, Berel, *Post-Holocaust: Interpretation, Misinterpretation, and the Claims of History* (Bloomington: Indiana University Press, 2005).

Lant, Antonia, *Blackout: Reinventing Women for Wartime British Cinema* (Princeton: Princeton University Press, 1991).

Lassner, Phyllis, '"The Milk of Our Mother's Kindness Has Ceased to Flow": Virginia Woolf, Stevie Smith, and the Representation of the Jew', in Bryan Cheyette (ed.), *Between 'Race' and Culture: Representations of 'the Jew' in*

English and American Literature (Stanford: Stanford University Press, 1996), pp. 129–44.

—, *British Women Writers of World War II* (Basingstoke: Palgrave, 1998).

—, '"Camp Follower of Catastrophe": Martha Gellhorn's World War II Challenge to the Modernist War', *Modern Fiction Studies*, 44.3, Fall 1998, pp. 792–812.

—, 'Under Suspicion: The Plotting of Britain in World War II Detective Spy Fiction', in Kristin Bluemel (ed.), pp. 113–30.

Lassner, Phyllis and Lara Trubowitz (eds), *Philosemitism and Antisemitism in Twentieth and Twenty-first Century Culture* (Newark: University of Delaware Press, 2008).

—, Ann Rea and Genevieve Brassard (eds), *Reading Sideways: Middlebrow into Modernism, The Space Between Journal* (special issue), 9.1, 2013.

—, and Mia Spiro, '"A Tale of Two Cities": Virginia Woolf's Imagined Jewish Spaces and London's East End Jewish Culture', *Woolf Studies Annual*, 19, 2013, pp. 58–82.

Lewis, Peter, *Eric Ambler* (New York: Continuum, 1990).

London, Louise, *Whitehall and the Jews, 1933–1948* (Cambridge: Cambridge University Press, 2000).

Luckhurst, Roger, 'The Contemporary London Gothic and the Limits of the "Spectral Turn"', *Textual Practice*, 16.3, Winter 2002, pp. 527–46.

Lyall, Sarah, 'Cloak, Dagger and Abuses of a New Era', *The New York Times Book Review*, 5 October 2008, pp. 1, 9.

Macdonald, Gina. 'Helen MacInnes', *Dictionary of Literary Biography*, 87, *British Mystery and Thriller Writers Since 1940*. First Series, 1989, pp. 287–94.

Macdonald, Kevin, *Emeric Pressburger: The Life and Death of a Screenwriter* (London: Faber and Faber, 1994).

Macintosh, J. J., 'Ethics and Spy Fiction', in Wesley Wark (ed.), pp. 161–84.

McCloskey, Barbara, 'Cartographies of Exile', in Alexander Stephan (ed.), 135–52.

Mackay, Marina, '"Is Your Journey Really Necessary?": Going Nowhere in Late Modernist London', *PMLA*, 124.5, October 2009, pp. 1600–13.

MacKenzie, S. P., *British War Films 1939–1945* (London: Hambledon and London, 2001).

McLaine, Ian, *Ministry of Morale: Home Front Morale and the Ministry of Information in World War II* (London: Allen and Unwin, 1979).

Marciniak, Katarzyna, *Alienhood: Citizenship, Exile, and the Logic of Difference* (Minneapolis: University of Minnesota Press, 2006).

Margolis, Rebecca, 'The Canadian Army Newsreels as a Representation of the Holocaust', in Hilary Earl and Karl A. Schleunes (eds), *Lessons and Legacies XI* (Evanston: Northwestern University Press, 2014), pp. 121–43.

Marwick, Arthur, *Britain in the Century of Total War* (Boston: Little, Brown, 1968).

Maslen, Elizabeth, 'Military Tales of Between the Two Wars'. Unpublished Talk to Probus Organisation, April 2010.Mazower, Mark, 'Introduction', Eric Ambler, *The Mask of Dimitrios* (London: Penguin, 2009).

Merry, Bruce, *Anatomy of the Spy Thriller* (Dublin: Gill and Macmillan, 1977).

Mitgang, Herbert, 'Helen MacInnes, Behind the Best Sellers', *New York Times Book Review*, 17 December 1978, p. BR22.

Monaghan, David, 'John le Carré and England: A Spy's-Eye View', *Modern Fiction Studies*, 29.3, Autumn 1983, pp. 569–82.

—, *The Novels of John le Carré: The Art of Survival* (Oxford: Basil Blackwell, 1985).

Montefiore, Janet, *Men and Women Writers of the 1930s* (London: Routledge, 1996).

Mosse, George, 'Toward a General Theory of Fascism', in Constantin Iordachi (ed.), *Comparative Fascist Studies* (London: Routledge, 2010), pp. 60–94.

Muller, Jerry Z., *Capitalism and the Jews* (Princeton: Princeton University Press, 2010).

Murphy, Robert, *British Cinema and the Second World War* (London: Continuum, 2000).

Neville, Peter, *Hitler and Appeasement: The British Attempt to Prevent the Second World War* (London: Hambledon Continuum, 2006).

Ofer, Dalia and Lenore J. Weitzman (eds), *Women in the Holocaust* (New Haven, CT: Yale University Press, 1998).

Oram, Malcolm, 'Eric Ambler', *Publishers Weekly*, 9 September 1974, pp. 6–7.

O'Toole, Fintan, 'The Real Men of England', *The New York Review of Books*, 6 June 2013, pp. 18–22.

Overy, Richard, *The Bombing War: Europe 1939–1945* (London: Allen Lane, 2013).

Palmer, William J., 'Spies and Their Novelists', *Contemporary Literature*, 47.3, Fall 2006, pp. 497–501.

Parry, Ann, '"Lost in the Multiplicity of Impersonations?": The Jew and the Holocaust in Post-war British Fiction', *The Journal of Holocaust Education*, 8.3, Winter 1999, pp. 1–22.

Payne, Stanley, *A History of Fascism 1914–1945* (Madison: University of Wisconsin Press, 1995).

Peach, Linden, *Masquerade, Crime and Fiction* (Basingstoke: Palgrave, 2006).

Perriaux, Sophie, 'Enlightened Humanism Defeated: German Writers, Writings, and Ideas', in Anthony Coulson (ed.), pp. 83–8.

Piette, Adam, *Imagination at War: British Fiction and Poetry 1939–1945* (London: Papermac, 1995).

Pistol, Rachel, 'Enemy Alien and Refugee: Conflicting Identities in Great Britain during the Second World War', *University of Sussex Journal of Contemporary History*, 16, 2015, pp. 37–52.

Plain, Gill, *Twentieth-Century Crime Fiction: Gender, Sexuality and the Body* (Edinburgh: Edinburgh University Press, 2001).

Pogorelskin, Alexis, 'Phyllis Bottome's *The Mortal Storm*: Film and Controversy', *The Space Between: Literature and Culture 1914–1945*, 6.1, 2010, pp. 39–58.

Prescott, Orville, 'Review, Pamela Frankau, *Ask Me No More*, *New York Times*, 10 November 1958, p. 27.

Priestman, Martin (ed.), *Cambridge Companion to Crime Fiction* (Cambridge: Cambridge University Press, 2003).

Raskin, Richard, 'From Leslie Howard to Raoul Wallenberg: The Transmission and Adaptation of a Heroic Model Source', *P.o.v: A Danish Journal of Film Studies*, 28 December 2009, pp. 85–104.

Rattigan, Neil, *This is England: British Film and the People's War, 1939–1945* (London: Associated University Presses, 2001).

Reeves, Nicholas, *The Power of Film Propaganda: Myth or Reality* (London: Cassell, 1999).
Remmler, Karen, 'Encounters across the Void: Rethinking Approaches to German-Jewish Symbioses', in Leslie Morris and Jack Zipes (eds), *Unlikely History: The Changing German-Jewish Symbiosis, 1945–2000* (Basingstoke: Palgrave, 2002), pp. 3–30.
Richards, Jeffrey, 'Foreword', in Estel Eforgan, pp. xiii–xv.
Robinson, Benjamin, 'Kaus Mann's Hotel Reservations', in Alexander Stephan (ed.), pp. 178–95.
Rothberg, Michael, *Traumatic Realism: The Demands of Holocaust Representation* (Minneapolis: University of Minnesota Press, 2000).
Rowe, Margaret Moan, 'Women's Place in John le Carré's Man's World', in Alan Norman (ed.), *The Quest for Le Carré* (New York: St Martin's, 1988), pp. 69–86.
'Sachs, Hans'. *Encyclopedia Brittanica*, http://www.britannica.com/EBchecked/topic/515273/Hans-Sachs (accessed 20 December 2014).
§Shane, Scott and Charles Savage, 'In Ordinary Lives, US Sees the Work of Russian Agents', *The New York Times*, 28 June 2010. http://www.nytimes.com/2010/06/29/world/europe/29spy.html (accessed 5 July 2015).
Schlesinger, Arthur M., *The Vital Center* (Cambridge, MA: Riverside, 1949).
Schweizer, Bernard, 'Rebecca West and the Meaning of Exile', *Partial Answers: Journal of Literature and the History of Ideas*, 8.2, June 2010, pp. 389–406.
Sedgwick, Eve Kosofsky, *Between Men: English Literature and Male Homosocial Desire* (New York: Columbia University Press, 1985).
Seed, David, 'Spy Fiction', in Priestman (ed.), pp. 115–34.
Sherman, A. J., *Island Refuge: Britain and Refugees from the Third Reich 1933–1939* (Ilford: Frank Cass, 1994).
Shneer, David, *Through Soviet Jewish Eyes: Photography, War, and the Holocaust* (New Brunswick: Rutgers University Press, 2010).
Silver, Brenda, 'Woman as Agent: The Case of le Carré's *Little Drummer Girl*', *Contemporary Literature*, 28.1, Spring, 1987, pp. 14–40.
Smith, Andrew, 'Rethinking the Gothic: What Do We Mean?', *Gothic Studies*, 4.1, May 2002, pp. 79–85.
Smith, Andrew and Jeff Wallace, *Gothic Modernisms* (Basingstoke: Palgrave, 2001).
Smith, James, *British Writers and MI5 Surveillance, 1930–1960* (Cambridge: Cambridge University Press, 2013).
Snowman, Daniel, *The Hitler Emigrés* (London: Chatto and Windus, 2002).
Snyder, Robert Lance, *The Art of Indirection in British Espionage Fiction* (Jefferson, NC: McFarland, 2011).
Snyder, Timothy, 'Holocaust History: An Agenda for Renewal', in Hilary Earl and Karl A. Schleunes (eds), *Lessons and Legacies* XI (Evanston: Northwestern University Press, 2014), pp. 357–68.
Sontag, Susan, *On Photography* (New York: Anchor, 1977).
Spiro, Mia, *Anti-Nazi Modernism: The Challenges of Resistance in 1930s Fiction* (Evanston: Northwestern University Press, 2013).
Spicer, Andrew, 'A British Empire of their Own? Jewish Entrepreneurs in the British Film Industry', in Nathan Abrams (ed.), *Jews in/and British Cinema*, *Journal of European Popular Culture* (special edition), 3.2, pp. 117–29.

Stern, Guy, *Literature and Culture in Exile* (Dresden: Dresden University Press, 1998).
Stephan, Alexander (ed.), *Exile and Otherness: New Approaches to the Experience of the Nazi Refugees* (Bern: Peter Lang, 2005).
Stewart, Victoria, 'Middlebrow Psychology in Gilbert Frankau's Novels of the 1930s', *Working Papers on the Web*, 11 July 2008, np.
Stone, Dan, *Responses to Nazism in Britain, 1933–1939* (Basingstoke: Palgrave, 2003).
Stonebridge, Lyndsey, *The Judicial Imagination: Writing after Nuremberg* (Edinburgh: Edinburgh University Press, 2011).
Suh, Judy, *Fascism and Antifascism in Twentieth-Century British Fiction* (Basingstoke: Palgrave, 2009).
Sutherland, John, 'Review, *The Heir Apparent: A Life of Edward VII, the Playboy Prince*', *The New York Times Book Review*, 1 December 2013, pp. 1, 20.
Telotte, J. P., 'German Expressionism: A Cinematic/ Cultural Problem', in Linda Badley, R. Barton Palmer and Stephen J. Schneider (eds), *Traditions in World Cinema* (Edinburgh: Edinburgh University Press, 2006), pp. 15–28.
Theweleit, Klaus, *Male Fantasies*, trans. Stephan Conway (Minneapolis: University of Minnesota Press, 1987–9).
Thompson, Dorothy, 'Refugees: A World Problem'. *Foreign Affairs*, 16.3, April 1938, pp. 375–87.
Tirohl, Blu, 'Forensic Photography, Film Noir, and Fellig: Scenes Excavated by the Night Prowler', *Photography & Culture*, 5.2, July 2012, pp. 135–48.
Toffell, Gil, 'Cinema-going from Below: The Jewish Film Audience in Interwar Britain', *Participations: Journal of Audience and Reception Studies*, 8.2, November 2011, pp. 522–38.
Tracey, Laura, 'Forbidden Fantasy', *Clues*, Spring-Summer 1988, pp. 11–37.
Turner, Graeme, *Film as Social Practice* (New York: Routledge, 2006).
Valman, Nadia, *The Jewess in Nineteenth-Century British Literary Culture* (Cambridge: Cambridge University Press, 2007).
Wallace, Margaret, '"Send Me Down" and Other New Works of Fiction', *The New York Times*, 1923–Current file, 13 July 1941, ProQuest Historical Newspapers, p. BR5.
Wark, Wesley (ed.), *Spy Fiction, Spy Films and Real Intelligence* (London: Frank Cass, 1991).
Wasserstein, Bernard, *Britain and the Jews of Europe 1939–1945* (Oxford: Clarendon Press, 1979).
—, *On the Eve: The Jews of Europe before the Second World War* (New York: Simon and Schuster, 2012).
Welky, David, *The Moguls and the Dictators* (Baltimore: Johns Hopkins University Press, 2008).
West, Rebecca, 'Obituary: Miss Pamela Frankau', *The Times*, 9 June 1967, p. 12.
White, Rosie, *Violent Femmes* (New York: Routledge, 2007).
Williams, Gordon, 'Propaganda into Art: Wartime Films of Powell and Pressburger', *Trivium*, 17, 1982, pp. 39–65.
Wolfe, Peter, *Corridors of Deceit: The World of John le Carré* (Bowling Green: Bowling Green State University Press, 1987).

—, *Alarms and Epitaphs: The Art of Eric Ambler* (Bowling Green: Bowling Green University Popular Press, 1993).

Wollaeger, Mark, *Modernism, Media, and Propaganda: British Narrative from 1900 to 1945* (Princeton: Princeton University Press, 2006).

Woods, Brett, 'Beyond the Balkans – Eric Ambler and the British Espionage Novel, 1936–1940', *California Literary Review*, 2 October 2008. http://calitreview.com/49 (accessed 5 March 2014).

Wyman, David, *The Abandonment of the Jews* (New York: New Press, 2007).

Young, James E., *Writing and Rewriting the Holocaust* (Bloomington: Indiana University Press, 1990).

Index

49th Parallel (Howard), 12, 43, 120, 121, 126, 130, 136, 145–60, 220

Above Suspicion (MacInnes), 35, 70, 81–93, 141, 218
Abraham, Karl, 42
Aciman, André, 46
Aldgate, Anthony and Jeffrey Richards, 132, 136, 146, 151, 154, 162n
Allingham, Margery, 69
Ambler, Eric, 2, 5, 8, 11, 12, 16–67, 69, 70, 72, 79, 80, 87, 112, 120, 149, 170, 172, 175, 179, 194, 217, 221; *see also Background to Danger*; *A Coffin for Dimitrios*; *The Dark Frontier*; *Epitaph for a Spy*
Ambrosetti, Ronald, 48, 59, 61, 66n
The Americans (TV series), 1, 26
Améry, Jean (Hans Meyer), 183
Andreas-Friedrich, Ruth, 90–1
Anschluss, 3, 132
antisemitism (general), 13n, 18, 19, 44, 45, 66n, 72, 74, 78–9, 87, 92, 113n, 125, 188, 200, 213n
  Britain, 74, 86,114n, 115n, 136
  criticism of le Carré, 201, 215n
  fictional representation, 11–12, 115n, 179, 181, 203, 207
  and history, 75, 77
  and liberal democracies, 183
  see also Fascism; Holocaust; Jews; Nazism
Arendt, Hannah, 6–7, 186–7, 211n, 213n, 218
Ask Me No More (Frankau), 113n
Asquith, Anthony (*Freedom Radio*), 162n
Assignment in Brittany (MacInnes), 35, 81, 92, 116n

Atkins, John, 210n
Atwood, Margaret (*The Handmaid's Tale*), 115n
Austro-Hungarian Empire, 10, 40
Axis powers, 10; *see also* Fascism; Nazism

Background to Danger (Ambler), 10, 19, 25, 26, 28, 35–46, 49, 51, 52, 60, 142, 158
Bakhtin, Mikhail (heteroglossia), 89
Balcon, Michael (*Jew Süss*), 136
Balfour Declaration, 163n
Banville, John (*The Untouchable*), 4
Barker, Jennifer, 137, 161n
Baruma, Ian, 87
Bathrick, David, 211n
Bauman, Zigmunt, 72, 86
BBC (British Broadcasting Company), 12, 119–22, 160n
Bildungsroman, 72, 168
The Black Laurel (Jameson), 186
Blitz, 123, 127, 129, 133
Bloom, Clive, 2
Bluemel, Kristin, 4, 13n
Blunt, Anthony, 4
Bold, Christine, 80, 82
Bond, James (Ian Fleming), 1, 9, 80, 113n, 170, 171, 173, 205, 206, 211n, 218
Borinsky, Alicia, 6
Bottome, Phyllis, 4, 13n, 51, 129, 162n
Boulting Brothers (*Pastor Hall*), 162n
Bourne, Jason (Robert Ludlum), 2, 9, 114n, 205, 206, 211n, 219
Bowen, Elizabeth, 189
Boyd, William, *Restless*, 113
Brecht, Bertolt, 43
Brenner, Rachel, 207

Brewer, Susan, 121, 123, 133, 160n, 161n
Bridge, Ann, 3, 5, 8, 11, 12, 63, 69, 79, 80, 94–101, 112, 149, 160, 175; see also *A Place to Stand*; *A Tightening String*
British Commonwealth, 130, 145, 150, 163n
British Council of Christians and Jews, 163n
British Empire, 4, 83, 150, 163n, 209n
British humour, 140–2
Brittain, Vera, 4, 115n
Britton, Wesley, 64n
Buchan, John, 17, 21, 64n, 65n, 146, 169, 181
Buckingham, Janet Epp, 163n
Burdekin, Katharine, 4, 88, 125
Buzard, James, 65n, 174
Byron, John, 106

The Cabinet of Dr Caligari, 23, 39, 43
Call for the Dead (le Carré), 10, 12, 168–201, 203, 206, 207, 218, 220
Cambridge Five, 4
Canada, *49th Parallel*, 145–60
Carlston, Erin, 9, 179, 200
Carroll, Rachel, 65n, 116n
Cause for Alarm (Ambler), 22, 25, 26, 28, 37, 41, 52, 65n
Chaplin, Charles (*The Great Dictator*), 156, 162n, 163n
Chapman, James, 126, 130, 135, 145, 146, 155, 160n
Childers, Erskine, 29
Christie, Agatha, 46, 69, 169
  Miss Marple, 63, 81
Churchill, Winston, 123, 161n
citizenship, 3, 9, 35, 73, 79, 80, 81, 90, 96–8, 125, 184, 186, 202
  American, 90, 100–1
  British, 37, 103, 175, 177, 192, 198, 205, 208
  Canadian, *49th Parallel*, 145–60
Cliveden Set, 65n
A Coffin for Dimitrios (Ambler), 18, 25, 41, 52–64
  The Mask of Dimitrios (British edition), 59, 60
Cohen, Deborah, 114n
Cold War, 2, 3, 5, 6, 8, 70, 94, 101, 102–12, 159, 166–215, 219; see also *Call for the Dead*; *Colonel Blessington*; *The Spy Who Came in from the Cold*
Colonel Blessington (Frankau), 5, 77, 101–13, 218
Communism, 2, 9, 10, 12, 19, 40, 45, 53, 66n, 67n, 79, 92, 97, 101, 103, 166, 177, 207–8
  British responses, 18, 180
  Communist espionage, 172–5
  East German communism, 5, 176–215
  Red Scare, 111
  violence related to Nazism, 3, 185, 189
  see also Soviet Union
The Confidential Spy (Greene), 10
Confino, Alon, 115n
Conrad, Joseph, 197
cosmopolitanism, 2
Coulson, Anthony, 13n
Creed, Barbara, 59
Cull, Nicholas, 160n, 163n

The Dark Frontier (Ambler), 26, 29, 30–5, 38, 39, 49, 60, 218
Delbo, Charlotte, 181–2
Democracy (general), 3, 12, 96, 97, 103, 119, 135, 137, 141, 145, 155, 160n, 179
  as middlebrow narrative, 124–5
  political philosophy, 123–4, 129, 138, 150, 157–8, 211n
  Western Allies, 50–3, 65n, 92–3, 146–7, 183, 203–4, 213n
Denning, Michael, 2, 3, 20, 64n, 82
The Devil We Know (Frankau), 11, 63, 71–80, 84, 101, 104, 106
Diethe, Carol, 65n
Doak, Robert, 116n
Dracula, 26–7, 29, 38, 44, 59–60; see also Nosferatu
Du Maurier, Daphne (*Rebecca*), 193
Dumas, Alexander (*The Corsican Brothers*), 197
dystopia, 5, 20, 23, 26, 35, 57, 58, 72, 88, 103, 104, 111, 115n, 125–6, 166, 172, 190–1, 202–3
dystopian history, 219

Eagleton, Terry, 213n
Eco, Umberto, 86, 108, 116n, 210n
Eforgan, Estel (Howard biographer), 118, 120, 125, 133, 134, 136, 144, 160n, 162n, 163n

Einstein, Albert, 43, 62
Elgar, Edgar, *The Banner of St. George*, 174–5, 198
Elsaesser, Thomas, 22, 23
Endleman, Todd, 114n
Engelmann, Bernt, 91
Epitaph for a Spy (Ambler), 5, 16, 25, 46–51, 76, 202
Esty, Jed, 13n, 114n
Everett, Glenn, 210n
Evian-les-Bains conference, 66n, 186, 212n
Expressionism (general), 5, 26–7, 29, 39, 46, 48–50, 52, 59–63, 102–3, 106, 107, 111, 137, 143, 158, 173, 204, 218–22
   German Expressionist film, 16–17, 21–2, 32–4, 62, 65n, 85, 133
   Gothic Expressionism, 17, 21–4, 36, 37, 38, 43, 57–8, 167, 190, 203, 218, 220

Facts and Fictions (Bridge), 94
Fascism, 2, 5, 9, 10, 11, 13n, 19, 20, 21, 23, 24, 25, 31, 35, 37, 40–6, 52, 53, 58, 60–3, 66n, 80, 87, 97, 102–5, 112, 114n, 115n, 116n, 180, 206, 220
   British responses, 16, 17, 18
   Fascist aesthetic, 32, 138–9
   Fascist ideology, 107–8, 161n; *see also* Umberto Eco
   Fascist violence, 3, 41–2, 46
   Hungarian Fascism, 5, 10, 93–4, 97, 100
   Italian Fascism, 28, 31, 32, 41, 45, 47, 116n, 184
   and Jewish science, 43
   women's roles *see* femininity
femininity
   Above Suspicion (MacInnes), 81–93
   femme fatale, 65n, 70, 193
   fictional representation, 1, 11, 65n, 80, 96, 143, 182–3, 190–4, 214n
   Jewish women and Nazi ideology, 182–4
   Madonna image, 75, 76, 101
   A Place to Stand (Bridge), 94–101
   women audiences, 148
   women's social roles, 20, 65n, 70–1, 81–2, 84, 100–1, 106, 138, 153, 193, 214n
Finkielkraut, Alain, 195

The First of the Few (Howard), 122, 160n
Fischer, Louis, 92, 199, 214n
Fleming, Ian, 169; *see also* James Bond
Fox, Jo, 126, 128, 139, 151, 160n, 161n
Frankau, Pamela, 2, 3, 5, 10, 11, 12, 63, 71–80, 101–13, 114n, 116n, 179, 217; *see also Colonel Blessington*; *The Devil We Know*
From the Four Corners (Howard), 130
Furst, Alan, 116n

Gardner, John, 210n
Gellhorn, Martha, 94
gender (general), 60, 80, 101, 109, 112
   gender-bending, 104
   and genre, 69, 80–1, 83
   heteronormativity, 65n, 116n
   heterosexuality, 77, 106, 143
   homo-social desire, 197
   Jews and gender, 183–6
   Nazi gender ideology, 112, 138–9
   persecution of homosexuals, 9, 66n, 200
   sexual abuse, 60, 182
   wartime films, 148, 193
   women characters *see* femininity: women's social roles
   see also femininity
The Gentle Sex (Howard), 122
Geraghty, Christine, 151
Gilman, Sander (*The Jew's Body*), 66n, 114n, 182, 211n
Ginzberg, Louis, 106
Gledhill, Christine, 160n, 193
Gledhill and Swanson, 120
Gluzman, Michael, 13n
Gonshak, Henry, 212n
Gopinath, Praseeda, 210n
Gothic style, 26–7, 36, 37, 38, 44, 45, 57–9, 62–3, 65n, 85, 173, 190, 193, 198, 202, 218; *see also* Expressionism
Greene, Graham, 4, 170
Grenville, Anthony, 90
Grierson, John (documentary filmmaker), 130, 163n
Griffin, Roger, 108, 115n, 116n
Grosz, George (Expressionist artist), 106

Haffner, Sebastian, 90, 91–2
Halberstam, Judith, 44, 214n

Haltof, Marek, 36, 38, 42
Hammel, Andrea, 7
Hammond, Andrew, 113n, 209n
Hansen, Miriam, 127
Hark, Ina Rae, 120
Harper, Sue, 147, 153, 161n, 163n, 193
Harris, Robert, *Fatherland*, 116n
Hayes, Peter, 163n
Heckner, Elke, 212n
Hepburn, Allan, 9, 13n, 104, 112, 113n, 116n, 182, 183, 189, 192, 207, 214n, 215n, 222n
Here Lies (Ambler memoir), 16, 17, 18, 19, 29, 46, 52, 66n
heteroglossia (Bakhtin), 89
Hindersmann, Jost, 214n
Hitchcock, Alfred, 20, 42, 142, 150, 158
Ho, Janice, 161n
Hoffman, Eva, 6, 7, 189
Holocaust, 5, 6, 10, 13n, 163n, 167, 168, 191, 194–6, 204, 220
  denial, 184
  representation, 183–9, 211n, 212n
Homberger, Eric, 66n
Hopkins, Chris, 66n
Hopkins, Joel, 19
Hopkins, Michael, Michael Kandiah and Gillian Staerck, 210n
Horn, Eva, 3, 176, 189, 211n, 212n
Horowitz, Sara, 184
Howard, Leslie, 3, 5, 12, 69, 70, 71, 79, 80, 87, 118–64, 175, 221
  Howard, Ronald, 118, 119, 156
  see also *49th Parallel*; *Pimpernel Smith*
humanism, 207
Huppaüf, Bernd, 31
Hutterites, 147, 152–3, 163n; see also *49th Parallel*
Huxley, Aldous, 4

I Find Four People (Frankau), 71

James, P. D. (*The Children of Men*), 115n
Jameson, Storm, 3, 13n, 88, 129, 161n, 186, 219–20, 222; see also *The Black Laurel*; *Then We Shall Hear Singing*
Jews and fictional representation, 2, 10, 38, 42–5, 71–9, 86–7, 136, 178–81, 188, 195–215, 220
  British Jewish film industry, 74, 136, 145
  and gender, 73–6, 114n, 178–9, 182–3, 195–9
  Jewish identity, 71–9, 109, 161n, 180, 185, 197, 208, 222n
  myth of wandering Jew, 44, 72, 78, 186–8
  see also antisemitism; Dracula; Holocaust
Jews in history, 6, 9, 13n, 20, 35, 65n, 66n, 67n, 72, 77, 79, 92, 115n, 125, 129, 195, 204, 207–15
  Britain, 71–4, 87, 91, 114n, 179–80
Journey into Fear (Ambler), 63
Joyce, William (Lord Haw Haw), 121, 156
Judt, Tony, 210n, 211n, 213n, 214n
Jung, Carl G., 29, 59, 61

Kaes, Anton, 23, 39
King, Holly Beth, 198
Koestler, Arthur, 159, 199, 210n, 213n, 214n
  The Mixed Transport, 159
Konuk, Kader, 1–2
Korda, Alexander, 136
Kracauer, Sigfried, 23
Kristeva, Julia, 107–8, 213n
Kushner, Tony, 13n, 65n, 66n, 87, 92, 114n, 135, 159, 163n, 168, 179, 183, 188, 210n

The Lady Vanishes (Hitchcock), 142
Lang, Fritz (German Expressionist filmmaker), 21, 34
Lant, Antonia, 139, 162n
Le Carré, John, 2, 3, 5, 7, 8, 9, 10, 12, 34, 65n, 70, 101, 102, 166–215, 218; see also *Call for the Dead*; *A Murder of Quality*; *A Small Town in Germany*; *The Spy Who Came in from the Cold*
Le Queux, Willliam, 20, 64n
Lewis, Peter, 54, 60, 63, 65n, 66n, 67n
The Little Drummer Girl (le Carré), 27
The Looking-Glass War (le Carré), 24
Luckhurst, Roger, 65n
Ludlum, Robert (*Bourne Identity*), 169, 204

McCarthy, Mary, 187
McCloskey, Barbara, 7
MacDonald, Gina, 115n
McEwan, Ian (*Sweet Tooth*), 113n
MacInnes, Helen, 3, 5, 10, 11, 12, 34,

50, 63, 69, 79, 81–93, 95, 96, 112, 115n, 120, 149, 160, 175, 179; see also *Above Suspicion*; *Assignment in Brittany*; *While Still We Live*
Macintosh, J. J., 218, 222n
Mclaine, Ian, 119, 160n, 162n
Mann, Heinrich, 43
Mann, Klaus, 64n
Mann, Thomas, 90, 154, 178
Marciniak, Katarzyna, 66n
Margolis, Rebecca, 163n
Marwick, Arthur, 65n
masculinity (general), 1, 4, 9, 25, 32, 57, 65n, 72, 80, 104–6, 156, 189
　British masculinity, 135, 172–6
　heroism, 2, 19, 20, 26, 34, 53, 63, 70, 80, 99, 102, 103, 105, 109, 148, 175
　matinee idol, 70, 132
　Nazi militarist masculinity, 178
　Nazi *ubermensch* (superman), 103, 138
　Nazi *untermenschen* (subhuman), 4, 84, 131, 139, 148, 196
　racialised, 72, 73, 75–6, 178–80, 195
　sexism, 138, 143
　see also gender
Maslen, Elizabeth, 18, 186, 212n, 222
Mass Observation, 53, 115n, 139
Maugham, Somerset, 169
Mazower, Mark, 55
Meistersinger, 42
Memory of the Camps (documentary), 160, 164n
Metropolis (Lang), 33–4
middlebrow, 2, 69, 113n, 125
Milosz, Czeslaw, 95, 98, 99, 116n
Ministry of Information (MOI), 12, 118–19, 126, 128, 133, 140, 145, 155, 160n, 161n; *see also* propaganda
Mitchison, Naomi, 4
modernism, 2, 4, 8, 13n, 45, 54, 56, 74, 86, 87, 113n, 114n, 116n, 138, 150
　anti-Fascist modernist art, 154
　and exile, 7
　medieval modernism, 85
　modernist films, 160n
Monaghan, David, 210n, 211n
Montefiore, Janet, 3, 10, 69
Mosse, George, 107
Munich Agreement (1938), 52, 53, 118, 131, 211n

A Murder of Quality (le Carré), 169
Murphy, Robert, 130, 135, 146, 162n

Nazism (general), 4, 8, 9, 11, 12, 13n, 21, 23, 34, 36, 47, 53, 54, 62–3, 65n, 70, 79, 80, 82, 86, 90, 114n, 115n, 118, 120–4, 158, 176–7
　Aktion T4 euthanasia program, 71, 113n
　concentration and death camps, 10, 45, 51, 52, 64n, 84, 88, 91, 94, 95, 114n, 131, 159–60, 161n, 167, 179, 182
　degenerate art, artists and book burning, 178, 211n
　Einsatzgruppen (mobile killing squads), 115n, 159, 163n
　Final Solution, 23, 84, 94
　Hitler, 4, 52, 60, 61, 64n, 65n, 82, 87, 89, 98, 116n, 123, 128, 140, 161n
　invasion of Poland, 83, 92, 100, 129, 131, 149, 220; *see also A Bridge to Stand*
　Kristallnacht, 133, 195
　Lebensraum, 83, 99, 159
　Nazi-occupied Europe, 18, 24, 161, 175
　race theory and ideology, 4, 35, 37, 61, 66n, 73, 76, 85, 95, 113n, 135, 137, 138, 142, 149–53, 160n, 195–6
　targeted victims, 4, 12, 18, 51, 66n, 85, 86, 121, 125, 134, 136, 137, 144, 147, 149–50, 158, 178, 221
　ubermensch (superman), 103, 138
　untermensch (subhuman), 4, 84, 131, 139, 148, 196
　violence, 3, 5, 148
　Wannsee Conference, 84
Neville, Peter, 65n, 115n
Night Train to Munich (Carol Reed), 142
Nosferatu, 43, 59; *see also* Dracula
Nuremberg Laws (Nazi Germany, 1935), 24, 35, 43, 44, 65n, 86

Oppenheim, E. Phillips, 17, 20, 29, 64n
Orwell, George, 85, 86, 197, 210n

Pabst, G. W. (German expressionist filmmaker), 42
Peach, Linden, 13n
Peking Spring (Bridge), 80

Pen to Paper (Frankau), 116n
Perriaux, Sophie, 6, 8
photography, 5, 24, 30–2, 38, 42, 48–50, 79, 163n, 172, 185, 214n
Piette, Adam, 13n
Pimpernel Smith (Howard), 12, 30, 51, 120, 122, 132–44, 146, 150, 151, 154, 162n, 221
A Place to Stand (Bridge), 5, 10, 70, 72, 85, 93, 94–101
Poe, Edgar Allan, 39, 204
Popular Front, 18, 67n
Portman, Eric, 152; *see also 49th Parallel*
Powell, Michael, 131, 136, 145–6, 155, 162n
Pressburger, Emeric, 131, 136, 145–6, 149, 150, 155, 162n
Priestley, J. B., 119, 123
propaganda, 6, 13n, 64n, 91, 135, 137–8, 142, 144, 150, 155–6, 160n
  anti-Fascist, 53, 85
  anti-Nazi films, 120–1
  British art and entertainment, 3, 12, 118–24, 127–8, 130–44, 145, 162n
  German propaganda, 121, 126, 138–9, 157
  influence, 134
  morale, 119, 126, 161n
  Programme for Film Propaganda, 145
  World War I, 121, 125, 127–8

race, 71, 73, 108, 114n
  race hatred, 72
  see also Nazism
radio broadcasts *see* BBC; Leslie Howard; propaganda
Rattigan, Neil, 121, 126, 132, 162n
realism, 4, 5, 20, 24, 25, 46, 55, 58, 65n, 102
Reed, Carol, 142, 158
refugee filmmakers, 133
refugees and fictional representation, 2, 5, 8, 9, 47–50, 94–8, 101, 136–7, 187–8
refugees and history, 2, 6–7, 13n, 17, 18, 25, 40, 43, 56, 60, 71, 73, 74, 77, 94, 129, 162n, 186, 202, 213n
  British internment, 135
Remmler, Karen, 212n
Rimington, Stella, 113n, 218

Robinson, Benjamin, 7, 194
Roosevelt, President Franklin D., 67n, 124
Russian Revolution, 7

Sayers, Dorothy, 69
The Scarlet Pimpernel (Howard), 134, 136
Schlesinger, Arthur, 211n
Schweizer, Bernard, 13n
Sedgwick, Eve K., 197
Seed, David, 13n
Shelley, Mary (*Frankenstein*), 59
Shneer, David, 214n
Shylock, 78
Silver, Brenda, 214n
Sisman, Adam, 212n
A Small Town in Germany (le Carré), 167, 185
Smith, Andrew, 26, 45
Smith, Andrew and Jeff Wallace, 214n
Smith, James, 211n
Snyder, Robert, 54, 65n, 66n, 67n, 214n
Snyder, Timothy, 7, 13n
Sontag, Susan, 24, 31
Soviet Union, 8, 10, 13n, 14n, 19, 37, 52, 53, 91, 95, 97–8, 115n, 177
  Katyn massacre, 94
  satellite nations, 97–8, 178
  spies, 11, 40–1, 52
  Stalin, 181, 197, 209
  see also Communism
Spanish Civil War, 3, 10, 18, 80, 154, 159, 184, 211n, 214n
Spender, Stephen, 21, 167, 177, 199, 211n
The Spy Who Came in from the Cold (le Carré), 12, 185, 201–15, 220
Stern, Guy, 189
Stevenson, Robert Louis, 197
Stewart, Victoria, 115n
Stone, Dan, 113n
The Story So Far (Ambler memoir), 53
Sullivan, Francis X. (*Pimpernel Smith*), 140
Sutherland, John, 211n

The Tailor of Panama (le Carré), 212n
Then We Shall Hear Singing (Jameson), 83, 161n
Theweleit, Klaus, 211n
The Third Man (Greene), 4, 27, 104, 112

Thompson, Dorothy, 6, 77, 79–80
A Tightening String (Bridge), 93
Toller, Ernst, 16, 64n
Tracey, Laura, 214n
Turner, Graeme, 21

The Untouchable (Banville), 4

Waiting for Orders (Ambler), 56
Wallenberg, Raoul, 134
Wark, Wesley, 13n
Wasserstein, Bernard, 43, 67n, 163n
Waugh, Evelyn (*Brideshead Revisited*), 193
West, Rebecca, 4, 85, 109–10, 129

While Still We Live (MacInnes), 82, 92–3
White, Rosie, 13n, 212n
The White Eagle (Howard), 128
Williams, Gordon, 152
The Willow Cabin (Frankau), 113n
Wolfe, Peter, 30, 46, 66n, 67n
Wollaeger, Mark, 148, 150, 160n
Woods, Brett, 18, 52, 64n, 65n
Woolf, Leonard, 133
Woolf, Virginia, 5, 6, 66n, 189
World War I, 7, 18, 24, 35, 47, 52, 121, 125, 127–8, 148, 154, 158, 161n, 189, 210n, 220

Yates, Dornford, 17

EU representative:
Easy Access System Europe
Mustamäe tee 50, 10621 Tallinn, Estonia
Gpsr.requests@easproject.com

www.ingramcontent.com/pod-product-compliance
Lightning Source LLC
Chambersburg PA
CBHW062136300426
44115CB00012BA/1943